Questions of Life
Answers of Wisdom

Volume 1

by the contemporary Sufi
M. R. Bawa Muhaiyaddeen
(Ral.)

The Fellowship Press
Philadelphia, PA

©1991 by the Bawa Muhaiyaddeen Fellowship
5820 Overbrook Avenue
Philadelphia, PA 19131

Library of Congress Cataloging-in-Publication Data

Muhaiyaddeen, M. R. Bawa.
   Questions of life, answers of wisdom / by the contemporary Sufi,
M. R. Bawa Muhaiyaddeen.
     p. cm.
   Includes bibliographical references.
   ISBN-0-914390-43-0 (v.1)
    1. Sufism. I. Title.
BP189.M69 1990   90-3822
297'.4--dc20   CIP

Printed in the United States of America
by The Fellowship Press
First Printing 1991
Second Printing 1994

Muhammad Raheem Bawa Muhaiyaddeen *(Ral.)*

About the Author

Muhammad Raheem Bawa Muhaiyaddeen (may God be pleased with him) was a man of extraordinary wisdom and compassion. For over seventy years he selflessly shared his knowledge and experience with people of every race and religion, from all walks of life.

Born well before the turn of the century, Bawa Muhaiyaddeen spent his early years traveling throughout the Middle East and India, examining the world's religions and a myriad of spiritual practices. Our record of his life begins around 1914, when pilgrims traveling through the jungles of Sri Lanka first encountered him. Awed by the depth of his wisdom, they asked him to come to their village to be their teacher. Some time later he did so, thereby beginning a life of public service—feeding, healing, and uplifting the lives of all who came to him.

The name Muhaiyaddeen literally means 'the giver of life to the true belief', and indeed Bawa Muhaiyaddeen did devote himself tirelessly to awakening faith in God within people's hearts. As a Sufi, he had that special gift of distilling and revealing the essential truth contained within all religions—the oneness of God. Thus, whenever he spoke, Buddhists, Hindus, Muslims, Jews, and Christians would sit together for hours listening to his wisdom.

In 1971 he was invited to come to the United States to Philadelphia, the 'city of brotherly love'. There, too, learned and unlearned, young and old, responded to his message of unity.

The next fifteen years, until his death on December 8, 1986, proved to be a time of maximum outreach. Speaking in person on university campuses, in churches, meeting houses, and private homes, as well as on numerous radio and television programs, he reached audiences around the globe, from the United States and Canada to England and Sri Lanka. He was interviewed by Time Magazine, Psychology Today, Harvard Divinity Bulletin, The Philadelphia Inquirer, and numerous other publications; over twenty books of his discourses and songs were published, as well as scores of audio and video cassettes.

In the midst of all this activity, Bawa Muhaiyaddeen continued to receive scores of daily visitors, answer their many and diverse questions, and touch their lives in a very personal way. Of all the religious scholars, world leaders, journalists, and soul-searchers who came to him, perhaps United Nations Secretary Robert Muller summed it up best:

> "I will never forget his words. They will be a message for the rest of my life. I hope that on the day he leaves earth, he will still be with us in spirit to help us succeed in our very difficult task."

Editor's Note

This is the first of many volumes of informal question and answer sessions with Muhammad Raheem Bawa Muhaiyaddeen (may God be pleased with him), a contemporary Sufi sage and mystic.

It is a spoken book—the sessions impromptu and the answers spontaneous. Many of the questions deal with life's daily problems, while others focus on the spiritual dimensions of human existence. Many of the answers are straightforward, others convoluted and mystical.

To make this wealth of information more accessible, the individual questions asked are listed at the beginning of each session, as well as in the table of contents. In the back of the book the questions are cross-referenced by topic, followed by an extensive subject index. In addition, there is a complete glossary explaining the foreign and esoteric terms that defy simple translation in English. Throughout the text you will find calligraphic circles ((ﷺ)) following the names of prophets, angels, and saints. These are traditional supplications and acknowledgements of respect, whose meanings can be found at the end of the glossary.

This book is addressed to everyone, from every race, religion, and walk of life. The reader, therefore, should be aware that although some answers may appear to apply to a particular religion, the truths contained within them belong to all of humanity. Likewise, references to male and female apply only to the body and the elements, not to God and the realm of the soul, for within wisdom and truth there can be no differences or separations of any kind, only oneness.

Bawa Muhaiyaddeen once said, "For every question, there is an answer." And indeed throughout this book and the volumes to come, he addresses our doubts, our confusions, and the heretofore unanswered questions of our hearts.

Preface

Imagine yourself seated before an ancient, wise, compassionate sage, a very small man with a kindly smile and a twinkle in his eye; one who has traveled the breadth of the world, searched the universe of the soul, and finally found the answer. Imagine that you are at the feet of such a one who has discovered the source of all answers. Feel the awe, the excitement, and ultimate humility of sitting before such a wise man.

And now, imagine just a bit further, that he turns toward you, embraces you with his smile and asks, "What would you like to know, my child?" If your mind were to become still and your heart were to melt and the questions your soul had been yearning to express poured forth, what might you ask, and what shape would the answer take?

This is a book full of such questions and answers, questions asked by people of all ages, all religions, all colors; people from varied walks of life such as students, physicians, carpenters, professors, plumbers, reporters, secretaries, rabbis, ministers, parents, children, and grandchildren, some seeing this wise man for the first time and others who have been with him day in and day out for many years.

This is a book of the spoken word, rich with answers covering a wide spectrum, from the most simple and practical advice to the most exalted and mystical experiences of the human heart and soul. It is a book overflowing with wisdom as it pours forth from the highest spheres of man's consciousness; the levels where man and God are united as one, where the I does not exist but has lost itself within that one compassionate almighty power which is God.

The answers come from Muhammad Raheem Bawa Muhaiyaddeen, an ancient Sufi sage whose wisdom, love, and compassion are so vast that they cut through racial and religious differences, through time, age, and tradition. Although he appeared many years ago from the jungles of Sri Lanka, no one truly knows where he came from or just how old he is. What we do know is that since the early 1900's, this extraordinarily wise and compassionate sage has been patiently and lovingly answering questions as he does in this book. It was his custom on most mornings to informally receive visitors. During this time he would answer any questions the visitors might pose. While reading through these pages, one may see a very simple question receive a long, eloquent, and profound answer; conversely, one may see a well thought out, seemingly complex question receive a one sentence reply. Yet within his words, so full of truth and divine wisdom, even the briefest reply can make a deep and lasting impression. And although the question came from just one, the answers are for us all.

If these questions and answers are read daily for just a short period of time, they can have a significant effect; for as one's heart opens, the power of these divinely inspired teachings will enter deeply within and greatly benefit all aspects of one's life.

May God protect us. May God grant His grace and peace upon us all. *Amīn*. May we all progress on the path of the one true Father, the Creator, Sustainer and Nourisher of all lives, that one incomparable power of truth, wisdom and justice. May God protect us and grant us His grace.

Howard Posner, M.D.

"My children, if there are any doubts in your mind, if there is anything that you do not understand, if there is anything pertaining to wisdom that you are unable to find an answer to, please open your heart and ask. It is your duty to ask your father. If your father knows the answer, he will tell you. If he does not know, he will ask and learn from you. Therefore, you must ask whatever is in your heart that needs to be answered and cleared."

Muhammad Raheem Bawa Muhaiyaddeen (Ral.)

Contents

About the Author   v

Editor's Note   vii

Preface   ix

SESSION 1

What are the false gods of the contemporary world?   3
What is our duty to the world?   4
What are the dangers associated with mantra meditation?   7
Can political education change the evils of the world?   8
Should there be equality between men and women?   9
When will the destruction come?   10
Can your students reach a state of oneness with you?   12
What will happen to that relationship when you die?   12

SESSION 2

*How does one endure the burdens of life and continue to meet
    all of his responsibilities?*   18
How do we dedicate ourselves to God?   20
What can I do about my self-deprecation?   22
How do I obtain the strength to serve God?   23
Is my desire for God just another veil?   23
Does disease come from God?   26

SESSION 3

Who is God?   31
What is the Bawa Muhaiyaddeen Fellowship?   33
What is marriage according to the will of God?   35
Does satan exist?   36
Can satan possess us?   36
Can satan be exorcised?   37

SESSION 4

An individual's questions on meditation.   41

SESSION 5

*How can we reach a balance between giving a child too much
   exposure to the world and overprotecting them?*   49
*Is there a point at which God or the spiritual teacher give up on
   someone who is on the path?*   50

SESSION 6

What is meant by the melting heart?   55
*Can we learn about God's qualities by observing them in one of
   God's representatives?*   56
*Two school teachers ask about controlling children with
   strength versus love.*   57

SESSION 7

Our attachments are intoxicants.   63
Is repetitive prayer the way to remember God?   70

SESSION 8

I'm out of work and need direction in my life.   75
*Please explain about the battles that surround Prophet
   Muhammad ﷺ.*   76
How do I remove doubt from my life?   80
Why does our faith waver?   81
How can we know if we have spiritually progressed?   82
How can I stop being afraid of loneliness?   84
*Are parents responsible for the karma and spiritual attainment
   of their children?*   86

SESSION 9

Please tell us something about Judas.   *91*
Must we all go through a crucifixion?   *94*
Why did God send Jesus (☉) *to the world?*   *95*
*Why did wise men even attempt to teach those who would only
    cause trouble?*   *96*
Is it good to be married?   *96*
*I met a karate teacher earlier and felt a connection toward him.
    Is that the right path for me?*   *97*
*If we haven't seen the roots of our problems, should we keep on
    cutting the branches?*   *99*
*In my work, the recommendations I make sometimes send
    people to jail. Is that passing judgment?*   *99*
Should we express our anger?   *100*
*My philosophy is opposite to that of someone I work with.
    How should I handle the situation?*   *100*
When students are difficult what should a teacher do?   *101*

SESSION 10

At the time of death, what happens to the soul and to the body?   *107*

SESSION 11

How will the sound of God be heard within us?   *113*
*What is the meaning of "A man of wisdom will know all three
    time periods"?*   *113*
*How can a disciple overcome the fear of relinquishing his own
    learning?*   *119*
A friend was mugged twice. What can you advise her?   *125*
How can we cleanse our lives?   *127*
*How can we tell whether it is wisdom or the illusory mind that is
    leading us?*   *128*
Were you ever in our state?   *129*
How can I overcome fear?   *130*

SESSION 12

*When Bawa Muhaiyaddeen talks, how can we know what level
to tune in on?* 135

Why does there have to be a day of destruction? 137

*A friend is paying us rent. How much involvement should he
have in household decisions?* 137

Where does duty for my family lie? 139

Why should anyone choose to have a child? 140

I was hurtful to my parents and now I want forgiveness. 142

SESSION 13

How can we escape from being food for hell? 147

What can I do in order to know myself? 149

*The discrepancy between my intentions and actions affects my
faith. What can I do?* 150

*Once when I was worried, something just popped inside me and
my mind was eased. What was that?* 151

Is it wrong to expect happiness? 152

*Things I thought I had finished with keep returning to my mind.
How can I prevent that?* 152

*Sometimes one needs to rush, sometimes to go slowly. How can
we be consistent?* 154

How can we be trusting in the company of many people? 154

SESSION 14

How can I prevent my arrogance from blocking my trust in God? 159

How can I overcome anxiety and sorrow to see God's light? 161

SESSION 15

Can you tell me who Jesus (ﷺ) is? 165

Why did Jesus (ﷺ) come? 165

Is Jesus (ﷺ) with us now? 167

How can we establish a direct connection to God? 167

What man can be righteous before God? 168

Why is man here? 169

Why do some people not love God? 170
Is Jesus God? 170

SESSION 16

How can I balance my spiritual life with my physical needs? 175
Could I have a name to guide my qualities? 175
Please speak about religious indifference. 176
Should we expect any more prophets? 182
I've studied singing. Should I continue? 184
How can we transform our thoughts into thoughts of God? 186
Who is the Messiah and has he come yet? 186

SESSION 17

My grandmother is ill. What shall I tell her? 191
Who is the true guru? 192
What is the Trinity? 194
Who is Jesus? 198

SESSION 18

What is the correct way to act when seeking employment? 203
Can determination be nurtured? 204
What wisdom will make our faith grow firm? 205
How can I cut the excessive attachment to my mother? 206
My mother only believes in this world. What shall I tell her? 208
How does the disciple see his teacher within? 209
How can we cut attachment to things that are wrong? 211
How much of our lives are predestined? 211
Is it true that no two snowflakes are alike? 212

SESSION 19

Is it our responsibility to bring others on the path? 217
How can I live a life surrendered to the will of God? 219

I sent my sister books and pictures and she intends to come here. What more should be said to her? 220

Is it right or wrong to give charity to religions? 221

What message do you have for some brothers who are in prison? 223

SESSION 20

How can I readjust my life? 227

What are the lights I see during meditation? 227

I have realized much inner growth, but I feel I should do more. 228

SESSION 21

How can I get rid of jealousy? 233

Why is the expression on the face so important? 234

SESSION 22

Where were you born? 239

How long have you been in the world? 239

How many children can you embrace? 241

What message would you like to address to the whole world? 244

What is the first step to freedom? 245

How can people understand that all are God's children? 246

What should we strive for in life? 246

SESSION 23

How to treat the illnesses of man. 253

How do fate and destiny relate to doing good works? 255

How does surrender to God fit in with fate and destiny? 257

What is man-God, God-man? 263

How do we make the connection to God? 267

What is meant by rasūl? 268

SESSION 24

What does 'Duty is greater than God' mean? 273
How can I make my faith grow? 273
Were you ever born? 276
How do energies attack man? 276

SESSION 25

What should we do when we see faults in others? 281
Should we perform duty which does not come from love? 282
If I'm paid to fulfill someone's evil purposes, am I culpable? 286
*How should I understand karma, accidents and destiny in
   relation to God's will?* 286
What does it mean to be with the guru for twelve years? 287

SESSION 26

How can we better our lives? 299
What does it mean to 'Bend the sky into a bow'? 301
What is the station of the elemental spirits? 303
How do the elemental spirits change? 306
Why is Jesus ☉ the most celebrated prophet? 307
What is the difference between a qutb *and a prophet?* 311
*Did God create the thymus gland as the center of energy
   for the body?* 313

Glossary 317
Questions by Topic 331
Subject Index 339

Session 1

———❧———

*Interview with David Freudberg for Boston
radio station WGBH:*

What are the false gods of the contemporary world?
3

What is our duty to the world?
4

*What are the dangers associated
with mantra meditation?*
7

*Can political education change
the evils of the world?*
8

Should there be equality between men and women?
9

When will destruction come?
10

Can your students reach a state of oneness with you?
12

What will happen to that relationship when you die?
12

Session 1

DAVID FREUDBERG: There are many madnesses within me, so I thank you for granting me this interview.

BAWA MUHAIYADDEEN: My love to you. May God protect us. Everyone in the world has been created with the same things in them that my little brother has. Except for God, everyone has what you have within. But even though everybody is in that state, each person tries to establish some kind of peace within himself. The day that we are able to attain true inner peace will be a good day for us.

DAVID: Bawa, throughout history, people have worshiped idols, false gods, false prophets. Would you describe the false gods of the contemporary world?

BAWA MUHAIYADDEEN: Now, at the beginning of creation and at the time when man first came into being, God took the forms of the five elements (earth, fire, water, air, and ether) and mingled them into the one fistful of earth that became man's body. The same elements from which man was made were also an integral part of every created thing. So even as he emerged, man had a connection through his own form to the world and to all of the creations.

Within man, God can be found, as well as the things which are opposite to God—demons, ghosts, satans, and animals. Everything exists within man: good and evil, heaven and hell, light and darkness, truth and falsehood, wisdom and ignorance. All the things in the world that man can see and understand, even the things he cannot see or understand, exist and function within him. They are the very things God used to make the earth-form of man.

God created the five kinds of lives (earth lives, fire lives, water lives, air lives, and ether lives) out of the elements and gave them to mankind; but He also gave man the gift of wisdom, which is the sixth kind of life, the life made of light. When man looks with his light of wisdom, he sees that Power which sees him. He sees the mysterious God as light without form, as an effulgence, as a mirror that reflects everything in existence. When he looks into that wondrous mirror with his wisdom, he sees himself there and knows his own true form. He sees that he is within the Mirror and the Mirror is within him.

This is God's greatest gift to man: the divine luminous wisdom that allows man to see that he exists within God and God exists within him. But man has lost that gift. Instead he has accepted evil, nurturing within himself all of the satans, idols, and animals which exist within the earth lives. Because he has lost his wisdom and failed to reach the state intended for him, he has resorted instead to worshiping the images of the ghosts and demons that exist within him. He worships what is opposite to God and acts in a way that is opposite to a true man's actions. When he does that, he is not a man, he is an animal. He may have the face of a man, but he is really in an animal state.

That is why it is so easy for him to exhibit animal qualities. Sometimes he takes the qualities of the monkey from within him, externalizes them, and then worships the very form he has made. Likewise, he makes the snake within him into an idol and worships it as a tangible form. He does the same with the qualities of satan. He takes them from within him, externalizes them, and deifies them. He even brings out the hell within him and worships that, too.

In this way, four hundred trillion, ten thousand spiritual qualities are conjured up by the mind and placed in front of him, like miracles. These miracles come from where they exist as qualities, actions, and intentions, as thoughts, desires, and illusions, and as ghosts and demons. But because he is unable to touch these shadow forms within, he externalizes them, making them into statues which he can touch and pray to and praise in song.

However, God bestowed upon man the conviction that there is only one God worthy of praise and He gave him the wisdom to see that he exists within God and that God is there within him as a mirror. Whoever cherishes that great gift will see his own true self. Such a true human being will see God's image within his own image, just as God sees true man within Him.

DAVID: As I understand your teaching, it divides life into two parts. One part is God. The other part is mind and body, which govern the world. And you have said that we have a duty to each part: we must meditate and concentrate on the part that is God, adopting His divine qualities of infinite compassion. But what is our duty to the world?

BAWA MUHAIYADDEEN: The light of wisdom, or the soul, is the only thing that has a connection to God and can worship God. Mind and desire keep circling around this body, which is the world. How is this done? Just as the hands of a clock keep rotating around all twelve hours, mind and desire rotate around the body over and over again, saying, "One o'clock, two o'clock, three o'clock," etc. In this way mind creates the passage of time. It keeps going around and around until the agreed upon time for the body is over. At one moment, thinking that everything is going well, it will smile and say, "This is a good day." But at another moment it might say, "This is a terrible day." It goes back and forth, changing and changing what it says.

Mind and desire are like that. They smile, dance, talk, and do all sorts of things, and while they go on rotating, they perform their four hundred trillion, ten thousand different tricks. This is their work. At one time, your mind will assume the form of a beautiful young woman, covered with makeup and jewelry, and say, "I want a handsome man to marry. I want to make love." Then your desire will try to embrace her. But as soon as you take hold of her, that beautiful woman will change into a vampire, grab your neck, and drink your blood—immediately transforming you. In this way, the two fangs of mind and desire will bite into you firmly and change you into a bloodsucking vampire.

During another of their rotations, mind and desire will take the form of gold or silver and make you say, "I want this, I want that, I want wealth, I want land, I want a woman." Sometimes the mind will take the form of a baby and beg, "Take me to the supermarket," where it will cry, "Buy me this, buy me that." Or it will say, "Let's go to the jewelry store." Once there, it will demand, "Buy me this necklace, buy me that gem." It will howl and howl until it gets these things, and then it will want still more.

This is how the mind operates, circling round and round, entangling man so that everything he desires grabs hold of him, urging, "Buy me this, get me that." Day and night, the mind's power possesses him, not allowing him to sleep, causing him to search and search for the object of his desire. Once he finds it, it grabs hold of him and drinks his blood, changing him into a vampire that in turn searches for other lives, grabs them, and sucks their blood. This mind and desire catch everybody and change them into vampires and demons. And so it goes.

Mind and desire make one round after another, trying to catch you. If one ruse does not work, they will go to the next one and take another form. They are capable of taking four hundred trillion, ten thousand different forms. For each of those forms that they create within, they also create statues on the outside; and for each of those statues, they create mantras, meditations, and methods of worship. They make them into gods: the god of earth, god of water, god of fire, god of gold, god of ether, god of wind, god of illusions, tree-god, sun-god, moon-god. Man praises them, sings songs to them, and treats them as miracles, but they are really only *shaktis*, or elemental energies, that have been created out of his own qualities.

In this way, man's beautiful form is changed, and the viruses that appear within its cells or energies are then disseminated to others, causing cancer and various other kinds of serious diseases.

A man caught up in the throes of mind and desire is separated from God. But one who is in the state of truth and wisdom will be able to look into the mirror of wisdom and then dissect and analyze the incessant circlings of mind and desire. It is much like understanding the workings of a clock. First one examines the parts of the clock that make the hands go round. What work do each of these parts do? Is it just as it appears to be on the outside, or is there some inner mechanism that is making things happen? Next, he removes each part of the clock, piece by piece, until he finally removes the center wheel, the mechanism that controls the working of the clock. Once this is done, the clock stops ticking, and its hands stop rotating. When the hands stop, time stops; the circling is finished. Like this, once the working of mind and desire are removed, the world leaves a man of wisdom.

Such a man discards that controlling mechanism which made the clock go round and replaces it with a new one. He then replaces all the old parts with new parts, with the qualities and actions of God, the love and compassion of God, the affection of God, the quality of loving all lives as one's own, the quality of trusting one's neighbor as oneself and regarding others' sadness and hunger as one's own. The man of wisdom replaces the old qualities with God's three thousand compassionate qualities and ninety-nine powers. Once those are firmly established, the clock will work again, and this time when it starts up, the hands will point only to the connection between man and God. This time his actions will be God's actions, his words will be God's words, and his prayer will be God's prayer. If a man can come to that state, then the world will automatically leave him, and all the work that he does will be God's work. This is selfless duty, duty that is not concerned with one's own hunger or sadness or happiness.

This is what a person with wisdom will do.

DAVID: In their search for spirituality, many people meditate by reciting mantras. They claim it gives them deep relaxation. You have said that there are dangers associated with mantra meditation. Would you explain that please?

BAWA MUHAIYADDEEN: I will tell you something from my own experience. A person who meditates will say to himself, "My meditation must be good." But he is really like a donkey who rides on the back of another donkey. He feels happy for a while; however, when the two have traveled for a short distance, the donkey on the bottom will be unable to walk anymore because of the heavy load. So the donkey riding on top will have to get down and take his turn carrying the tired one. Not only will the donkey underneath have to carry the one on top, he will also have to endure his kicks.

Similarly, all the meditations that people perform are being done through ignorance, through lack of wisdom. I really do not know whether anybody ever realized any peace through meditation. The stubbornness of the mind may make a man claim to have peace, but only the wisdom of truth knows whether he actually does. As his clock goes around and around, one second passes and the next second comes. He may be meditating and experience some comfort for a moment; but the next moment he thinks, "Oh, I am meditating. I am at peace." The minute that thought comes to his mind, his ego is functioning and he loses this peace. Then once more he loses himself for a second, but just as soon, he is aware of himself again. Thus he is not free from sadness for even one second. Such meditation is like the unceasing waves of the ocean. None of this is real meditation, for it is only when the I is no longer there that one is truly meditating.

There is only one point in meditation; until one is able to give up himself for the sake of others, there is no meditation. Meditation starts only after all comforts, sorrows, and disappointments are transcended. Peace comes only when he has no more happiness or sadness. Until then there is no meditation, or *tiyanum*, there is only *tiyenungul* (a Tamil word meaning evil thoughts). These evil thoughts are his meditation. *Tiyanam*, true meditation, is to discard all evil qualities, to remove all thoughts, and then to sacrifice the self. To completely dedicate yourself to God is true prayer. If you do not do that, there is no real prayer or meditation.

DAVID: The world is full of evil: wars, bigotry, greed, to name a few. Bawa, do you see a role for social change through political education about these evils?

BAWA MUHAIYADDEEN: Now, in the world there are two battlefields; one is the political battlefield, the other is the religious battlefield. On the one, wars are waged for the sake of politics; on the other, wars are waged over religions and races. People die in these wars. Nothing exalted will ever come out of them.

In God's kingdom there is no fighting. He rules over both the kingdom of hell and the kingdom of heaven, giving each of His creations what is due to them, but taking no share for Himself. God is One. He proclaims, ''My religion is to recognize all lives as one's own life, all religions as one's own religion, all languages as one's own language, all vision as one's own vision.'' It is in this state that God conducts His kingdom. He has no partialities, no religious differences, and no prejudices based on skin color, whether it be black, red, white, or yellow. In His kingdom there is no fighting.

If politicians would rule their countries the way God rules His kingdom, that would be very good. Then you would see some progress in this world. But as long as they do not, no real change can occur.

The same thing is true of religions. God is One, but when people go to their place of worship to pray, they take all their differences with them, thinking, "My religion, my race, my sect." Each person is tenacious about his own beliefs, so what do his mind and desire do? They point out these religious differences to him and then he attacks and ridicules and rejects others. He tries to eliminate all those who do not belong to his religion. So, even though he claims he is going to pray, he is not worshiping God, he is only worshiping those lethal weapons he carries with him, the instruments of war that separate himself from others. They are what he holds onto. That is what he calls religion. That is not worshiping God!

In these modern times, all the religions proclaim, "My scripture, my religion, my sect, my language..." These are the weapons with which man can attack or murder his own brethren. These are the atomic bombs he takes with him. Such weapons should not be carried into a house of God. If one can discard all these and go to pray in a state which recognizes that we are all the children of Adam ⊛, that we are all one family, that we are all one race, and one religion, that there is only one God, and that He alone is worthy of prayer—then, even before that person prays, even before he enters his place of worship, he will have realized peace. Only those who surrender those weapons will experience peace. That is prayer. Anything else is not true prayer.

DAVID: Should there be equality between men and women?

BAWA MUHAIYADDEEN: What is the difference between man and woman? The only difference is the body. There is no difference in their life, or in their wisdom, or in the light of their eyes. There is no difference in their love. There is no difference at all in their qualities or actions, in their speech or learning, in their mind or desire, in the light or the truth within them.

What is a man? A true man is one who has no torpor or desire. Therefore God is the only true man, since the rest of us have both torpor and desire.

The only real difference between man and woman lies in certain anatomical parts. But when it comes to what they really are, there is no difference. Therefore, if we would regard only that essence, that truth within, then we would see equality between man and woman. That would be good. Man and woman are two lights, the sun and the moon; the sun has heat and the moon has coolness. Man is the sun and woman is the moon. If both can be united, they will work together and live in harmony.

If either meets with an accident, will it matter if the body is male or female? Won't there be an equal chance of losing an arm or a leg? So what do we mean when we talk about equality? It is the inner equality that really matters. There should be equality in the love between them; there should be equality in their affection and in their lives. There you cannot see any differences. That is what matters.

Now, a truck is big, and the engine within it is small. The truck can carry a huge load, but without an engine, the truck is useless. Would you then say that the truck and the engine are equal? Would you consider them equal?

It is the same way with a male and a female. The man is big and he can be loaded up like a truck. He can carry the world and many things of the world, even a kingdom. But we have to remember that what makes the truck move is a very small engine. The woman is that engine.

DAVID: I think you are going to make some of our women listeners happy.

BAWA MUHAIYADDEEN: Truth has got to be told, whatever it is.

DAVID: To switch to a subject that is perhaps not as happy: I've heard that you foresee a great disaster in America, and I wonder how soon you expect this, and what will happen?

BAWA MUHAIYADDEEN: I never mentioned America alone. According to the signs shown to me, there are things now apparent in the world which indicate destruction. Certain signs which I can now see happening were revealed to me by my divine teacher. I was told of forty-one signs that would precede destruction, and out of them I have already seen thirty-seven. All that was told to me has come to pass, except for four remaining signs. Now they too are beginning to occur. Because everything is happening just as it was revealed to me, that tells me the destruction is near.

Some of those thirty-seven signs are: True faith in God will be diminished and forgotten and be replaced by mantras and false prayers throughout the world. The poor will become rich and the rich will become poor. Kings who were at one time rulers will become lowly, while the lowly will rise to the state of kings. Fathers may consort with their daughters and daughters with their fathers. Also, a mother may consort with her son and the son with his mother. Even after giving birth to seven children, a woman may leave her husband and take another husband. Men will change into women, and women will change into men. Marriage between a man and another man will occur, as well as marriage between one woman and another. People will live like animals. Women, who used to be covered by many yards of material, will reduce that amount of material to one foot. All the places on the body that should be covered will be exposed. All shyness and bashfulness between man and woman will be lost. Respect and good conduct will become extinct. Good people will be ridiculed and treated as though they were bad, and those who are bad will be accepted and praised as good. There will also be racial wars, religious wars, and wars fought over land. These things could happen everywhere—in all countries, in all cities, and even in small towns. Machines made of the elements will fly through the air and be seen in the skies. Man will fly into space and even into outer space. Some men will try to wage war against God, saying, "There is no God." They will manufacture armaments and devastate everything through fire and atomic energy.

Such changes will come to pass. At that time, all devotion to God and the virtues of respect, modesty, shyness, and fear of wrongdoing will be gone. A wife will not obey her husband, and a husband will not have love for his wife. Some will leave the good path and go on the evil path. People will begin to worship devils and demons. They will call whores virgins and virgins whores. They will call learned ones fools and regard the unlearned as scholars. They will call the wise ones ignorant and the ignorant ones wise.

Many such signs of destruction have been revealed to me, and I can see that they are now coming to pass throughout the world. It is because I have seen all this that I said the destruction is at hand. As this state draws nearer, there will gradually be destruction through earth, fire, water, and air. I have said all this before. The exact moment and time I cannot say.

DAVID: What are the remaining four signs?

BAWA MUHAIYADDEEN: That I will talk about later. They are very forceful things that will happen in the future. I have spoken about them in my books.

DAVID: Bawa, during the last few days I have been interviewing many of your children on tape, and there is great wisdom that comes through them. They love you very much. In those tapes we have tried to put into words what is the teaching process that has taken the form of Bawa. So my last two questions concern that.

Firstly, does a child of Bawa, a student of Bawa, reach a state of consciousness in which the person is no longer separate from Bawa?

BAWA MUHAIYADDEEN: Now, electricity is drawn from water, then it passes through a motor and travels through a copper or aluminum wire insulated with rubber. When you turn on the switch, the bulb lights up. If you want the electricity to travel into the bulb, there must be some connection established between the electricity and the thing it powers. For example, if you want to cut something with an electric saw, the electricity has to first flow into the saw. This connection is necessary in order for anything that is electrically powered to operate. Once the connection is made, the results can be seen. But if the bulb doesn't light up or the machinery doesn't run, does it matter to the electricity? No, it is not concerned with that. It will go on being what it is.

In the same way, if there are children who want to learn, then there must definitely be a connection established between the child and the current. The bulb may be very beautiful, but whether it be white or green or red, if there is no connection to the current, it will never light. Furthermore, if a child tries to touch the current directly (rather than letting the electricity flow into the bulb), the current will throw him and give him a shock. If he says, ''I am a great person,'' and goes off on his own, then no matter how beautiful that bulb is, it will not connect to the current. But the current does not become sad. The current is only concerned with trying to create light.

DAVID: Bawa, you have told us before that your body is very old.

What will happen when it dies?

BAWA MUHAIYADDEEN:　What has to die will die, and what has to remain will remain. Supposing you dig a well and the water dries up. Just because the well went dry, you cannot say that there is no water there. You cannot say that the spring is dead, for if you dig down one more foot, water will again spring up. If people will only dig a little deeper, they will find the water there. Of course, they can say, "There is no water in the well any more," and go away. But those who have real thirst will dig a little deeper, and they will find water there. What is will always be. That which dies is dead and gone, but that which is will always be.

DAVID:　Thank you, Bawa.

December 8, 1978

Session 2

A visit from Rabbi Zalman Schachter
and students from Temple University:

How does one endure the burdens of life
and continue to meet all of his responsibilities?
18

How do we dedicate ourselves to God?
20

What can I do about my self-deprecation?
22

How do I obtain the strength to serve God?
23

Is my desire for God just another veil?
23

Does disease come from God?
26

Session 2

RABBI SCHACHTER: I want to thank Bawaji for seeing us today. I know he has a great deal of work.

BAWA MUHAIYADDEEN: All the children come here with problems or with something on their minds, and we have to comfort them. One might come weeping, another might come in anger, another might come hungry, and still another might come feeling sad or disappointed because he didn't get something he wanted. As each child comes we have to look into his state. If he is filled with sorrow, we have to comfort him and relieve his suffering. Not only do we give peace to the children, we also embrace and console them. We have a lot of work. Sometimes when I look at the faces of the children, I see that they are a little tired, so I cook for them and give them something to eat. There are so many things like this that must be done. This is the reason I sometimes feel tired.

RABBI SCHACHTER: An *insān kāmil*, a true man, presents Allah as a father to us.

BAWA MUHAIYADDEEN: The slaves of God, the slaves of Allah, must continually perform the duties and functions God has placed upon them.

Allah has given the world to everyone, as common property. Heaven, this world, the world of the souls, and the hereafter have all been placed in the hands of man. Having given all this, God has said: Do whatever you wish to do. Build your house wherever you like—in the world of the souls, in this world, or in the hereafter. My children, I have given you everything. It is all common property, and you are free to do as you wish. Each of you must do whatever you have to do. I have discarded darkness and hell and thrown them far away. They are not within Me. But darkness and hell are within you, so you too must try to discard them. Live with peacefulness and equality. This is what Allah has said. If you can establish such a

17

state, then you will know true peace.

RABBI SCHACHTER: The burden God has placed on my shoulders is very, very heavy, without any letup. My body is now telling me to treat it right, so it will be able to continue serving. I would like to ask Bawaji for some help and enlightenment in order to understand how to give the proper amount of time to all the things I need to do.

BAWA MUHAIYADDEEN:God has placed many parts in the body. We must give Him the responsibility for seeing that each part of our body performs its duty. Every part must be handed over to God.

Our eyes do many things. Sometimes they bring good things to us and sometimes they bring evil things. We must hand the eyes over to God and say, "O God, let these gems, these eyes which You have given me, remain Your property. Please make them Yours and take the responsibility for all the things they do, good or bad. Please accept the responsibility for the work they do; make them discard all that is evil in this world and take in only what is good. Please do not let this be my responsibility."

The ears hear so many sounds: good sounds, evil sounds, musical sounds, sounds of desire, sounds that fascinate us. You must say, "O God, please take the responsibility for these ears and give me ears that will discard all evil sounds and hear and absorb only Your sounds. May they be Your responsibility; do not make me responsible for the evils they bring. Let these ears be Yours."

The nose has the ability to perceive both good and bad smells. Sometimes it accepts the good, but at other times it accepts the bad. You must say, "O God, You have given me such a beautiful nose and placed within it a tiny piece of tissue which gives the perception and awareness of smell. Please take responsibility for it, and give it the power to discard evil smells and take in only Your fragrance."

The tongue can say things that are moral and things that are immoral. It can utter good speech and bad speech. It can say evil things and cause anger. The tongue has so many different propensities. You must say, "O God, in what a subtle manner You have made this tongue. Please accept the responsibility for it. You are the One who must speak through this tongue. You must guide it onto the good path and help it to acquire patience, tolerance, and peacefulness. You must give me a tongue that can bring grace, peace, and equality. I am not able to do that. Whatever has to be said, You must say. Whatever has to be tasted, You must taste. You are the One who must make this tongue realize good tastes instead of bad tastes. I am Your slave whose only duty is to be the instrument that performs Your duties. That is all. To carry out those duties is Your responsibility.''

Say this and hand over all responsibility to Him. Allow Him to act as the conscience of the tongue. Allow Him to see, allow Him to hear, allow Him to smell, and allow Him to speak.

God has also created the *qalb*, the innermost heart. It is a secret within which are contained four hundred trillion, ten thousand different kinds of gases, forces, cells, spirits, demons, ghosts, occult powers, and miracles. All of the eighteen thousand universes are contained within it. All the treasures of the world of the soul, this world, and the hereafter are contained within this small handful of earth that forms the *qalb*.

Seventy thousand veils of darkness hide this heart which God has given us. Each of these veils is separated from the next one by a vast space containing millions of animals, reptiles, and insects. Between each veil are countless dogs, cats, snakes, scorpions, ants, and many vicious creatures. We must tear away these veils one by one, and drive off the animals that lurk behind them.

All of the things that we see in the outside world are present within us as shadows. The qualities of monkeys, rats, dogs, elephants, foxes, and lions have taken subtle forms inside our hearts. As soon as any quality that is in man's mind emerges, it takes a subtle form within the *qalb* and is born and reborn. The mind is capable of performing endless miracles. It becomes an elephant, then a rat, then a lion, a snake, a fairy, a jinn, a ghost, a satan, and all sorts of blood-drinking demons.

Sometimes the mind is like a baby. Sometimes it is like an old lady. Sometimes this same mind is like a beautiful young woman called maya, or illusion. Sometimes it is like an elephant, and sometimes it is like a bull that draws the world behind it and plows. The mind can take on so many different forms. That is its work. It gives birth to millions and millions of energies. Each thought or intention that passes through it creates a form out of these energies. This is what is called rebirth—the qualities within us giving form to rebirth after rebirth.

First the mind creates the qualities, then it externalizes them, making them into visible forms and worshiping them as gods. All of these poisonous reptiles, deadly animals that kill, all the things that fascinate and confuse us, are merely outer forms of the qualities and thoughts that come to the mind. These are the gods that we see around us. Man's mind makes gods out of elephants, horses, rats, snakes, eagles, vultures, cows, goats, tigers, scorpions, the sun, the moon, and the stars, demons, and blood-sucking vampires, and it worships them. His mind makes earth, fire, water, air, ether, and illusion into gods and worships them. It makes the monkey pranks within him into a monkey god and worships that; it makes the cow within him into a cow god and worships that; it makes the quality and poison of the snake within him into a snake god and worships that. His mind makes forms out of all the thoughts and qualities that come to it and worships them all. That is what the mind does.

If we want to discover the man within, we must split open this mind and tear away each of the seventy thousand veils that are there. Then we will be left with only one veil, and we will become true human beings.

The body is the one veil which separates a true man from God; all the other veils must be torn away. All the forces of the mind, all the miracles, must be cast off so that they can no longer deceive us and turn us into snakes, scorpions, dogs, foxes, demons, and crazy men. We must tear them out by the roots and throw them away. Only then can we establish the connection with God. The heart is the mirror which can help us to form that connection of devotion to God; we must see ourselves in that mirror and speak to God.

RABBI SCHACHTER: Can Bawaji suggest what we should do in order to dedicate the eyes, the ears, the tongue, and the heart to God? What does Bawaji suggest we do every morning upon arising?

BAWA MUHAIYADDEEN: Every breath must remind us of God. Every look must be spent searching for God or looking at God. Every word must be the speech of God. Every taste must be in search of

His taste and remind us of Him. Every thought must be of God, and every intention and action must be His.

We must always think and act in this way. Just as God looks at every heart and understands and then comforts its sorrows, so must we try to alleviate the sorrow and suffering in the hearts of others. Just as God treats all lives alike, so must we. We must think of His attributes and put them into action. We must take on the duties and the qualities of God.

True prayer is having good thoughts, good conduct, good qualities, and the actions of God. Prayer is not like the speech of a parrot. Some people go to church or the mosque and recite and recite without understanding. Then they return home and do whatever they please. They may go two, three, or even five times a week and recite prayers they have learned by heart. That is just the work of a parrot; it can talk, but it doesn't understand what it says. Such talk is of no use. If a cat comes and threatens it, what will the parrot do? Will it say, "Help! A cat is coming"? No, it will squawk in fear. In times of danger, the parrot will forget all the words it has learned and return to its own inherent sounds.

In the same way, when circumstances change, when disease comes to man, or when the Angel of Death comes, man will only squawk in fear. He will forget to perform the prayers he learned. But there is a true and lasting prayer that will not be forgotten in times of illness or danger. Yearning for God in every thought, directing every breath toward the point that is God, thinking of Him each time we act, and intending no harm to anyone in our actions—that kind of prayer will bring peace.

RABBI SCHACHTER: We promised upon coming here that we would not strain Bawaji too much, but I would like to ask the students if there are any questions they want to ask.

BAWA MUHAIYADDEEN: If you would like to ask something, please feel free. You have come all this way. When you go to a lake to bathe, you must bathe. If you travel a long distance in search of a restaurant and you finally find one, you must go in and eat. You shouldn't leave without eating and then say that the restaurant was unsatisfactory. If your car has too much air in the tires, it will start jumping around. So you must let out some air until the pressure is just right. Then the car won't bounce and the ride will be comfortable. In the same way, if there are too many thoughts within your mind, it will jump about because it is overinflated. If you release these thoughts and sorrows and reduce the pressure to the proper level, the mind won't jump. So please let out whatever you have been holding back in your minds. Please tell us what you have within your hearts. Then the weight will be less. To the best of our ability, let us work together.

STUDENT: I suffer from doing wrong. Sometimes I hate myself just for having too many thoughts. What do I do then?

BAWA MUHAIYADDEEN: You shouldn't try to cross a river holding on to the tail of a water buffalo, should you? A buffalo loves mud, so when it reaches the middle of the river where there is a lot of mud, it will lie down. If you were clinging to it, can you imagine what your plight would be then?

Don't hold onto your mind and expect it to help you cross the river. The mind is ignorant. Like the water buffalo, as soon as it sees mud it will lie down. That's what your difficulty is. There is no use in hating yourself. Instead, find the right thing to help you cross the river and hold onto that. If you hold onto wisdom, you can cross the river safely.

When you have a cold, it is easy to hold a tissue right up to your nose and blow. But if you try to bring the tissue all the way round behind your head to blow your nose, you will find it very difficult, even if you use both hands. God has given you a nose that is right in front of you, eyes that can see, and hands that can reach. So, whatever you have to do, look at it with your wisdom and do it in the most straightforward way. That will make it easy. But if you fail to use your wisdom and go all around your head trying to do something which you could do directly, it will certainly be much more difficult.

To make our life easier, Allah has given us all of His treasures and wealth, His qualities and actions, His powers, His solace, and the subtlety of His wisdom. He has placed so much in our hands. If you use what He has given you, it will be very easy to conduct your life properly, without despair or suffering. But if you try to conduct your life through karma and maya, you will experience difficulties. It will be like reaching around behind your head to blow your nose. Instead, seek that subtle wisdom and let it guide you. Then your life will be much easier.

STUDENT: Each of us has a unique way that we can serve God. Yet this world seems to make it difficult for me to be strong in serving in my way.

BAWA MUHAIYADDEEN: That is right, my brother. There are many flowers on a single rose bush, and each one has a fragrance. There is only one bush, but the fragrance comes into each rose that blooms. In the same way, the fullness that is God dwells within every heart, and as soon as the rose of your heart blooms in its purity, that fragrance will come into you and you will recognize it yourself. Do whatever your duty is.

STUDENT: My heart is so full of desire for love and beauty and desire for God. And yet the desire itself seems to me to be just another veil.

BAWA MUHAIYADDEEN: That is certainly true. This desire seems to be a veil between you and God. That veil exists in every man. That is the history of the world, a very ancient history. But man also has a story within him, the story of man-God, God-man.

All of mankind are the children of Adam (ﷺ), whether they be black, white, or any other color. They are all one family. No matter how many languages, religions, paths, or differences exist in this world, there is only one family and one God. That is how it is. That love for all must come to dwell within you.

God does not see any differences, does He? He accepts every religion. God is the same to everyone. He is Father and Mother to everyone. We, too, must realize this state. As long as we fail to realize this, arrogance will seize us, and then our karmic connections to illusion, fanaticism, and bigotry will cause us to see differences and to discriminate against others. So even though you have love and desire for God, it is that desire which stands as a veil between you and Him. If you can discard it, then nothing will stand between you and God. The moment this veil recedes, you will see one God, one family, and one prayer. If you reach that state, there will be no more veils.

One more thing, my child. If we look into our own story, we will see that there is only one story. Our story is God's story, and God's story is our story. There is only one secret and one treasure. Man's secret is God, and God's secret is man. Man's treasure is God, and God's treasure is man. Man and God both dwell in the same place. We have to realize this, my child. Even though many prophets came and told us that there is but one God and one truth, we have divided into many religions, philosophies, and languages. All these differences and separations exist among us. The prophets did not come here to create separations. Furthermore, none of them ever claimed to be God or asked anyone to worship them or pray to them. They simply relayed His commands. All of them said, "Trust in God. Have faith in God alone. I have been sent to tell you this." And then they gave all responsibility to Him. But in spite of what they told us, we continue to have all these divisions and differences.

The prophets came to re-establish our connection to God. And what is the connection between God and us? It is having His qualities, His actions, His conduct, and His peace. It is acting with His equality, treating all lives as our own, without discrimination or mistrust. It is showing love to all, seeing their sorrow as our own, and comforting them. It is performing duty to all equally, showing no 'self-business' (selfishness). We need to establish such a state.

There is only one story for man and God. It exists as a secret, a great mystery within man. If you can come to understand this, you will discover that your Father and you are in the same place. God and the human generation are in the same place; two do not exist there. There is only one family and one God. When you realize this, you will see equality and peace all around you. You must reflect upon this. This is the true story of man.

But the world has another story, a history written on the earth. Although God's kingdom belongs to everyone, man has attempted to make it his own by waging wars. This is the history of the world. For the last two hundred million years, this world has known caste divisions, religious bigotry, racial differences, color differences, and sectarianism—based on philosophies, languages, and politics. Motivated by the love for land, woman, and gold, by mind and desire, men have tried to capture territories and even the wealth of God. This is the reason for so many wars and so much destruction throughout this yuga. It is the cause of battles between kings, battles over religions, battles between castes, and battles among those who have adopted different philosophies.

The whole earth is a battleground. If you read the vast story written upon it, you will see how many murders have been committed in the name of some tradition. There has always been fighting, and millions have died as a result of these religious and political struggles. No one has ever died from performing God's actions. There is no war story in that. Yet the story that the earth holds, the story that has been written over the last two hundred million years is one long war story. Many of these stories are depicted in the great epics and in the *purānas,* the Hindu scriptures. A ruler is killed and someone captures his kingdom; then that new ruler is also killed.

A war starts every time man tries to capture God's kingdom and make it his own. Everything is the property of God—our lives, our eyes, our houses, our possessions, and our freedom. How can we think that anything belongs to us? This very body is God's property. Even the soul is His, so what is there that we can call our own? God is our only treasure, and we are God's treasure. The only thing that belongs to us is God's love, and we must take it with us when we return to Him. Nothing can compare to the love that God shows, and there is no limit to His grace. Those who turned away from this love and developed instead a love for land, or gold, or woman, have conducted wars as a self-business. We must reflect on this with our wisdom.

God does not like murder or brutality. He does not want people to hurt each other. He wants us to live with peacefulness, tolerance, and compassion. These qualities are His light form. God sees no differences between one language and another, between this caste and that caste or this race and that race.

My child, we must reflect on these differences. How do the cows in the east differ from the cows in the west or the north or the south? It is true that some may be black, some white, some brown, and some yellow. But they are all cows. They all respond when you speak to them in the language of their own land, whether they live in

Hindu countries, Christian countries, or Islamic countries. And they all give the same kind of milk. Does a cow in the west give a different kind of milk than the cow in the east? Does it give a different kind of milk according to the language or religion of its owner? Does the color of the milk change with the color of the cow? No, there is no difference. Milk is milk.

In the same way, God's truth is one. No matter what your religion, color, or race, no matter what language you speak or philosophy you follow, the milk of truth and love drawn from God's innermost heart is one. It brings peacefulness and tranquility. Without difference or discrimination, God gives this milk in trust to all people, but the religions take it by force. If they would only draw gently, the milk would be white. Instead they torment and stab, so what do they get? Blood, not milk. Murder and blood. That is all that can be drawn from selfishness. When those who love land, gold, and sensual pleasures want to draw milk, they murder for it. But the milk drawn directly from God is the milk of truth.

No matter where you are or what religion you follow, there is only one milk, one truth. God is One, devotion is one, worship is one, and the human family is one. As long as we fail to establish this state of unity, we will not progress. Arrogance, karma, and illusion will block us. These three qualities will destroy us.

With your wisdom you must try to establish God's qualities. That is the only way you will find peace and tranquility.

STUDENT: Does disease come from God?

BAWA MUHAIYADDEEN: Fatal diseases are born with us. The soul is a pure ray that comes from God, but the body, which houses the soul, is composed of earth, fire, water, air, ether, and illusion. This body is an outgrowth of the thoughts and intentions of the father and mother. Every thought, intention, energy, yearning, look, sound, and every action of the father and mother are made into cells which join together to form the body of the child. All these things in the parents merge and become the tissue of the fetus, which takes form as the house of the body. God's point is located in the center of that house. If we can learn to control the body and eliminate all of the evil thoughts and intentions which are our diseases, only that point of God will remain.

The element of fire in our body manifests as anger. The element of water is creation and the thoughts associated with creation. The air, spirits, vapors, and miracles are the deceptions and illusory tricks that come from maya and desire. And the thoughts and anger that arise from our unfulfilled desires are our diseases. Each thought, each intention, turns into a disease. They are inherent in this body. Every wrong food, every wrong action, turns into an illness. In this way we create and increase our own diseases. These are the things that kill us. And if we take anything in excess, even honey or nectar, it can be poisonous to us. But if we take everything in the right proportion, no more poison will come into us. With our wisdom, we must strive little by little, section by section, to dispel the illnesses that are in this body.

The body is a dark house. If you light a lamp, as it burns ever brighter, the darkness will recede little by little. Firmly place the truth as a lamp in your innermost heart, and with the light of that lamp, you will be able to see God within. You will be able to read His actions and His duties. Then your diseases will recede gradually, just as the darkness leaves a house. But if you live without lighting a lamp in that house, your dark thoughts will become the cancers that will kill you.

RABBI SCHACHTER: I want to thank Bawaji for allowing the word of God to touch our souls and our hearts once again.

BAWA MUHAIYADDEEN: May He keep you well so that you may be of help to these children for a long time and teach them good wisdom. May God give you a life of peace. May He make this life long. May God protect you and bless you all with long life. May He give peace to all these children. *Āmīn.*

RABBI SCHACHTER: We wish that God also will give strength to Bawaji so that we may come here from time to time, when our hearts need to be set straight.

BAWA MUHAIYADDEEN: May God help us all.

February 27, 1979

Session 3

A college student interviews Bawa Muhaiyaddeen
for a course in comparative religions:

Who is God?
31

What is the Bawa Muhaiyaddeen Fellowship?
33

What is marriage according to the law of God?
35

Does satan exist?
36

Can satan possess us?
36

Can satan be exorcised?
37

Session 3

STUDENT: Who is God?

BAWA MUHAIYADDEEN: Do you have faith in God?

STUDENT: Yes.

BAWA MUHAIYADDEEN: I, too, have faith in God. We cannot see Him as an external form. God exists within us at a particular point. He has no attachments or blood ties. He has neither wife nor children, house nor property. He has no race, religion, or separations of any kind. He has no doctrine. His religion is truth. God has no color. He is not black or white or yellow. We cannot say that He was born or even that He appeared on a certain day. We cannot say that He is living happily or that He has a self-image. We cannot even say, "God was revealed to us in a spiritual form. We saw Him like this, we saw Him like that, we saw a miracle." God has no form. He casts no shadow. He bears no similarity to a goat, a bull, or to any other thing that has been created. He is not like the sun or the moon or the stars. He cannot be compared to anything.

God is a power, a point existing within all creations. The rays of that power called God exist in each created life. In all the universes nothing is equal to Him. He rules as the One Power. God is absolute plenitude. His form is compassion. His nature is to look at the lives of others and see them as His own life, to feel their hunger and their suffering as His hunger and His suffering, and to do His duty accordingly.

The grace of God comes to all lives in creation. His justice is perfect. He does not discriminate between high and low or rich and poor. It may be the wish of a rich man to search for karma and acquire the world, and the wish of a poor man to search for *dharma,* the duties he was born to do. Toward both men, God shows the same qualities of patience, tolerance, peacefulness, and tranquility. He regards every life with good thoughts and performs His duty toward each with love, compassion, generosity, charity, justice, integrity, and with the three thousand qualities of His grace and the ninety-nine powers of His duties. He puts His duty into action in the world of the soul, in this world which is the world of hell, and in the world of heaven which is the world of God.

God is a treasure without form or self-image, a treasure that can give peace and tranquility to human life. He exists as the inner patience, contentment, trust, and praise known as *sabūr*, *shakūr*, *tawakkul*, and *al-hamdu lillāh*. He is the power of compassion, the power that exists in good thoughts. He is the One who resplends as the treasure of wisdom within wisdom. God is the radiance and the beauty in a pure and open heart. He is the resplendent light in the face of one who has beautiful qualities. Just as there exists a point on the tongue which perceives taste and a point of light within the eye which can see, God exists as a point in the wisdom of life. He is the point within faith. He is a power.

Man will say one thing and do something else; his actions are often the opposite of his words. But God's words are in complete harmony with His actions.

If a man can conduct himself in the same way that God conducts Himself; if he can open his heart so that his qualities, actions, and words are all in harmony; if he can perform his actions and duties as God does, without attachment or differences between the I and the you, or separations between races, colors, and religions; if he can do God's duty with peace and tranquility—if man can do all that, then the beauty of the heart and the light of wisdom will come into him. That beauty and light will show in his face.

In that state, the power of God will arise within man, and when it does, he will perform the duty of God perfectly. He will not harm any creation in the world or kill any life at all. He will not hurt a single heart. He will regard all lives as his own life and realize the hunger of others as his own hunger. He will dedicate his life to performing duty to all other lives. There will no longer be any difference between his actions and his words; they will be one. Such a man will know the power of God within him as the light of wisdom within wisdom.

God is a power, and that power can be seen within you. But if the power of His qualities, actions, and duty does not exist within you, then God will not be seen in you, nor will you see God. Even if you spend millions of years meditating in the jungle or thousands of years praying and meditating in a church or a mosque, you will not see God until you bring His qualities into your behavior, until His actions are your actions.

A man who can attain that high state of perfection will become a representative of God, and it is through his qualities, actions, and duty that God's qualities, actions, and duty can be seen and understood. God has no other form. His actions are His form. When man acts with His goodness and His compassion, God can be seen. He works within good conduct, good behavior, and peacefulness. He can be seen within a man who trusts Him and praises Him. He can be seen within a man who has His duties, His actions, and His beautiful, peaceful qualities of compassion and patience. When this state functions within a man, God can be seen.

God is the power of those qualities. That is what is called God.

What is your second question?

STUDENT: What is this Fellowship?

BAWA MUHAIYADDEEN: The word fellowship sounds like the Tamil words *pelai,* which means fault, and *sūpi* which means to suck. The baby mind sucks at the faults and desires in the heart of man as if they were milk. It likes all things which are evil.

The Fellowship is here to tell that baby mind:

Correct yourself.
Correct your faults.
Bring peace to your heart.
Destroy your arrogance and show love and compassion.
Destroy the karma to which you are connected.
Destroy your own hunger and erase the hunger of others.
Cut away your selfishness and help all lives.
Do not earn wages for your own good; dedicate your
    life to the good of others.
Do not live by taking the property of others;
    show them the way to live in contentment and equality.
Come to a state of peace.

God has given His kingdom to all His creations so that each one can live in contentment. All the animals in the jungle and the creatures in the ocean are contented; the birds of the air are contented; and even the sun, the moon, and the stars live contentedly in the sky. Man alone has lost his contentment because of his selfishness, his desires, his greed, his arrogance and pride, his trickery and treachery, and the differences he sees between the I and the you.

To man, who is never satisfied, the Fellowship says, "All other lives live happily, O man. Why can't you? God has given you a kingdom of freedom. Realize that in His kingdom everyone lives contentedly. O man, why do you destroy the contentment of others? Learn to live in contentment. Give up your jealousy, ignorance, and selfishness. Act with the qualities of God. Imbibe wisdom and live like a man. Show the compassion of God to all lives, so that they can exist as one life, in contentment and unity. Live in the state of God's peacefulness, the state of love, compassion, freedom, and equality. Resolve to live in this state. Then the place where you live can be changed into heaven, into the kingdom of God.

The Fellowship says, "O mankind, understand this. We are human beings, are we not? Man is the noblest of God's creations. But you have abandoned your human face, preferring to show instead the face of a dog, a donkey, or a snake. Sometimes you even turn your face into that of a demon or a ghost. You put on the masks of tigers, lions, elephants, bears, vultures, monkeys, and eagles. You put on the masks of four hundred trillion, ten thousand animals. Don't you know that each one of these is out to kill the other? Why are you fond of these masks? You wear them in your heart as well as on your face.

"O man, you were born beautiful. God gave you such a beautiful face. And of all hearts, God gave you the most beautiful. He endowed you with seven kinds of wisdom. Animals were given only three levels of wisdom—feeling, awareness, and intellect. But God gave you four more levels—judgment, subtle wisdom, divine analytic wisdom, and divine luminous wisdom. And God gave you a connection to Him. He placed His kingdom within you and placed you within His kingdom. Your life is within Him, and He lives within you as your life. Your secret is within God and God's secret is within you.

"O man, you should be a representative, a king, and a friend to all lives. God gave you special abilities so that you could protect others, but having received such power, what have you done? You have abandoned your true state and your beauty and have taken on the faces of animals and demons, preferring these to your human face. You have forgotten the beauty of God and the beauty of man and have lost the qualities of God and the qualities of man. You have uprooted the truth of God and the truth of man. You have lost the abilities God gave you.

"O man, try to understand this. Try to change into a true human being and try to live in that way, serving all lives. Let your actions fit your words. Let your speech be put into action in the form of duty. Let your outer behavior match your inner qualities. With those qualities you can rule the kingdom of God and show others how to live in that kingdom in equality, peace, and tranquility. That is a life of freedom. Realize this, O man."

The Fellowship teaches so many things. It explains what a life of human freedom is. It shows the way to realize the faults of man and to avoid them. It teaches and illustrates the qualities of God. That is the function of the Fellowship.

STUDENT: What is marriage according to the law of God, and what is the life of a married man and a married woman?

BAWA MUHAIYADDEEN: When dogs marry, the whole world knows about it. When elephants marry, the entire jungle is informed by the sounds of their trumpeting. The marriage of cattle or goats is known to all because of the noises they make. The marriage of a snake is made apparent by the way it jumps, rolls around, and hisses. And no one can sleep when a cat marries, because it howls all night long. All the marriages of the animal world are made public by the sounds and actions which accompany them.

But the marriage between a man and a woman should be recognized by the consideration and love they show each other. Their sex life should remain private and should be performed with good conduct. Marriage is a unity in which a man and a woman are joined together as one, heart to heart. Their hearts are one, their love is one, and their qualities are one. They should live together in happy unity.

If two people conduct themselves like this, it is a true marriage. When the wife grows old or when she has any physical or mental illness, the husband must continue to have the same love for her and perform the same duties as he did when she was young and well. Until she dies, he must maintain that duty, that unity, and that love. And the wife must care for her husband in the same way.

If both husband and wife can lead a life of love, good conduct, good qualities, and good thoughts as long as they both live, it will be a good marriage. They must share in profit and in loss, in suffering and in happiness. The sadness and joy of one should be the sadness and joy of the other. Although they have two bodies, they must have only one life. Although they have two minds, they must have but one heart.

If such unity can be established, that is marriage. But if that state is not correctly established, the marriage will be like an animal marriage.

⟨∾⟩∾⟨∾⟩∾⟨

STUDENT: Is there a devil? What is the devil, or satan?

BAWA MUHAIYADDEEN: Yes, there is. There is not just one satan, there are many. One who ignores the qualities of God and tries to ruin another person is satan. Murder is an act of satan. Trying to destroy someone's life and livelihood is an act of satan. All evil thoughts are satanic. All the bad qualities, all the evil qualities, all the qualities of the monkey mind, all the qualities of the snake and the rat, all the animal qualities are satanic. All distinctions, differences, and separations are satanic. Anything that can hurt or separate mankind is a quality of satan. Anything that creates trouble among men is a quality of satan.

Satan is darkness and ignorance and evil qualities. As we dispel the millions of evil qualities within, we will be filled with the qualities of God. Then satan will automatically leave us.

⟨∾⟩∾⟨∾⟩∾⟨

STUDENT: Can satan possess us? Can he take over our body?

BAWA MUHAIYADDEEN: Yes, satan can possess your body. The body is not connected to God; it is connected to satan, to evil qualities. The body is made of earth, fire, water, air, and ether; and satan is within those elements. Satan runs in the blood, nerves, tissues, and bones. Satan is everywhere—in our arrogance, karma, and maya, and in the mind. The mind is a baby that asks for everything, and the moment you buy it what it wants, it cries for the next thing. When it enters a shop, it will ask for everything there. These qualities of self-gratification, pride, and arrogance within the baby mind are satan.

But the body, which is connected to satan, is not the only form you have. You also have a light form, a form of peacefulness and beauty, which is connected to the qualities of God. Satan tries to possess the physical form in order to ruin the light form within.

STUDENT: Is there such a thing as an exorcism to get rid of satan?

BAWA MUHAIYADDEEN: You cannot drive off satan that way. These qualities are huge demons, jinns, and evil spirits. Exorcism will not chase them away.

STUDENT: How would you get rid of them?

BAWA MUHAIYADDEEN: Only God's qualities and wisdom can burn the evil qualities and overcome satan.

STUDENT: Thank you.

March 22, 1979

Session 4

An individual's questions about meditation.

41

Session 4

QUESTION: Could Bawa speak about meditation?

BAWA MUHAIYADDEEN: Meditating in this world is difficult. Man is capable of doing almost anything, but meditating is very difficult for him. If he realized what meditation really is, he would not meditate.

QUESTION: He would not meditate? Why not?

BAWA MUHAIYADDEEN: Because if he understood what meditation is, that in itself would be meditation.

QUESTION: Because then he is not separate from it? When you don't know you are meditating, is that when you are truly meditating?

BAWA MUHAIYADDEEN: That is correct. It is only because man does not know himself that he thinks he is meditating. He thinks he sees forms on the outside but they are really qualities and energies within himself that he has manifested externally. There are four hundred trillion, ten thousand such energies, or *shaktis,* which function within his body. He turns these *shaktis* into mantras and then calls that meditation.

Man's body is composed of the five elements of earth, fire, water, air, and ether. He also has mind and desire, the desire for earth, woman, and gold, and the sixty-four arts and sensual pleasures. Also within him are numerous animal qualities that kill and eat one another: dog qualities, eagle qualities, vulture qualities, elephant qualities, and the qualities of demons and ghosts.

These are man's inherent qualities, which he manifests on the outside as forms. Then he places his faith in them without realizing that he is worshiping his own qualities. He addresses each one he brings forth, asking it, "What do you want?" Then it asks for whatever it desires.

All of man's lecturing, discoursing, and prayers are directed to those qualities.

QUESTION: So, it is mirroring one's own consciousness rather than seeing something which is outside the self?

BAWA MUHAIYADDEEN: Yes, it is one's own qualities that are seen as though they were outside.

QUESTION: But if one looks at everything as one's own self, then everything outside is also one's self, so isn't it the same thing?

BAWA MUHAIYADDEEN: Everything that is outside is within us, and everything that is within us is also outside.

QUESTION: So what is real? That which we see outside we see only because we experience it inside. Is that also real?

BAWA MUHAIYADDEEN: The real actors are all inside; what we see outside are only scenes. The world is a stage, and everyone is acting out his own part. It is this acting that is referred to as meditation. If we will stop the acting and try to discover who we really are, then we will be able to discover God and find the connection between man and God. That is the secret: to discover our true selves. There is no meditation beyond that. One who knows his true self no longer has any desire for earth, woman, or gold. He has no desire, no selfishness, no illusion, no torpor, no religious or racial or caste differences, and no blood attachments. He sees everyone as a member of God's family. In that state he is the way God is. That is the state of true man.

Just as the sun belongs to all beings, a true man also belongs to all. God belongs to all, truth belongs to all, grace, wisdom, and justice belong to all, and God's qualities are needed by all. God's kingdom is common property, to be shared by everyone.

A true man is also common property to all beings. He has no need for meditation; that is only an act. All that remains for him is duty, and there is no selfishness in that duty. He treats all lives as his own life, regards the suffering of others as his own suffering, the hunger of others as his own hunger, the illness of others as his own illness, and the happiness of others as his own happiness.

That is the true state. To be in that state is prayer. Prayer is not merely speaking some words; it is putting those words into practice.

Everything else is an act. Meditation is also an act.

QUESTION: So then true meditation is really a state of being, rather than actions?

BAWA MUHAIYADDEEN: Neither your actions nor the state you are in are meditation.

Look at the way a dog behaves. When it snows, this dog feels cold and thinks, "Oh, it's freezing! I can't bear this cold! Tomorrow morning I must buy a blanket to cover myself." He passes the whole night with this thought. When dawn comes it is still very cold, but once the sun rises, the weather grows warmer and the snow begins to melt. After a while the sun becomes so hot that the dog cannot bear it. He runs to a tree and sits in the shade with his tongue hanging out. Then he says, "I would have wasted my money if I had bought that blanket. Look how hot it is now! I can't bear this heat! What I really need is an umbrella to protect me from the sun. I'm glad I saved my money. Tomorrow I will buy an umbrella."

The meditation we perform is like that. As soon as some difficulty arises, we start to meditate, saying, "Oh, I must solve this problem tomorrow." But the moment the situation changes and another problem comes along, we cannot bear the new difficulty, and like the dog we say, "Ah, no, no! Not a blanket! I need an umbrella!" This is the work of the mind.

An elephant gets dirty and thinks, "Oh, my legs are itching, my body is itching, and I am covered with dirt. I must take a bath." He wades into the river, draws the water up into his trunk, and showers it over his entire body. But as soon as he is completely clean, he digs into the river bottom, sucks up some mud with his trunk, and sprays it all over his body. After having washed so carefully, he covers himself with mud once again. Only then is he satisfied that his bath is finished.

Our meditation is like that elephant bath. We sit there, wash away the dirt we had, and then rub mud all over ourselves again. That is all we are doing. What we call meditation is like the antics of the dog and the elephant. It is nothing more than the work of our thoughts and our desires. That is not meditation. True meditation has only one focus.

If you want to understand meditation, you must first become a true human being. You must have God's actions and God's qualities, His compassion, His patience, tolerance, forbearance, and tranquility, the state of not hurting any other life, and the state of not killing or eating any other life. If you can establish such a state, you will become a true human being. You will see God within man and man within God. That is meditation. That is true prayer. God's qualities must be present in your actions. That is true prayer. Anything else is like the dog's way of thinking or the elephant's way of bathing.

An eagle flies way up in the sky amidst the clouds, balancing on the air currents. And yet, all the while it is poised on high, its attention is on the earth below, searching for snakes, rats, chickens, cats, and fish. The moment it spots something, it folds its wings, swoops down, snatches its prey and flies back up to a tree, where it can sit and eat its meal.

This is the way man's desires and passions cause him to behave. He looks upward, thinking he is praying or meditating, but his attention is actually focused on some intention, some thought or desire, some attachment he has, or perhaps on some illness or suffering, or on his poverty. Just as the eagle swoops down for something it wants, the moment man thinks of something he yearns for, or of some difficulty he is facing, he follows that thought, and his state of prayer is gone. Is this true prayer? No.

A vulture flies around, trying to pick up the scent of a corpse. The moment it detects that scent, the vulture traces it to the source. Then it dives down upon the carcass, tears at its flesh, and devours it. Similarly, our mind flies about searching for the scent of things we desire. As soon as it picks up the scent, it swoops down on that thing, tears it to pieces, and eats it. This is the way the mind behaves. It is like a vulture, like a dog, like an elephant, an eagle, a tiger, a lion, a monkey, a buffalo, a crocodile, a fox, a rat, a snake. The mind is like a donkey laden with burdens. Each of the four hundred trillion, ten thousand different qualities within the mind has its own particular desire. The moment that quality sees what it wants, it swoops toward it. That is not prayer.

QUESTION: Isn't there another aspect of the mind which can love God? I mean, there is a lower mind which goes after all these things, but isn't there a part of the mind which can really advise?

BAWA MUHAIYADDEEN: The mind has four hundred trillion, ten thousand veils, and each one has an energy within it that pulls at whatever it sees, just like a magnet pulls iron. If an energy sees the earth, it will pull the earth toward it. If it sees water, it will pull the water toward it. If it sees air, it will draw the air toward it. This is how the energies of the mind work.

We have to split this mind open and go beyond it, and at that point we will find seven doors which must be opened. We must cut our way through each one and go inside. Beyond all of them we will find the flower garden of the innermost heart. We have to go into that flower garden. *Āmīn.*

April 5, 1979

Session 5

How can we reach a balance between giving a child
too much exposure to the world
and overprotecting them?
49

Is there a point at which God or the spiritual teacher
will give up on someone who is on the spiritual path?
50

Session 5

LOU WILSON: How much should we subject a child to the world? Is it good to take children to places such as amusement parks? How can we reach a balance between giving a child an overdose of the world and overprotecting him?

BAWA MUHAIYADDEEN: What one learns in childhood is etched on stone. Whatever qualities are shown to a child while he is young are the qualities which will become strong when the child is older. They will be permanently recorded like an imprint on a photographic plate. All the fathers and mothers must realize this.

If you teach young children qualities that will make them good, those qualities will be impressed upon their hearts. If you impress upon them faith in God and in God's grace, if you instill in them the yearning to find God, and if you show them qualities filled with truth, then those are the things that will be impressed deeply upon their hearts. Then the children will come to see the good in your qualities and actions, and they will develop the same ones. For the rest of their lives, their wisdom will continue to grow from what was etched on stone when they were young.

But if you take young children to amusement parks, lakes, and shows, it is these things that will come back to them when they are older. Then it will be much harder to change them.

The world will always be available. No matter what you go to look at, the world is just a passing show. Sometimes the show changes, then it comes back again. It will be there later for them to look at. But unless good qualities and good conduct are impressed upon the children's hearts now, it will be difficult later to search for them and dig them up.

Therefore, while children are young you must give them good wisdom, good qualities, good thoughts, and good behavior. You must teach them tolerance and peacefulness. Chisel these qualities upon their innermost hearts. Impress them firmly. Then, later on, when they go to school, to work, or various other places, the words and the good qualities that were imprinted at the beginning will keep coming back to them. Whenever they face some kind of difficulty or danger, they will remember and think, "Trust in God. That's what my father and mother always told me."

Even if the children go astray later on, those good thoughts will return to them. It is possible that by thinking of those words they might be corrected; they might change. Whatever good they learn while they are young will be a great help to them in their later years. So what qualities should you teach them now? And what kind of wisdom should they learn? The mothers and fathers must think about this and try to teach the qualities and wisdom that will benefit them.

BILL CONNELLY: Is there a point at which God or the sheikh will give up on someone who is on the path to God?

BAWA MUHAIYADDEEN: A *kāmil sheikh,* a realized teacher, will not abandon a child. However, the child himself might give up. While the *kāmil sheikh* is climbing upward, he will say, "Hold onto my hand," but the child may let go. As they are climbing up the mountain the child will certainly feel tired, so the sheikh will say, "All right, just hold on carefully," and as he climbs he will pull the child up with him. But if the child says, "O my God, I can't climb!" he will fall. Or he might find the path too difficult and think about finding another path. Or he might be attracted to a beautiful woman or be drawn to gold, music, dancing, or something else and let go of the sheikh's hand.

While the sheikh is moving upward, the child may hear other sounds. Earth will call to him. Gold, gems, sensual pleasures, and satan will call to him. Elemental miracles, or *siddhis,* will try to attract him. Racial and religious differences will pull on him. Voices will try to divert him, saying, "I am an angel. I am Rama. I am a celestial maiden." Sounds will beckon from all four sides, promising, "I will make you a king. I will make you a great poet. I will make you a messenger of God. I will even make you God." The voices will lure him with so many promises. If the child turns toward these attractions and fascinations, he will be diverted from the path.

All the while, the sheikh will not look back. He will see what is happening and say, "Come, come, come," and he will keep on climbing. If the child doesn't turn around, if he continues to follow behind the teacher, he still may succeed in climbing, even though many other sounds are calling him. Every time the child turns this way or that to look at something, the *kāmil sheikh* will call, "Come, come, come along. Don't stop to listen to all those sounds, don't stop to look at that. Come quickly." He won't turn around to see whether or not the child is coming. He will just say, "Come, come, come." And all the while, voices will be calling from all sides, "Look at this beautiful thing. Look at my beauty. Look at me. Look at my breasts." But the sheikh will not pay attention to any of them. He will continue to say, "Come, my child." If the child is distracted by the sounds and the visions and stops to say, "Oh, what lovely beauty! Oh, what happiness! I want this, I want that," the sheikh will not wait. He will keep climbing.

Some children will resist the temptation to look around and will continue to climb behind the teacher. But even for those children, more trouble lies ahead on this slippery mountain of the mind, which is seventy thousand miles high and has seventy thousand different kinds of slipperiness.

This is the mountain that we are trying to climb now. It is a hard, black rock, so hard that no matter how much you try to break it, not even one drop of water will come out. There is no compassion at all within that rock. It is composed entirely of selfishness and the possessiveness which says, "My property. My house. My fame. My wife. My child."

As you try to climb up this mountain with the sheikh, he will say, "Hold on! Be very careful, it is extremely slippery!" And if you hold on firmly to the *kāmil sheikh,* with one hand he will lift you up, and with the other hand he will lift himself. He can climb this mountain. But if you don't hold on firmly, every time you climb up one foot, you will slip back three feet. If you let go, that is your own choice, and you will fall. But as long as you are willing, the sheikh will try to lift you up as much as possible, depending upon the extent of your faith and your yearning.

The sheikh will never let go, but you might let go by your own choice. If you desire praise and some praise comes to you, at that moment you might release your grip on the sheikh's hand. Or if there is something you desire or aspire to, at that time you might let go. But it will be you, the child, who lets go, not the *kāmil sheikh*. He will never release his grip as long as you are holding on. He wants you to climb that mountain, for he knows that only if you climb all the way to the top can you talk with God directly.

So, hold on firmly at every turn, as you meet with each obstacle. Don't let go. As the sheikh lifts you and carries you upward, if your mind grows bigger and bigger, if the I expands and becomes huge with the feeling of "I am great," if others praise you and feed your vanity more and more, if your fame and titles and honors increase, if your wealth increases, and if your desires grow stronger—if your attachment or affection for all these things increases, if you become bigger, then you might let go of the sheikh's hand.

But if your mind shrinks, little by little, you will not release your hold, and it will be easy for you to climb. If you become small, he can lift you up and carry you easily. Try to become small. Then the sheikh will pull you up. That will be good.

April 8, 1979

Session 6

What is meant by the melting heart?
55

Can we learn about God's qualities by observing them in one of God's representatives?
56

Two school teachers ask about controlling children with strength versus love.
57

Session 6

QUESTION: Bawa mentioned the melting heart yesterday. What does he mean by that?

BAWA MUHAIYADDEEN: If you have the desire to eat a fruit, then you will naturally have the determination to search for one. In the same way, if you want the fruit of the innermost heart, the *qalb,* you will want to search for the place where that fruit exists. As soon as you have firm determination and certitude in wanting Allah, as soon as your heart wants that taste and has that state of faith, certitude, and determination, or *īmān,* then at that time the fruit of your heart will soften and melt.

DR. MOHAMED AJWAD MACAN-MARKAR: Will that melting state be shown outside, like weeping, tears flowing down, or anything like that?

BAWA MUHAIYADDEEN: It is possible. When the heart melts, if it is really melting, you might cry. But if the heart doesn't become soft, there will be no tears.

There are many different things that melt the heart. Sometimes when you feel very sad you might weep. Or if somebody beats you, your eyes might fill with tears. If you have a strong desire which is not fulfilled, tears might come then also. Such tears are called crocodile tears. They are created by the mind and by desire. But the tears that come from a strong desire for God are different. They come from a melting heart. When that kind of heart connection is made, everything melts. The tears that come then are entirely different.

However, when the heart is made to melt by those other desires, what happens is similar to what happens when milk is made into butter; the blades keep churning and churning until some curds float upward and form the butter. In the same way, when desires enter the mind, they churn it up and keep churning until they form butter for the mind. But when the desire that enters you is for Allah, then it is faith and wisdom that keep churning and rotating inside the grace of God, until His light is formed.

The first kind of churning takes the butter that is extracted from the mind and body and gives it to the mind. In the second kind of churning, wisdom extracts God's light from His grace, and the butter that comes from that churning is given to grace. That light, that *rahmat*, is wisdom's food. It is like that.

What else did you talk about yesterday?

DR. AJWAD: I said that we have never seen God. Bawa talks of God's qualities, but since we have never seen God, we do not know what those qualities are. The only way for us to learn is to look at Bawa as God's representative, to watch what he does, and to look at his qualities and say, "This must be what God's qualities are like."

BAWA MUHAIYADDEEN: If you observe one of God's qualities, you must take that quality into yourself. Once you absorb it, you must bring it into your actions. After it comes into your actions, you must reveal that action to others. If you can do that, it will be good. Through that action you can see God.

DR. AJWAD: We can see your love through your actions.

BAWA MUHAIYADDEEN: Not through my actions, through yours. You must take the quality of love into yourself and put it into practice. That way you will demonstrate it to the other children. In other words, you are offering it to the hearts of the others. If you do it that way, then you are putting love into action, and within that action you will see God.

DR. AJWAD: So if we wish to see that love, first we have to see it demonstrated in Bawangal's actions, and then we have to go in the reverse direction to find out what that love is. Is that correct or not?

BAWA MUHAIYADDEEN: If you see a good quality, take on that quality yourself and use it. If you see a good action, take on that action yourself and use it. You yourself must take on that quality or perform that action and then spread it among others. If you do this, you will be able to understand the resonance of Allah, and that resonance will give you the explanations you need. Then both you and the others will benefit.

But if you do not take that quality into yourself, if you do not put it into practice, then it is like writing on water with your finger. You write, but when you turn around and look again, the writing is gone. You only saw a finger, not the writing itself. Similarly, you might have observed the sheikh, but you did not see the real action, because you did not put it into practice yourself.

QUESTIONER: In several discourses Bawa mentioned how divine love can control anything, even an animal. I work as a school teacher, and I am in a position where sometimes it is my duty to control the children as I do my own child. Now I have always tried to work with them with love. But I am seeing through experience that the love that I could give, the love that is in my heart, is really not enough to control them. And when I try using force or fear or any such method, it seems to work. When I see other people who hardly seem to have love, people who just use force and strength—that really works very well.

BAWA MUHAIYADDEEN: That is all right. If the love is perfect within you, if the love that fills your heart is selfless and knows no partiality, if your whole life is filled with that love for all, then all lives will be overcome by it and bow down to you.

But if the love in your heart is based on selfishness, if it has any anger or arrogance in it, or if it is based on racial differences, then that is not true love. Whether a child shows you love or bites and hits you, your love should always be the same. If you have a compassionate love which is the same toward all, then everyone will bow in respect to you.

If you had that clear love, you would be pure. You could never become angry or hasty or impatient, and you wouldn't have the feelings of I or mine. You would not feel jealousy or revenge. When you have such things in you, that is not really love; others will not bow to that kind of love. Only when you have the perfect type of compassionate love will all lives be bound by it and obey you.

Now let us look at your young son. He cries and rolls on the ground and shouts and throws things because he does not understand. He does not have clarity of wisdom. When he cries, what do you do? You comfort him.

In the way that you comfort your child no matter what he does, you must show that same kind of love when you deal with the children at school, even though they might be shouting, howling, and fighting. Then they will be controlled by your love. But you have not shown them that kind of love.

If you beat them, what happens? Then they are controlled only by the fear of your beating, not by your love. Whatever is controlled by fear at one time can jump out at another. The moment it realizes that it can attack, it will.

Those who are controlled by love will not be like that. They will be submissive to that love, and as they grow they will continue to show respect. But if you try to control children by laws or by beating or through anger, then as they grow, those same tendencies will grow with them, and one day they will attack.

This is the difference between the two loves. Think about it and act accordingly.

QUESTION: I am a Special Education teacher. I work with children who have emotional problems and other problems. They always say, "Why do you care? Nobody else ever cared about me." At times they might not pay attention to what I say, but they will fight over who gets my affection. So when one needs more help than another, I have to deal with that. But then the other one will get angry and want to fight with me. Then a third child comes up to me, and the one that wanted to fight me will start to fight that child. So what do you do when you give your all, and it still does not seem to be enough?

BAWA MUHAIYADDEEN: For what purpose did you go to that school?

QUESTIONER: Because the children have emotional problems and learning problems.

BAWA MUHAIYADDEEN: You went there to teach. Do they have the wisdom of a teacher? If they did, they could teach you. But since they are at a lower level, they have the qualities of ignorance, playfulness, and naughtiness. They might bite or pinch or scold or cry. These are their qualities. That is why they need to learn from you.

So what must you do? You must be a supervisor, a master. And a master must have patience. If a dog has eight puppies, they bite each other trying to get at her nipples for milk. If she escapes from them and lies down somewhere else, they chase right after her and continue to bite at her. Even then the mother manages somehow or other, doesn't she?

Like that, you too must have patience and compassion. When they start pulling at you from all directions, you must be able to bear it all. That is the way a teacher must act.

QUESTIONER: I don't like to scold them. They are high school children and when I do scold them, they get so upset that they become violent. They are not supposed to have this violence in them, but they do. How should I deal with them? I am patient with them. I talk nicely to them. I go through this every day.

BAWA MUHAIYADDEEN: The times are changing. Parents themselves are not acting correctly nowadays. The children are in a degraded state because the father and mother have not brought them up properly. The parents' bad qualities have come into the children. That is why they are troublesome.

You are called a teacher because you can change those qualities and make the children peaceful through the qualities of God. Since it was through love and lust that their parents gave birth to them, it is with love and wisdom that you have to bring them up. You must be both a father and mother to them. That is the only way they can improve—through wisdom, love, and patience. That is what your job is.

April 9, 1979

Session 7

---

*A visit from members of a spiritual community,
some of whom are recovered alcoholics:*

*Bawa Muhaiyaddeen addresses the group
about our attachments which are intoxicants.*

63

Is repetitive prayer the way to remember God?

70

Session 7

BAWA MUHAIYADDEEN: My children, I give you my love. I give you the love from my heart, lots and lots of love. May God protect all of you. I am happy that you were able to come.

My brothers, my children, you have traveled a long way to come here. That is the way God brings people together in unity. May He create unity among all who are on the good path. May He unify all of us in truth. That kind of friendship is very good. If we can achieve a friendship within truth, our life will be worthwhile.

When we look at the world, we feel love for everything we see. Our mind loves all that it sees—trees, shrubs, flowers, fruits. It desires earth, fire, water, gold, the jungle, the world, and illusion. These things attract the mind. In the same way, the body is attached to hunger and searches for food to appease that hunger. The body has many other attachments and desires as well.

But there is only one desire, one attachment, which needs to be fostered—the desire for truth without selfishness. If we meet in friendship which is selfless and true, that kind of friendship will bring victory to our lives. That is the only attachment which will give us liberation. All the other things we desire or are attached to will someday turn and attack us. They are diseases which will eventually kill us.

But the attachment to God and truth is different. If the light of wisdom within us can nurture an attachment to truth and to God, who has no attachments, then the unity of that friendship will give us liberation, and we will know victory in our life.

My children, you have come here so that you may meet us and we may meet you. But only when we meet in that one place, in that station called truth—only on the day when we both form an attachment to the truth within us will we find peace and tranquility. Until then our lives will be restless, like the waves in the ocean.

I give you my love. Now, my children, please tell us the purpose of your visit. Is there anything you would like to ask?

SPOKESMAN FOR GROUP: Three of us were alcoholics and are now members of Alcoholics Anonymous. Others of our group are also attempting to turn their lives and their wills over to the will of God.

BAWA MUHAIYADDEEN: Very good. People who use brandy, wine, and other kinds of alcohol, or opium, marijuana, and other drugs become intoxicated, and their lives are destroyed by that. Other people become intoxicated by their love for land, and their lives are ruined because of that. Others drink the alcohol of arrogance and karma or the alcohol of illusion and illusory things, and they fall into that trap. Still others drink the alcohol of sex, or of gold and wealth. There are sixty-four arts, sixty-four sexual or sensual pleasures.

So many intoxicants exist, and everybody is drunk. The causes may differ, but everyone is drunk on one thing or another. They are all living in a state of torpor and hypnotic fascination. No one is living in a state of clarity except that One, my God. I have not seen anyone in this world who has not taken up one or another of these intoxicants. All are drunkards. So who can correct whom?

Only if we correct and reform ourselves and develop the wisdom to realize what we are can we help those we care about. We do need to give them love and teach them the meaning of love, the meaning of wisdom, and the meaning of faith in God, but we can only do that if we have these things within ourselves. We cannot thrust them upon others; they have to develop from within. Only then will the light of wisdom shine in them.

This is not something we can do for another person. Each individual must look at the difficulties and troubles that he has undergone and realize what profit and loss they have brought him. Each one must understand this for himself and then free himself from that state of intoxication. That is the only way his state can truly be changed. I cannot change others, nor can you.

Within each one of us there is a connection to God. We must understand what that connection means and perform our duty in the same way God does, without selfishness, attachment, or partiality. We must have the compassion which sees no difference between the I and the you. We must be filled with the compassionate qualities of

God, who creates all lives and dwells equally among them, protecting, nourishing, and permeating each and every life.

If we can eliminate the evil qualities of envy, falsehood, treachery, deceit, trickery, bigotry, fanaticism, and arrogance; if we can end the discrimination against black, white, or yellow, the differences between the I and the you, the discrimination between my religion and your religion or my caste and your caste, dispelling all these evil actions and qualities from us and replacing them with the fullness of compassion and love; if we can drop the battle sword we hold within our hearts and abolish the atomic bombs of arrogance that are capable of killing other lives; if we can lay down all the weapons that our minds harbor and all the weapons that the religions hold onto, and then stand with empty hands upraised and hearts surrendered to God, saying, "My God, there is nothing that happens through my efforts or my actions. It is all Your will. There is nothing that I can achieve or do"; if we can put an end to all the wars we are waging and serve God in the way that He serves, without partiality or favor, loving all lives as much as we love our own; if we can treat the hunger of others as our own hunger, the suffering of others as our own suffering, and the illnesses of others as our own; if we can treat the hearts and bodies of others as we would treat our own; if we can develop that kind of feeling and awareness within and dedicate ourselves equally to all lives, high or low, always doing duty without showing favoritism; if we can open our hearts in this way and always perform our duty impartially, as God does; if we can eliminate all evils and surrender our hearts to Him and our lives in loving service to others—only then will that love create a clarity within all the lives that we touch. If we can be in such a state, always doing the duty and service of God, that will be very good.

This must not be simply a matter of words. That is not enough. These qualities must permeate our actions and change our behavior. And even beyond that, these qualities must be found within our duty, and we must perform that duty with the compassion which can penetrate all other lives. If we can serve in that way, then our duty will become the duty of God. However, first we must open our hearts and come to that state ourselves. Then the work becomes very, very easy.

Let me tell you a story. A crazy man and a drunkard were sitting under a tree, and off to one side sat a wise man who had realized God. Now, to any onlooker, all three men appeared to be in the same state, for they were all blabbering away. Crowds began to gather around to watch the fun. They looked at the three men and said, "Oh, look at these lunatics blabbering away!"

After a while, the man who was drunk got up. Muttering to himself, he swayed and tottered down the road, zig-zagging here and there and bashing into people like a car with no brakes. Everyone watched and said, "He's drunk. He's acting crazy!"

Then the crazy man got up. As he walked along the road, he stooped to pick up a scrap of paper, looked at it, smiled, and cried out, "Oh, the bank has sent me a check! Oh, oh, oh! This is my check! Oh! Oh! This company belongs to me!" He picked up each scrap of paper he saw, turned it around, and pretended to read it. Then he smiled with glee and exclaimed, "Oh, this is mine! This belongs to me!"

Next the realized sage stood up. He had not walked far when he saw a dry leaf lying on the road. He picked it up, looked at it, and sadly nodded his head, murmuring, "Oh, what a shame. Mmmmm, look what has happened to you." He shrugged his shoulders and gazed upward, raising his hands to the heavens. "What is the use of all this?" he asked. And as he looked around at other things, he kept repeating, "Oh, what is the use of all this?"

Since the wise man was making the same gestures as the other two, he appeared to be just like them. So the people looking on thought that all three men were crazy. The first one muttered to himself and bumped into people as he stumbled down the road. The second one picked up scraps of paper, talked to the air, and waved his hands about. The third one talked to a leaf and kept looking at the sky and gesturing. But what was really behind each one's actions? The drunkard was desperately in love with a girl and had a very unhappy family life, so he had turned to alcohol as an escape. The second man had a mania for possessions and wealth, so every scrap of paper reminded him of money and banks. Because of this one burning desire which tormented his mind day and night, he eventually became crazy.

The third one, the sage, loved only God. He kept wondering,

"What is the use of this world?" Even a dry leaf made him pause and reflect. "How beautiful you were when you first came! What a lovely green color you had. We looked up at you and were fascinated by the glossy shine on your surface. But after a while your nature began changing and your color turned to yellow, then to brown, and finally you became all shriveled and dried up. Now we look down on the ground and see you lying there dead. Soon you will be fertilizer for the earth. This is the world. The same thing is bound to happen to everything in the world. You are a creation of God, and every creation suffers the same fate. Everything that is born grows, then propagates, and finally ends up like you. How beautiful a child looks when he is first created. How beautiful his baby sounds are. And he is so lovable when he goes off to school. But after he has finished studying, how arrogant his actions become! O leaf, everything changes, just as you have changed. Even man's state changes. What a wonder! This is the fate of everyone and everything."

And in his realized state, the wise man looked up to the heavens and declared, "God is the only One who is not bound by that condition. He is the only One who does not suffer change. Everything else, every created thing, has to change. The only thing that was never created is that One, that mysterious Power. That will never change."

To the world, all three looked crazy, but behind the actions of each was a different inner meaning. The world looks only at the outside, but God is the One who looks within and knows.

Similarly, all the preaching we do and the advice or wisdom we offer, all the religions, scriptures, doctrines, and philosophies we adhere to, and all the different books we read might appear to be alike. You may look at a book and say, "This says the same thing that all the others say." But there are differences deep within, in the thoughts that lie behind each statement. The real meaning is known only to God.

Prayers, preaching, philosophies, and all the things that we learn might look alike to the world. Wise men, drunkards, and crazy people may appear the same on the surface. So may truth. But the only one who will be able to tell the difference is one who has reached the stage where he really knows the truth. Only one who is in the station of God can see the difference. We have to reflect on this.

Anybody can pray and worship, anybody can go to a church or a mosque, and anybody can study and preach. They will all look the same from the outside. But if we could look within, we would see that each one had different thoughts, even though they led to the same kind of actions. The difference lies hidden within the state of each individual. When the world looks at them, it sees them as the same, but when God looks, He knows the difference.

My love to all of you.

QUESTIONER: We are people who have been released from one kind of intoxicant. I have been sober for thirty-three years, but we still have trouble with these other intoxications.

BAWA MUHAIYADDEEN: Everyone here has used some kind of intoxicant. Some have used LSD, marijuana, or alcohol, while some were intoxicated by sex, and some were hippies. There is not one person here who has not been involved in one thing or another. About five thousand or more people have come here, and they have all been in that state, every one of them. Now they are married and they have jobs. Those who had run away from their parents have made peace with them and are living happily, serving their parents, serving God, and taking care of themselves. Each one of them was in that state for a long time, but over the past seven or eight years, they have gradually reformed and are now living like human beings. So don't worry too much. We all have to clear ourselves.

There are ninety-six different types of crazinesses and obsessions. If we overcome one obsession it does not mean that we are clear, because another will come along and capture us. We may struggle hard to overcome that one, and then along comes still another. At one time we are obsessed with sex, after that we become obsessed with our children, and when we overcome that, we become obsessed with our jobs. Next the obsession for wealth overtakes us, and when we overcome that, we become obsessed with buying a house. Whenever we think we have succeeded, another obsession will appear.

There are ninety-six such obsessions, and before we are through with them all, we are dead. It is impossible to completely rid ourselves of them. Until the obsession for God eclipses all others, until we can clear our own hearts, we will not be free. Unless we surrender to God, unless we experience the state of true surrender, we will never be rid of these obsessions. We will never be free. People may say, "I got over this, I got over that," but inside they are still crazy with these obsessions.

When an elephant goes to the river, it goes with the idea of washing itself. But after it finishes bathing, it digs into the river bottom, then sucks the mud up into its trunk, squirts it all over its body, and throws it at the other elephants. So they all end up covered with mud. A buffalo also goes to bathe and comes out muddy. The elephants and buffaloes think they are clean, but can you really call that a bath?

We are exactly like that. We wash off the dirt we carry with us, but right away we pick up the same dirt and cover ourselves all over again. To say we have bathed is easy, but that kind of bathing will never work. It is within that we must make ourselves clear.

QUESTIONER: Even if you find some freedom, it is very easy to be retrapped continually, every day.

BAWA MUHAIYADDEEN: That is why we must become clear within.

When a seed sprouts, it needs contact with the earth. It needs earth, fire, water, air, and ether to grow. Even though the seed is tiny, a whole tree is contained within it—branches, leaves, flowers, ripe and unripe fruits, and even the taste and color of the fruits. But after a while, what happens to the fruits? They fall to the ground, because they too have that connection to the earth. One seed gives rise to many fruits, yet all the fruits and seeds must eventually fall back to the earth.

In the same way, as long as we maintain our connection to earth, as long as we are connected to our desires, as long as we have attachments to the state which is governed by hunger, disease, aging, and death—those attachments will ultimately pull us down. No matter how high we throw a stone into the air, it must come down. No matter how much we have studied or prayed, no matter how much we have tried to rise above the earth, no matter how much wisdom we preach or how high we fly in the air, that connection to the earth will finally bring us down again. Only when all those connections are severed will we no longer come back down to the earth.

QUESTIONER: That's our problem. Every day, down we come.

BAWA MUHAIYADDEEN: May God protect you. Until you pluck out the roots, the tree will continue to grow, shooting out new branches and leaves. Only if you pluck the roots out at the bottom will the tree shrivel and dry up.

I give you my love, much love from the depth of my heart.

QUESTION: My problem is in remembering God. Is repetitive prayer the way? Praying without ceasing?

BAWA MUHAIYADDEEN: Look at the ocean: the waves roll without ceasing. But do they know peace? No, because of their constant movement they can find no tranquility or rest. At one time, the wind will blow from the west and push the water toward the east. Later, the wind will shift to the north and push the water in that direction. The wind is constantly causing the currents to move in four different directions, pushing the water to a place where there is less water. High tide follows low tide. The ebb and flow of the tides never ceases. The ocean interacts with the five elements of earth, fire, water, air, and ether, which are always moving and changing. Thus it is kept in constant motion. Does the ocean acquire any peace from this? No.

So, what is the point of saying the same thing (mantra) over and over unceasingly? How can that help? We have to know the one thing called truth; we must know that still point. And once we have found the point of truth, we must die within it. Our faith and certitude must surrender and die within that truth. We must make our selves die. Our desire for earth, woman, and gold; our selfishness, anger, hastiness, and sin; our connection to hunger, disease, and old age must die and leave us. All these thoughts must die. And when there is only one point left, then we must die within that point.

In that state you will not hear anything. If someone taps you on the shoulder and says, "Hello, hello!" you will not hear it. Even if someone shouts at you, you will not hear it, because you will be in that state of one-pointedness. Everything else will have died within you.

An electric current cannot flow through dry wood. But the current of illusion will flow through you and pull you in different directions if you have all these thoughts in your mind. Only if you become an inert log of wood will these worldly things stop affecting you. At that point, the breath is speaking to the breath, the soul is speaking to the soul, light is speaking to light, wisdom is speaking to wisdom, and grace is speaking to grace. Only in that state will you achieve peace. All the meditations, mantras, and book knowledge in the world are of no use at all.

You must learn wisdom. You must learn the truth. You must search for the story of God. It can be found everywhere. His wonders can be seen everywhere. He is not contained within a form. He has no house or property. He was not born and He will not die. He is a power, the power which controls all the other powers we can think of. He is the only power that can create, and then protect and sustain what He has created. We must learn the wisdom which teaches His qualities, the wisdom of truth and of divine knowledge. This is what we must seek. If we can gain that wisdom, then we will attain peace and tranquility.

My love to all my children. May God bless you with His mercy and compassion.

Āmīn.

April 11, 1979 A.M.

Session 8

I'm out of work and need direction in my life.
75

*Please explain about the battles that
surrounded Prophet Muhammad ﷺ.*
76

How do I remove doubt from my life?
80

Why does our faith waver?
81

How can we know if we have spiritually progressed?
82

How can I stop being afraid of loneliness?
84

*Are parents responsible for the karma and
spiritual attainment of their children?*
86

Session 8

QUESTIONER: I need direction in my life.

BAWA MUHAIYADDEEN: What do you do for a living?

QUESTIONER: I'm out of work now.

BAWA MUHAIYADDEEN: You must get a job. You must earn the kind of qualities and conduct that will protect you. And you must follow the path of God. Search for that path with your innermost heart, and then you will be able to progress in the correct way. All of this is essential for you. So, find the path of truth and perform your duties as you go along that path.

God has given you eyes, ears, and legs. You are not lacking anything. Therefore, do not beg or rob or tell lies. One person never has to become a slave to another. You need freedom to be able to worship God and to live your life freely. Even your body needs that freedom. So, carry on your life cultivating good qualities, good behavior, independence, and freedom. The one thing you must find and acquire is wisdom. Conduct yourself like that.

Is there anything else you need?

QUESTIONER: I want to try to find a job now, and I'm interested in what kind of work I should do. I want to get a construction job because of the money.

BAWA MUHAIYADDEEN: When people do not work, their strength diminishes. Their blood changes, they become obese, and their hearts grow weak. This causes diseases of the nerves, diseases of the bones, pains in the hips, and many other diseases. It also causes laziness.

There is work for us throughout our entire life. All the exercise we need comes from the work we do. There are lazy people who eat the food earned by the labor of others. Then they go out jogging for exercise. Only lazy people need to run along the road to get

75

exercise. A man who works hard doesn't have to jog, because he is always exercising his hands, his legs, and his entire body. In the course of his work the whole body gets exercise.

Don't be one of those lazy people. If you become like that, if you never do any work, then your body will fill with water, and you will get fat.

Any other questions, my children?

QUESTION: I have heard Bawa say that there is no fighting on the path to God. For some years I have had difficulty trying to understand the meaning of the wars which are said to have surrounded Prophet Muhammad (ﷺ). Could Bawa explain that for me?

BAWA MUHAIYADDEEN: Prophet Muhammad (ﷺ), the *Rasūlullah*, the Messenger of God, never fought any physical battles.* He was given the victorious sword of *īmān,* of faith in God, certitude in that faith, and the determination to reach God. This is the only sword that was given to Muhammad (ﷺ).

At the time that Prophet Muhammad (ﷺ) came into this world as the Seal of the Prophets, the people were worshiping statues and idols in a shrine called the *Ka'bah,* in Mecca, Saudi Arabia. They worshiped 330 million different idols as gods and prayed to statues of 48 thousand *rishis,* or sages. They also believed in various animal gods such as snakes, eagles, and vultures. In those days there was an idol called *kunūd,* which satan actually would enter into and cause to speak. He would also make devils and spirits speak from within various statues. So voices would actually be heard coming from them, and the people believed these acts to be miracles.

Whenever Prophet Muhammad (ﷺ) was nearby, these statues tumbled down and shattered to pieces. Still the people insisted on making more idols to worship. In the times of the earlier prophets, some of the statues had been broken. When Muhammad (ﷺ) came as

---

*For further explanation see *Islam and World Peace: Explanations of a Sufi* by M. R. Bawa Muhaiyaddeen.

the Seal of the Prophets, the moment he set foot in the *Ka'bah,* all of the statues shattered at once. In this way, God stopped the voices and satan's mouth was sealed.

Because Prophet Muhammad(ﷺ) asked the people to stop worshiping these idols and to have faith in the one God, they chased him from the land, leaving him with no place to live. They made him suffer many agonies.

Once Muhammad's(ﷺ) followers were being pursued by a huge army bent on hacking them to bits. In those days Muhammad(ﷺ) had only thirty-three followers. Originally there had been just four, then the number increased to thirty-three. How could such a small group have possibly fought against so many hostile forces? Surely that is not believable. But they never needed to defend themselves, for their enemies ended up disagreeing, fighting among themselves, and killing each other. The swords they carried with the intention of killing the Prophet(ﷺ) were turned upon themselves. Thus it was their own evil qualities that brought about their suffering and finally resulted in their death. Whatever each man did, his own actions returned to kill him. If a man took his sword in hand, that same sword killed him. This is what happened.

Throughout the ages so many have called out the name of God and then committed murder. They have robbed and told lies in the name of God, searched for wealth in the name of God, and built houses in the name of God. In their arrogance, they have prayed and then killed in the name of God. Is God at fault? Is God guilty for all these things that have been done in His name? No.

In the same way, Prophet Muhammad(ﷺ) is not guilty of all the evils committed in his name or in the name of Allah. The only war that Prophet Muhammad(ﷺ) ever fought was the war against the forces within himself. The only sword that Prophet Muhammad(ﷺ) ever used was the sword of faith, certitude, and determination, the sword of *īmān.* He never killed anyone with that sword. He used it only to kill those inner qualities of his which came to spoil and ruin him. That sword was the word of God.

One day when Prophet Muhammad(ﷺ) was resting and praying, a captain of the guard named Ikrimah approached, intending to kill him. The Prophet(ﷺ) was surrounded by twenty or twenty-one sleeping men, and his sword lay by his side. Ikrimah crept up, seized hold of that resplendent sword, and lifted it into the air. Just at that moment the Prophet (ﷺ) opened his eyes. Ikrimah warned him, "Not a sound, Muhammad! All the others are asleep. I have your sword, and I am going to slay you with it. Let's see if your magic and mesmerism and all your tricks can help you now. Let's see if that God of yours can save you. Where is that God you say is beyond imagination and cannot be seen by anyone? Go ahead, call on Him and ask Him to come and save you."

"He will come," the Prophet (ﷺ) said.

Then Captain Ikrimah raised the sword above the Prophet (ﷺ). He was about to strike but was suddenly seized by a violent trembling throughout his entire body. His hand shook so hard that the sword fell to the ground. Then the Prophet (ﷺ) picked up his sword and said to Ikrimah, "Now I am going to slay you. Why don't you call on your god? Let's see if he can save you. After all, he is close by in the *Ka'bah*, less than two hundred miles away. You asked me to call on my God, and I said, 'He will come,' even though He is far beyond what you can see. He did come, and the sword fell from your hand. But your god is close by, so go ahead and call on him to come and protect you." Then the Prophet (ﷺ) raised his sword. But Ikrimah's god did not come.

At once the captain fell at Muhammad's (ﷺ) feet. "Please protect me!" he cried. "I acted out of ignorance."

The Prophet (ﷺ) lifted him up with both hands and embraced him. "You see, there is no fight between the two of us," he said. "In the presence of God, you and I are brothers, children of the same father and mother. There is no reason for us to fight. There is only one difference between us. You picked up my sword and told me to call upon my God to save me, and He did. But when I threatened to slay you and told you to call upon your god, you ended up clinging to my feet. What is the real meaning of this? What is the real battle?

"The real battle is between wisdom and ignorance, not between you and me. The real battle is between your ignorance and the truth which is God. If you had been engaged in that inner war, then God would have come from any distance, no matter how far, to help you. Look at this sword. It is only useful in an outer battle; it is useless in the battle that is waged within. The swords you carry are the swords of the gods in the *Ka'bah,* the swords of ignorance. There is no fight between us, my brother.''

Then the captain of the guard begged Prophet Muhammad ﷺ to teach him to recite the *Kalimah,* the affirmation of faith. ''This is the path to God,'' the Prophet ﷺ told him. ''This is the path you must take. There should be no killing on the outside. All the battles must take place within us, where our real enemies are. They are the ones you must slay.''

In this way, the Prophet Muhammad ﷺ instructed the people of his time not to kill. But even after his time, people continued acting according to their own understanding of his words. They did what they interpreted as right. Can we blame God if a person uses the name of God to justify all the sins he commits for reasons of his own? It is not God's fault. God is concerned with justice, righteousness, and good qualities. That is what He is always trying to teach us. But do we listen? No, we continue to act upon the dictates of our mind and desire.

Even today, everyone is fighting. They fight for the world, for women, and for positions and titles. These are their wars. They murder, they rob, they lie, they commit every evil act imaginable. Filled with enemies inside, they bring forth those inner forces and fight them in the world. They wage wars against truth, against goodness, against love, and against good qualities and good conduct. That is the world.

And the fighting goes on. The one who has no wisdom fights outside in the world, but the one who has acquired wisdom will avoid all this outer conflict and turn inward to wage war against his own evil qualities. Instead of fighting in the world, we must reform ourselves and finish the battle within.

We must understand that on the path of the one God there is righteousness and a feeling that all lives are one's own life, that everyone's hunger is one's own hunger, and that all illnesses are one's own illnesses. On that path there is the understanding that we are all one family and that all children are as children born to us. There is only one God, and we are all His children. We must worship Him and only Him. If we realize this within ourselves, then all the fighting will stop, but as long as we do not have the clarity of wisdom to realize it, the wars will go on.

It is not easy to extract the truth from the histories we read. If you wash a cow's udder with water and pull it gently, you will get milk, but if you try to jab it with a knife or pull with force, what you will get is blood. There is no use in shouting, "What's this? I thought there was milk here, but all I got was blood!" Instead, you must realize that blood can be changed into milk. How can that be done? Through gentle actions. Once the milk comes, if you churn it, you will get butter. If you let it ferment, you will get even better butter. And if you melt the butter, you will end up with ghee.

Like this, every history has to be churned before we can extract its true meaning. We should not just look at the printed words. Every word, every meaning, must be churned within. Truth does not come forth unless we keep churning, going deep within. We can only find the sweet taste that lies within a fruit after it has evolved from a seedling to a flower to an unripe fruit, and finally to a ripe fruit with the proper color.

In the same way, you have to churn every action in order to find the wisdom which lies within. You must dig deeply within every point in order to find its true meaning. In all the learning that you do, you must not just look at the words. Many different meanings exist for each word. Go on boring deeper and deeper to find the power that lies within those words. What you will ultimately discover is that power and the light of God. The moment you see that light, all other things will vanish because they are merely forms, external manifestations of the inner meaning. Only if you churn and go within will you find that light and the source of all meaning. This is how you must come to understand divine knowledge, or *'ilm*.

RICK HACKETT: Bawa has said that you can't have any doubt in God. I find myself plagued by doubts in myself, and I do not know how to deal with them. I have doubts about my wisdom and my capacity to make decisions.

BAWA MUHAIYADDEEN: The primary problem is lack of faith in God. A man who has no faith in God cannot have faith in himself. If someone has developed faith in God, he will say, "Your will be done, O God. Whatever I do is Your action, not mine."

God is the One who is responsible for everything. When you hand over all responsibility to Him, He accepts the results, because He is the Creator, and He protects and nourishes what He has created. It is He who gave you your very life. He gave you a brain and the ability to think. He gave you eyes, ears, a mouth, hands, and legs. And He never fails to give you your food and clothing. Your father and mother may forget you, but God will perform His duty toward you without ever forgetting. He is the only One who will always remember.

If you do not have faith in God, who has done so much for you, then you cannot develop any faith whatsoever in yourself. If you do not have faith in God, then every one of your thoughts may bring danger and evil. Every thought that arises within you could kill you. This is the state that will result. But when you have faith in God, then all the responsibility becomes His. When something happens, you will have patience. If something more difficult happens, you will have inner patience. In the face of greater trouble you will feel contentment and gratitude. And for even greater trouble you will surrender totally to God, saying, *"Tawakkul 'alallāh*—There is nothing I can do; everything is Your responsibility." Finally you will give all praise to God, saying, *"Al-hamdu lillāh!"* This is true faith

At the point that you hand over all responsibility to God, that faith in Him will operate. If you have the faith that only God can do what needs to be done, then you will have peace of mind. But as long as that faith is missing, your life will be like a bit of straw tossed about in a gale.

SUSAN SOLLEDER: Why is it that our faith sometimes feels so strong and one-pointed, but at other times, when a difficulty or an illness arises, it almost disappears, or at least it seems to?

BAWA MUHAIYADDEEN: When you have faith, there will be no difficulties or troubles. But the moment you lose your faith, troubles will assail you.

When you swim in the ocean, you are bound to face certain difficulties. There will be many currents and waves and the storms and gales of satan. One wave will knock you over, another will buffet you about, and yet another will crash on your head. But still the water continues to keep you afloat. God keeps you balanced.

Yet instead of trusting that buoyancy, instead of feeling comforted by the knowledge that you are still afloat despite all the buffeting, you cry out, "Oh my God! This wave is beating me! And the wind is blowing me about!" When fear creeps into you, you lose faith in that buoyancy and stop paying attention to your balance. Then you begin to sink. Your loss of faith causes the accident or the danger. It is the cause, not the result.

❦

ROSE MARIE KJELLBERG: How can we know whether we have progressed or not?

BAWA MUHAIYADDEEN: It is easy to find out whether one has progressed. Do you have desire?

ROSE MARIE: Yes.

BAWA MUHAIYADDEEN: That means you have not progressed, you have gone backward. Do you have anger?

ROSE MARIE: Yes.

BAWA MUHAIYADDEEN: That means you have gone even further backward. Do you have envy within you? Do you feel jealous?

ROSE MARIE: I think so.

BAWA MUHAIYADDEEN: That means you are still further back. Do you and your husband quarrel?

ROSE MARIE: Not too much.

BAWA MUHAIYADDEEN: Even if you fight a little bit, that puts you a little further back. This is how you can find out whether you are progressing or not.

ROSE MARIE: That isn't very encouraging.

BAWA MUHAIYADDEEN: There is hope, so don't be discouraged. Don't worry. You must try to surmount these things. Go forward, leaving them behind.

God does not see any difference between one life and another. He permeates every life, dwelling within, as the life within that life. He sees no difference between one religion and another or between one color and another. He has no selfishness. He gives food equally to all His creations. He performs His duty, satisfying the hunger of all lives. He does not feel happy when they do right, or angry when they do wrong. He looks after and provides for all His creations, whether they commit faults or not, whether they do good or evil.

There will be a Day of Judgment, when each person will be judged according to what he has gained for himself through his own actions. God has said, "It is not My duty to judge them now. Let them do what they want. When Judgment Day comes, each one will be given what he searched for. What he receives will depend upon his state. I will give him a deed of ownership for whatever he has constructed during his lifetime."

At any moment, a man can give up everything he has and become completely free. Even though this state can be attained in one second, some people might not reach it in a thousand years. But if we can discard our attachment to earth, gold, lust, possessions, our body, and everything we have gained so far, if we can throw all this away and say, "My God!" then we can surrender to God and be liberated then and there. We can surrender to God even up to the last second before the Angel of Death comes to take us. Even at the very moment when life is about to depart, if we take that one step forward, if we turn away from all these things and go toward God, we will have won. Then God will embrace us and say, "My child!" He will not judge us before Judgment Day. After that, everything is finished, but until the Angel of Death comes, there is still time to surrender.

So do not worry. Be comforted by the thought that we still have time. During that time we have to keep moving, we have to walk, we have to run. We cannot stand still.

Now, when you set out on a journey, you may take along a heavy lunch basket. After a while you might leave behind some of the things you are carrying and say, "Oh, we don't want to be loaded down with these," but you will still hold on to your food. As you progress further, even that begins to feel heavy. "All right," you say, "let's eat some of this now and throw the rest away." But then you think, "We must at least bring the water." Soon that also becomes heavy, and you might say, "*Aiyō, aiyō,* even this water is too heavy to carry! I can't walk!" Then you discard the water to make your load still lighter. Next the coat you are wearing to protect you from the cold begins to be burdensome, and so you throw that away too. You continue walking with just a flimsy shawl over your shoulders, but soon even the shawl is too much. So you throw that off and walk on. After a while, sweat starts pouring down your face, so you have to take off your shirt and leave that behind also. Next, the shoes you are wearing to protect your feet become a nuisance, so you kick them off. Now you are walking in your socks. But even they feel like a burden, sticking, itching, and annoying you in all sorts of ways. So, you pull them off. Then the hat on your head becomes a dead weight. Because you are suffering under that weight, you get rid of it. Now all you have left is a loincloth to cover your backside. With only that small loincloth you suffer and struggle on until you reach the end of your journey. That is how it must be done. But there is still more. As you go even further wearing just the loincloth, you will cut away the attachments you have to everyone and everything.

In this way, one by one, you must discard all of the things you have acquired for yourself. This is what you must do on the journey to God. Then you will say, "Oh, now everything is gone. I have given up everything. God, you are the only One for me, the only One I need."

Then God will come and lift you up, saying, "Come, come." He will lift you up and say, "Hold My hand, I will take you." And He will take you. So do not be discouraged. You still have time. But keep walking. Do not stand still. Up until this time, you have been carrying so many dead weights, so many burdens. Only when they all have dropped away from you will God appear, saying, "Come," and take you along.

JANET AMES: For a long time I have felt a deep loneliness within me. It has always been very scary to me, so I have tried to fill it through relationships with friends or family, but none of them seem to take away that loneliness. They only seem to bring pain or disappointments. How can I stop feeling that loneliness, or stop being afraid of it?

BAWA MUHAIYADDEEN:　Let's say you go to a supermarket in order to buy a lid for a certain pot. The salesman may have stored the lids in one place and the handles in another. He might not even have the items right there, he may only have a list of the catalog numbers. So if you tell him, "I have a certain kind of pot. Can you give me a lid that matches?" it may take him some time to find the right lid. While he looks, you need to be patient. Don't be impatient and walk away, saying, "What's the mattter with him? He is taking too long. How much longer can I wait? I don't want it after all." If you leave, you will never obtain the correct lid. You have to be a little patient.

The salesman might bring five or six lids. He might even need to check the list and try ten or fifteen different lids before he finds one that fits the pot. As soon as one matches, he will say, "Ah, this one is yours. Now you can take it." Until that lid is found, the only thing you must do is wait patiently.

There is One who created you. The One who created the pot also created a lid for it. The One who created the male also created the female. They are all in this supermarket of the world. You only need to be a little patient. You must hand over all the responsibility to God and wait patiently, just as you have to wait when you ask the salesman to fetch a lid for your pot. When the time comes, you will get the right lid. But if you become impatient and ask the security guard to fetch a lid for you, or if you ask the supermarket manager's wife, or someone else's wife or child, you will be wasting your time. How can they bring you the proper lid? They cannot. You will only feel the pain of having wasted your time.

Because you were suffering so much, you went to others and explained your state to them. But you did not get what you wanted. With each person you turned to, you wasted more time and suffered more pain.

If you hand over all responsibility to the One who is responsible and then wait patiently, it will work out. Do you understand? Good.

Be like that. Trust in God. Hand over the responsibility to God and wait patiently. Everything will come your way. Let the One who created the pot bring the right lid.

QUESTION: If a parent or parents are responsible for the physical well-being of their children, are they not responsible for the karma of their children or the spiritual attainment of their children?

BAWA MUHAIYADDEEN: A photograph of the father and mother is snapped at the time of conception. At that time, the parents might be in any form—perhaps a dog or snake form, perhaps a monkey, crane, horse, or donkey form. While they are in that state, a photograph is taken of all their qualities. When the film is developed, all of their qualities and actions can be seen on it. That photograph becomes the child.

Your child then comes into this world of hell and grows on milk which is made from your blood. Your blood, your qualities, and your sounds are taken by the child as nourishment for growth. That is the way the body grows. Its awareness and intellect develop from these sources. Animals grow in the same way. This connection is called karma—that which comes from you and is imprinted within the body of the child.

You fulfilled your intentions, and just as you transmitted that karma to your child, now you must give the medicine required to transform it. If you can give your child the elixir that will change that karma, transform that seed, and get rid of bad qualities, then he will develop good qualities, good actions, wisdom, patience, inner patience, and contentment. If you can change yourself to that state and guide your children to the same state, then their karma will change.

On the other hand, if you hold onto your karma and continue feeding it to your children, they will never change. The roots will spread out and take firm hold. After that, it will be difficult to cut them away or uproot them. It is through your evil qualities that you created that karma. But your good qualities can cut away that same karma. If you transform yourself with good thoughts and good qualities, with wisdom, and with the grace of God, karma can be cut away.

Āmīn. That is all for today. Please go and have your dinner.

April 11 1979 P.M.

Session 9

Please tell us something about Judas.
91

Must we all go through a crucifixion?
94

Why did God send Jesus ⊛ to the world?
95

*Why did wise men attempt to teach wisdom
to those who would use it to cause trouble?*
96

Is it good to be married?
96

*I met a karate teacher and felt a connection to him:
is his way the right path for me?*
97

*If we haven't seen the roots of our problems,
should we keep on cutting the branches?*
99

*In my work, the recommendations I make
sometimes send people to jail.
Is that passing judgment?*
99

Should we express our anger?
100

*My philosophy is opposite to that of someone
I work with. How should I handle the situation?*
100

*When students are difficult,
what should a teacher do?*
101

Session 9

RAZINAH RAHMAN: Could Bawa tell us something about Judas?

BAWA MUHAIYADDEEN: Every one of us is a Judas. The good One is God alone. Everyone else is a Judas. Anyone who does not accept the words of Allah and the commandments of Allah is an enemy to God and a Judas. Anyone who does not take Allah's truth and act upon it is a Judas. Anyone who does not accept Allah's prophets and take their words into his heart is a Judas. Anyone who considers anything equal to Allah is a Judas. Anyone who betrays God's qualities, actions, thoughts, and conduct is a Judas. Anyone who does not have the patience, forbearance, and peacefulness of Allah is a Judas. Anyone who does not treat his neighbor the way he treats himself is a Judas. Anyone who steals the property of others through trickery or treachery and then gambles it away is a Judas. Anyone who forgets his conscience or falters and acts contrary to that conscience is a Judas. Anyone who eats flesh and drinks blood is a Judas.

Some people eat the hearts of others. Some people torture others. Some people eat the flesh and drink the blood of others. They are all Judases. Even the earth will not accept man's blood; it will always try to push it aside. The earth will absorb anything else—oil, water, or whatever is poured on it, and it will absorb blood mixed with water, but it will reject pure blood. It will not drink that. If man drinks the blood which even the earth rejects, he is a Judas.

When we reflect, we will see that those who do not follow the words of God, those who do not accept the truth or walk along the path of righteousness, those who are hypocrites, and those who live for their own selfish purposes instead of comforting others with compassion are all Judases. Those who murder truth and wisdom, those who murder the prophets, those who murder fetuses in the womb, those who murder good intentions and good behavior, those who murder *imān,* or absolute faith in God, those who murder love of God and devotion to God, those who murder the words of God and destroy God's wealth of divine knowledge known as *'ilm*—they are all in the state of Judas.

Those who, in the name of God, do business for their own benefit are also Judases. God has no relationship or connection whatsoever to earth, gold, or sensual pleasures. God is alone, and to that One belongs all wealth. He is the one Father, the compassionate One, the King above all kings. To the learned He is the One who is most learned, the One who knows all things. He directly understands the heart of each person and answers that heart directly. That is God.

Those who do not walk on the straight path of God's qualities, His actions, His conduct, and His love, those who do not trust in God, but follow their own minds and desires, those who have lost their sense of justice because of selfishness and attachments—these are the ones who really hurt God's truth. They all belong to the category of Judas.

These are the people who harmed the prophets of God. You cannot say that it was any particular race or nation. We are all the children of Adam ☺. Mankind is one family, one religion, and one race—the human race. You cannot single out the name of one group and say they did this or that. It is the individual who has gone on the wrong path who belongs to the category of Judas. If he drinks the blood which the earth has rejected and eats the flesh which even cows and goats do not eat, then he belongs to that category.

Those who do not trust God, who reject Him and try to murder Him or try to murder His prophets and His truth, can all be considered Judases. Such people are in the majority in the world today. We cannot and must not say that they belong to a particular race. If we look at this with wisdom, we will see that all mankind is one race. Jesus ☺ was a Jew, and the one who betrayed him is also said to have been Jewish, but that is only a label. There is but one race, the human race. To speak against particular religions and races, to keep on talking this way, attempting to divide man into separate groups—this kind of divisive talk only results in a lack of unity, a lack of wisdom, and a lack of the compassionate qualities of God.

Those negative qualities are the form of the evil mind of Judas. The individuals who have that evil mind are like Judas; they betray God. Anyone who betrays God and His prophets to satan is Judas. But those who do not have an evil mind, those who do not have the karmic quality of murder or the intention of harming others, those who do not have the quality of ridiculing God's words—such people are the messengers of God.

If you analyze with wisdom and with truth, you will see that there is only one human race, and all mankind belongs to it. Every child born is a child of Adam (☀), no matter which mother gives birth to him. Although a name may be given to a particular ethnic group, you cannot call men by that name. That is not correct. All men belong to the community of mankind. They may have different bodies, speak different languages, eat different foods, and behave in different ways, but they are all one life. That life is the sixth life, the light life.

Therefore, whoever has faltered or gone the wrong way can be called Judas. If we look at ourselves and reflect, we will realize how many times we have murdered, how many times we have injured and betrayed others, and how much wrong we continue to do every day. Anyone who can realize that will know who he is and whether or not he is a Judas. Anyone who examines his own heart and conscience and realizes his own state will discover who it is that betrays God or the prophets to satan. He will know who it is that creates the differences of my religion and your religion. When he examines his heart, he will realize who it is that hurts the hearts of others.

Jesus (☀) said, "Do unto your neighbors as you would do unto yourself." Anyone who can avoid hurting others will become one of those who follows God and the prophets. He will realize that all people belong to one family and that everyone's hunger is his own hunger, everyone's happiness is his own happiness, and everyone's suffering is his own suffering.

Each one of you must put down the sword you have drawn for battle. Throw away your guns and swords and remove what is in your heart. Do not keep these weapons with the intention of killing others. Remember that the other man also possesses the same weapons, and if a fight should erupt between you, the one who is weaker will die first. The one who is clever may win now, but he too is sure to suffer later. In any case, both will ultimately die.

Lay down the guns that are in your heart. If you can drop these weapons and hold fast to the patience of Allah, there will be no more fights or murders. Hold onto the weapons of inner patience, contentment, and absolute trust in God; the weapons of *sabūr, shakūr,* and *tawakkul 'alallāh.* Hold onto Allah's compassionate qualities and His tender love. Try to develop that love and carry it within your heart. Almighty God lives within the compassion of a melting heart.

Once you look within and conduct yourselves correctly, doing harm to no one, then you will become the children of God, the messengers of God, and the princes or prophets of God. Then you will be able to give tranquility and peace to all lives, and you will know a state of peacefulness within.

But those who carry weapons with them, those who betray others, those who have treachery, deceit, and revenge, and those who say, "My race, your race," are all in the state of Judas. They have the qualities of betrayal. These qualities were separated from God and the truth and were given to satan, to ghosts and demons, and to satan's other followers. Each one of us has these qualities that betray. If we want to become true human beings, we should reflect upon this and try to understand the meaning of the state of Judas.

QUESTION: I wonder if Bawa sees that we must all go through a crucifixion, as Jesus ⟨ﷺ⟩ did?

BAWA MUHAIYADDEEN: Even now you are nailed on a cross. If you look at yourself, you will realize that your body is the cross, and you have been nailed to it with the five nails of earth, fire, water, air, and ether. The nail of desire has been driven into your forehead, and the nail of the mind has been driven into your heart. And there you can see the blood pouring out.

Now you must resurrect yourself. Get up from that cross. In your present state you are living only half a life. Do not remain in a state of dying but not yet dead. Let your evil qualities die, and let the qualities of God be reborn within you. Three basic desires must die:

love for earth, love for sensual pleasures, and love for gold. When these three die, it will be like the passing of the three days, and after that you will be resurrected. You will rise up as the soul of God, having the qualities and actions of God.

QUESTION: Why did God send Jesus to the world?

BAWA MUHAIYADDEEN: God sent everyone to the world. He sent the sun, moon, and stars, the donkeys, horses, and all the other animals. He sent all of the prophets to this world, including Jesus ⊛. They came in order to understand themselves and then return to Him. Jesus ⊛ came, attained self-realization, and returned. We, too, have come for the same reason, to understand our own faults, correct them, and then return to God.

Creation is no big wonder, but there is a secret in it. We have to understand this secret of creation and then go back. We have to understand ourselves, experience whatever we must, gather together whatever we gain from those experiences, and then return.

Look at a pond. Everybody comes there to get water. There is no use in asking why elephants, rats, and cats come to the pond. Everybody needs water. The world is like that pond. It is God's work of art. And just as the animals come to the pond because they need water, we come here because we need to look at God's creations in order to understand our own qualities and actions.

When the truth is revealed, anyone with wisdom will weep. But those who have no wisdom will oppose the truth when they hear it. Those who are filled with arrogance, pride, and love for gold, wealth, and pleasure, those who love learning and worldly miracles, or *siddhis,* and those who have religious bigotry and fanaticism will not accept the truth. People with no wisdom will beat you if you disclose the truth to them. How much they beat you will depend upon the amount of truth you reveal. And finally, you will be tortured and chased away. You will not even have a place to live.

So to whom should we disclose the truth? The prophets, the wise men, and all those who chose the righteous path had to undergo much torture and suffering because they disclosed the truth to the wrong people. This was the reason for their suffering.

The small babies here are the ones who have truth in their awareness. They have not yet been caught by attachments. The world has not yet ensnared them. Until they reach the age of three or five or seven, they will smile and beam with happiness and love when wisdom is taught to them. They do not have the arrogance of the I or the arrogance of religion. That is why God is very loving toward little children. Even snakes and venomous serpents have love for them. If an infant is kicking its legs and arms and accidentally strikes a snake nearby, the snake will not bite it. Even if a child grabs the snake or puts it in his mouth, a good snake will not harm him. However, if an evil snake like us comes along, it will not discriminate in its choice of victims. It might bite anyone, even an infant, because an evil snake does not know right from wrong or good from bad.

There is no point in teaching the truth to those who have no wisdom or to those who have arrogance. If you disclose the truth to a religious bigot, he will shout, "My religion! Your religion!" and attack you. But if you preach the truth of God to one who has wisdom, tears will flow down his cheeks. The prophets and wise men preached to people who were arrogant and bigoted, and so they suffered.

DR. ART HOCHBERG: When the *gnānis,* or wise men, preached, didn't they know that the people they were preaching to had no wisdom? Did the *gnānis* make this mistake out of arrogance or because they themselves lacked wisdom?

BAWA MUHAIYADDEEN: The realized sage, or *gnāni,* is one who does not see any difference between the you and the I. (Bawa is punning in Tamil on the word *gnāni. Nan* means *I* and *nī* means *you.*) Because the *gnāni* has no blemish or fault within him, he cannot see any faults in others. To him everyone will seem equal, and in that state, he might reveal the truth to all. As a result, he could run into a lot of trouble.

NANCY SHABASON: Is it good to be married? I want to ask Bawa if he thinks it is necessary for me to marry.

BAWA MUHAIYADDEEN: Yes, marry. Married life is a great secret. There are many secrets within married life. Married life is also full of problems. You might have to climb high mountains, you might have to travel through deserts and jungles and cities, you might have to walk in the rain or journey by boat on the seas. You might even have to swim at times. Poverty and other difficulties will come. All this is what we call life, and these are the journeys you have to undertake in your life.

True marriage exists when two partners become one and journey together as one. When they travel by sea, the husband must be the boat and the wife must be the one who steers. When they climb a mountain, the wife must be the walking stick and the husband the climber. In the rain, the husband must be the umbrella and the wife the one who carries it. When they cross the desert, one must be the camel and the other must be the rider. Often the positions will have to be reversed. That is what married life is like.

In all circumstances, there should be unity between the two of you. In your actions, in your conduct, in your qualities, in your food and drink, in the duties you perform, in wealth and in poverty, in happiness and in sorrow, you must be in unity. These times must be shared by both. If you can find a husband with whom you can conduct your life in this way, that will be a true marriage.

Life is a journey that keeps taking you to different places. If a wife and husband can make that journey as one, it is very good.

QUESTION: Can I ask a question?

BAWA MUHAIYADDEEN: If you ask a question, ask one that has wisdom in it.

QUESTION: I don't know if it has wisdom or not. I would like to ask about the karate teacher I was with earlier. I felt that when I met this teacher, it was an emotional experience or something. I felt that he was my guru, my heart, or my path. Was that the right way to go?

BAWA MUHAIYADDEEN: You asked the same question the other day, didn't you? Now you bring the same question again—

karate teachers, gurus. Let God be your friend. Let Him be your guru. Let Him be your teacher. Let Him be God.

But if you want to accept whatever your mind thinks is correct, go ahead. Taste it and find out what it is like.

A man who goes to a bar will gaze at his bottle of beer and say, "Oh, my god, when I drink one glass of you, how much strength and energy you give me! When I drink another glass, I begin to dance. How strong you are! When I drink a third glass, you make me sing. Then you make me drink the fourth glass and cause me to become violent, so I start fighting and beating up others. When you make me drink the fifth glass, I start jabbering and blabbering. On the sixth and seventh glasses, you make me stagger and my head turns around and around. With the eighth glass, you make me grab at every woman that passes by. And by the time I take the ninth glass, my god, you put me to sleep.

"Can there be any god greater than you? You have done so many things for my life. Look at me. See how peacefully I sleep on the street! I have no bed and no blanket, and I have no clothes on my back. I don't even have my checkbook or my wallet, because someone came along and stole them, but I still feel peaceful. O my god, what peace you have granted me." This is what the man says at the time.

But when he wakes up and looks in his pockets, he remembers that his wallet is missing, and he cries, "O my god!" Then back he goes to the bar again.

His guru, his god, is in the bar. If you ask this person to get married and stay home with his wife, he will not accept it. He will say, "This is my true guru. This is my god. Can't you understand that?"

To such a man you can only say, "Very well, go ahead."

He will insist, "This god taught me so many lessons. He taught me strength and knowledge, he taught me how to murder, and he taught me how to grab women."

The world is like that. Everyone has his own god. The man who teaches karate is like a god to you. If that is the truth you have found, then I have to say, "All right, follow that god." But if one blood vessel gets blocked, that's the end. It's all over.

QUESTIONER: The other day Bawa said that instead of cutting only the branches of the tree as we have been doing, we should start cutting the roots. But we have not seen the roots yet. We have not been able to recognize them. He also said that if the tree becomes dried up like a block of wood, the current will not be able to pass through it.

BAWA MUHAIYADDEEN: All right. You can continue cutting off branches, because if the tree is huge and you start by cutting the roots, you might completely upset the tree and cause a lot of accidents. So cut off the branches first. It takes time, but that does not matter. Keep on cutting the branches. When only one branch remains on the tree, you can tie a rope around the trunk to support it and then start cutting the roots. It will take some time, but keep on cutting. There is no hurry. Do it gradually.

MICHAEL ABDUL MAJEED: I work in a juvenile court, and sometimes I have to send people to jail by my recommendations. Is that judgment?

BAWA MUHAIYADDEEN: You cannot pass judgment on someone, you can only say what you observe. You can say, "Now he is good," or "I haven't seen him doing anything bad." Or you can say, "Yes, he is drinking."

There is a proverb in Tamil which says, "If someone conducts himself honestly and straightforwardly, the world will consider him an enemy." But one who has murdered a thousand people will be considered a great one in the world. Because people fear him, they will praise him. Fearing that he might murder them, they will call him good. But one who is really going on the true and straight path, one who has never murdered anyone, will be considered an enemy by the majority of the world, by all those who are false. If you cling to truth, you will be an enemy to this world, which is a stage. This is how it is. So do your duty without being concerned about that. Give all responsibility to God, and then whatever comes will be God's work. Conduct your life with wisdom.

SHAMS HAHN: I work in a mental health clinic with people who have been in hospitals. My supervisor believes in anger and feels that people should express their anger. When she sees that I disagree about something, she says I have anger but am not expressing it. I cannot explain my feelings about anger to her in a way she can understand. I really don't know how to deal with her. She believes that people should express their anger, so she makes them get angry. She thinks that something is the matter with me because I do not express anger when I disagree with her.

BAWA MUHAIYADDEEN: Tell her that both of you are correct. Say to her, "When you show anger, then I should try not to show anger. When I show anger, you should not. One person must look after the patients with love and try to comfort them, while the other person can certainly bring out their anger and then try to correct it. However, if both do the same thing, no mental patients will come to the clinic."

MARQUITA CLARKE: I also work in a mental institution, and I am having a problem with the doctor who runs the unit. She finds it hard to get along with me, because although I am the head nurse, I am not the bossy type, the kind that gives a lot of orders without understanding what is going on. So she gets very angry. I don't return the anger, I just walk off, because I know eventually she is going to shout and scream.

BAWA MUHAIYADDEEN: Tell the doctor, "Those who have no wisdom and those who have destroyed their brains come to this hospital. Since they have no wisdom and since they are living here, we must be like parents who have given birth to children without wisdom. We have accepted responsibility for the problems that their parents failed to treat or cure. We have taken on a responsibility which even their parents refused to take. Therefore, we need to show even greater love and peacefulness than parents would. We have accepted the responsibility of being like parents who are prepared to dedicate their entire lives to their children. So, rather than showing them anger, we must show them love. Only then will they reach clarity and feel comfort."

Tell the doctor, "Love will comfort the patients as well as ourselves. If we are angry when we are trying to help mentally ill patients, their illness will only grow worse. First their fear must leave them. Because of things that happened to them when they were young, they live in fear and anxiety that these things will happen again. And that fear and anxiety are worse than the illness itself. So, we must treat them in such a way that their fear will disappear. Then we must feed them with compassion so that their awareness can awaken. Within that awareness, they can try to find love and learn to show that love to us. Once they have that love, we can treat them with love and that treatment will cure them."

Tell her, "We both must be like parents who are prepared to make sacrifices in order to see that the children's lives are corrected. Even though you are a doctor and have learned a great deal, it is still important to show the qualities you would exercise in safeguarding a child."

Tell her that you had these qualities even when you were young and that is why you show kindness now. And ask her to forgive you if there is a fault in you. Tell her, "You are a very learned person, a great person. Please forgive me." You can also mention that a few years ago you met someone with great love and devotion for God, who told you that mental patients should be treated with compassion and love. If she insists in knowing his name, then say, "It was Bawa Muhaiyaddeen who told me this, and his advice penetrated my heart."

JEENET LAWTON: Does this also apply to high school teenagers?

BAWA MUHAIYADDEEN: This is for the treatment of mental patients, not for high school students.

JEENET: Then how should we treat thirty teenagers? When I try to be loving and patient, they walk all over me. They laugh at me, they have no respect, and they don't do the work. But when I am strict (and it is very hard for me to be that way), they rebel and get angry and nasty. So I don't know what to do. When high school students resist learning and act playful, what should a teacher do?

BAWA MUHAIYADDEEN: If the one who is getting a haircut sits properly, then the barber will cut his hair correctly. So, first of all, as soon as you enter the class you must pray to God for two minutes. Your intention must be toward God. Say to your students, "Everyone please stand up and pray to God within your hearts." That should be the first thing you do. You, too, should stand up and pray to God. After that, preach to them about something. For about five minutes, speak some loving words on a particular subject.

Tell them, "I have been teaching you for some time. My very precious children, you are the students and I am the teacher. Unity and harmony must exist between a teacher and her pupils. God and His children must also live in unity. And our hearts must be in unity with truth. We should establish this state of unity in our hearts and within our love. This is necessary for our lives. We should conduct our entire lives in unity.

"Children, you must have faith in your teacher. Only then will you develop understanding and knowledge from the lessons she teaches you. The teaching and the learning must blend together, and so must our minds and our wisdom and our love. Once such a relationship is established, it will bring us victory.

"Next, let us think about our lives. Whatever efforts we make now while we are young will become an integral part of our lives. If we develop good qualities now, they will become a permanent part of us, even in times to come. If we develop wisdom from the start, that wisdom will never leave us.

"Your school days, these days of learning will pass by very quickly. The time is short. We are born, and we spend the first year or two with our mother. At that age, we do not have much understanding. In the years from three to five, we become playful. We like to play with toys, and we also begin to learn a few letters and words. Then we enter school. During those years from the age of five when we begin our studies until the age of eighteen when we finish high school, we must obtain most of the knowledge we will need for our lives. But this is also a time when many accidents can happen to us. Some of these accidents come from associating with certain friends, others result from our desires or our youthful games. Such things may interfere with our studies and interrupt the progress of our lives.

"Therefore, you must change your playful ways. You must

acquire knowledge and learn the qualities of wisdom during these years. You must complete the work and fulfill the purpose for which you entered school. This period of schooling lasts for only a short time, but it will give direction to your lives and be helpful to you for the rest of your days. If you are not successful, if you do not strive hard to learn good qualities, and if you fail to learn your lessons properly, then your whole life will be a disaster, full of sorrow and difficulties. It is during these young and formative years that you must progress rapidly and learn the qualities of compassion, patience, tolerance, and peacefulness. You have to strive and learn your lessons the hard way.

"Even if the teacher has certain qualities that are difficult for you to deal with, still it is good to go to him and try to gain clarity about the lessons. You must try to show interest and learn more from him. Only then will your life end in success. Do not waste your school years. After you have graduated from high school, you will have many years in which to play, but now is not the time for that. This is a very important period. It is the time for learning lessons, so do not waste it.

"During these high school years you have so much wealth in your hands—the wealth of wisdom, the wealth of learning, the wealth of life, and the wealth of good qualities. This is the proper time to gain those treasures. They will be the wealth for your future. Once you get your diploma, you will find it to be helpful throughout your life. What you do now is an indication of what you will do in the future, of whether you will succeed or fail. It all depends upon your performance during this short period of time. Understand this well and act correctly. This will help you to achieve victory in your life."

Every day you should talk to the children like this. Start with a prayer, and then teach them good qualities and a certain amount of wisdom. If you do this, you will find that your students will be more subdued and they will start listening to you.

JEENET: I can say all those things except the prayer. That is against the law.

BAWA MUHAIYADDEEN: All right, even if you are not able to speak about God, speak about good qualities.

April 13, 1979

Session 10

At the time of death, what happens to the soul and to the body?

107

Session 10

DR. MOHAMED AJWAD MACAN-MARKAR: What happens to the soul and the body at the time of death?

BAWA MUHAIYADDEEN: There are three periods in man's life when there is a certain beauty displayed on his face: when he is a child, during adolescence, and at the time of death. At each of these three times there is beauty.

DR. AJWAD: How can there be beauty after the soul leaves the body?

BAWA MUHAIYADDEEN: How do you know that the soul has left? Did you ever see it when it was within the body? You did not see the soul within the body, you did not see it leave, nor can you see it now. So how could you see the soul at death? Have you ever seen it?

DR. AJWAD: No, I haven't.

BAWA MUHAIYADDEEN: The soul will be where it has to be. At present it is doing a job and working, but after death the soul rests—until the body is taken to the grave. The state after death is like the state that results from receiving anesthesia. Between the time you die and the time of burial, it is as if you inhaled chloroform. The eyes can see everything, the ears can hear everything, and the mouth knows what to say, but the tongue is not able to speak. Everything is perceived and understood. All the secrets are known within, but the breath has ceased. You can see all the people around you, those who are crying, those who are laughing, and those who are eating and drinking. You can see everyone shouting, drinking, and dancing. You know all this because your awareness, intellect, and wisdom are still functioning. You know everything that is going on, but the corpse is not able to speak or move, nor can the eyes blink.

While you are lying there, your awareness will make you say, *"Aiyō!* I am a crazy fool. Now look at all this. These demons have been deceiving me." And wisdom will say, "You fool! You gave up God for the sake of your relatives and blood ties. Look, just look at the state of this lifeless corpse, lying there like a block of wood. Look at the state you have come to. Look at these donkeys. See how they jump, sing, and dance? See them all eating and drinking? Look at the way the corpse is lying there, and look at the way the donkeys are jumping. This is what you believed in, isn't it?" Wisdom will come and talk to you this way.

From the time of death until the body is taken to the grave, wisdom will point out each thing, one by one, saying, "Look at this." It will show you everything that has happened from the time of your birth until the day you were given this anesthesia. The record of your entire life history will be shown to you: what wrong you did, what justice you showed, what you hoarded, what you looked at, what you stole, all your comings and goings, how you scolded someone unnecessarily, and every word you said. Even the times you said one thing on the outside but meant something else inside—all of that has been recorded. Every expression, all your facial grimaces, rolling your eyes, twisting your head to catch a look at someone, sitting around and whispering certain things and making faces—it all has been recorded on the reels of your life. Nothing has been left out.

All the while, wisdom will be pinching you and saying, "Now look. See what you did that time?" And those reels will run until the body goes to the grave. Whether it be for one day or several days, the reels will run over and over again. You will be lying there totally immobile, looking upward toward the sky, watching those reels. But inside, floods of tears will be shed.

Those reels will show your entire life history without missing even one point. They will serve as evidence of all the dances and dramas you performed on the stage of your life. Your entire history will be revealed to you, and you will not be able to utter one word in reply. You will not be able to speak a single word of protest, for your mouth will be closed and your breath and speech will be stopped. As long as that anesthesia lasts, whatever the two witnessing angels on your shoulders have recorded will be revealed. You will not be able to deny anything, because the proof will be there before you. You will know yourself, you will know your good and bad actions, you will know everything. You will see your destiny.

If you have absolute faith, certitude, and determination that such a state will indeed come, and if you really understand this state through wisdom, then you will be fearful of the judgment that you will be given according to the proof shown on those reels.

What I am saying is the truth. If one understands this truth, then he will give up his religious differences and racial differences. He will give up all of these differences and focus on that one point of God.

DR. AJWAD: After the corpse is buried and the last man walks seven strides from the grave, then what happens?

BAWA MUHAIYADDEEN: Once your body is in the grave, the effect of that anesthesia is removed. Then God will say, "Arise!" and then the questions will be asked: "What did you do? What work have you done?" This inquiry will take place in the grave. You will be placed alone in a single room and will be questioned. After the questioning is over, a judgment will be given to you. This is your *qiyāmah,* your last day. Until the day of your final judgment, you will experience awareness in this room, all alone. If you have done good deeds, then you will be rewarded. But if your actions have been evil, then you will be punished by being burnt in fire, beaten with sticks, or by other means.

The effect of the anesthesia having been removed, the portions that belong to earth go back to earth. The *rūh,* the soul, belongs to the universe of the souls. But your mind and desire become the spirit of the elements, the *rūhānī,* and since that spirit body is within your physical body, it belongs to the earth. Look at the way fire contains heat. Heat is the energy, the essence, within the fire. Without that heat, fire belongs to the earth. Or look at the way coolness exists within water. Without that coolness, water belongs to the earth. And gas, or vapor, is the force within air. Without that, air belongs to the earth.

Similarly, within the body, which is a form made of earth, there is something that has no form, the *rūhānī,* which exists as a shadow. It is like a vapor. That essence is what reveals the form. Thus there are two aspects intermingled in the body. The physical form is the one that works and eats and goes in search of what we desire in the conscious world. This form, like the fire, can be seen, but the other (the *rūhānī*) like the heat, cannot be seen. In our dreams, when we see ourselves, it is not our physical form that we see; it is another form, the form which is awakened on the Day of Reckoning by the command, *"Kun!* Be! Arise!"

What prays and worships is yet another form, the light form, the form of wisdom, the *rūh*. It is not actually a form, it is a power. When the physical form and the shadow form are destroyed, that power is what surrenders to God and unites with Him. *Āmīn.*

April 20, 1979

Session 11

How will the sound of God be heard within us?
113

*What is the meaning of "A man of wisdom
will know all three time periods"?*
113

*How can a disciple overcome the fear
of relinquishing his own learning?*
119

*A friend was mugged twice.
What can you advise her?*
125

How can we cleanse our lives?
127

*How can we tell whether it is wisdom or
the illusory mind that is leading us?*
128

Were you ever in our state?
129

How can I overcome fear?
130

Session 11

DR. GANESAN: Last night Rajes asked, "When God speaks from within, how will that sound be heard?" Then this morning, Michael Green asked, "What is the meaning when someone says that a *gnāna guru,* a man of great wisdom, knows about all three times or periods?" Now that everyone has gathered here, Bawa wishes to answer both of these questions.

BAWA MUHAIYADDEEN: God is not something that is in a form. He does not take any form or shape. God does not conform to any concept of our mind, such as a religion, a color, a caste, or a race. He is not a form of fire or water or air. He is not like the jinns or fairies or angels, nor is He anything like the various idols that people create. He has no connection at all to thoughts or miracles or sorcery or occult powers or any such things.

What is called God is a power, a power with neither beginning nor end, neither birth nor death. God is a vast, magnificent power that is beyond *āthi* and *anāthi,* beyond the beginning and the end, a power that transcends all the *vēdas* and *vēdāntas,* all the religions and scriptures. It is a power that remains in the realm of peace and tranquility at all times. It is the purest power that exists in all of creation. It is the original, natural power. All other things are created, the things that move and the things that do not move, the things that speak and the things that do not speak.

This power called God exists beyond all the seven *shaktis,* or energies, of earth, fire, water, air, ether, mind, and desire, beyond all miracles and energies, beyond all creations and the seeds of those creations. It knows and understands all of these things and controls them. It keeps all creations within itself and also mingles within them, manifesting itself within trees, flowers, shrubs, sun, moon, stars, animals, and man. The grace of that power lies concealed within everything, looking on, providing the food for everything.

People call this power countless millions of names. Depending upon each person's understanding, depending upon the level of his intellect and the amount of wisdom he has, he will have a certain name for God and perform certain prayers. God is not hurt when man calls Him by the name of a particular energy or *shakti*. He does not get angry. He remains tranquil at all times. Whether a person wants Him or not, God remains in a state of peace and tranquility, performing equally for every one of His creations the three duties of creating, protecting, and sustaining. With endless forbearance He tolerates all the faults of those He protects and sustains.

Such a power is called God. That power has no form of its own; it is the life that moves within all creations. Out of all colors that we see, the most beautiful, natural color is God's color. God is the beauty beyond all beauties, the beauty greater than all the beauties of nature or created things. God is the most distilled essence of all beauty, the life of all that we call nature, the life that is most pure.

God is such a beautiful power, a power beyond all that we know. That power permeates and dwells within everything, functioning beyond the highest attained wisdom, beyond the wisdom of liberation, beyond the wisdom of *gnānam*. That power stands shining beyond all of these. That power and that grace dwell as the wisdom within wisdom within everything created. It is that power we call God.

Such a power cannot be seen by the eyes, it can only be seen by the eye of wisdom. It can be known and recognized only by the wisdom of truth. But to one who has no wisdom, it remains unknown. To one who follows mind and desire, it will seem as though God dwells somewhere unknown. But once true wisdom dawns and shines within a person, then the place where God dwells will be known to him.

What is called God is One. God is only One. He is without beginning, without birth, and without death. There is nothing equal to Him, nothing comparable to Him. He has no roots, no seed, no form. And yet there is no place where He is not. He permeates everything, showing no differences and not discriminating against anything.

If one acquires that same nature, if he dies within God, loses himself, and disappears within that Power, then such a person can be called His *'abd,* His slave, His representative, His messenger. Once he merges with God, then only God exists. How does he merge with that Power? His body is God's, his life is God's grace, and his resplendence is God's power. The heart of this slave becomes resplendent, and within that resplendence is the soul and God's grace. This is the connection with God.

If a person can form this connection, then all the different energies are cut away from him, all thoughts are cut away, all the qualities of selfishness, anger, sin, impatience, hatred, treachery, and cunning—all the artificial things, the things which have been grafted on, are cut away. All of his differences are cut away: the differences between the I and the you, the differences of color, religion, race, and philosophies. All these are cut away, and his state is changed.

And in that changed state, his sound, his thoughts, and his intentions become that power. His remembrance of God, his prayers, worship, *'ibādat, dhikr,* and *fikr* become that power. His looks, speech, laughter, and taste become that power. His peacefulness, his potentiality, and his happiness become that power. Everything turns toward the peace and tranquility of that power.

There is no distance between God and the one who develops that power, because where God is, the slave is, and where the slave is, God is. The slave is hidden within God and God is hidden within him, just as the fragrance is hidden within a flower. Although the flower remains a flower, its fragrance, its beauty, is God. And although a man who reaches this state may continue to live as a man and keep the form of a man, his innermost heart and God will be one. His body will be like a tree on which the flower of his heart blooms. The flower and God will be hidden within each other, and in that place the speech of God will be heard. All of God's intentions will be told there. The three periods of *awwal, dunyā,* and *ākhirah,* of the beginning, this world, and the hereafter will be explained there within the heart. What has happened, what is happening now, and what is yet to happen—all this will be heard there. All of God's words will come there, all of His actions and qualities and good and virtuous thoughts will come there. The words and sounds that come will be those of God, because His power and His grace are connected to that heart.

If this connection between God and the heart does not exist, and if a person prays while he is in a state built out of his own thoughts and intentions or while he is in a state influenced by various *shaktis,* or by the four hundred trillion, ten thousand miracles, or by the sun, moon, and stars, or by the fire, water, or air of his mind, then he will not merge with God. Instead he will be far away from God, and his prayer will be a prayer to something that has form.

It is only by merging with that which has no form that man can really lose himself. Only in a state in which there is no mind, no desire, no discrimination, no differences of race or religion, no I or you—only when none of the four hundred trillion, ten thousand differences exist can he merge with God. Only at that station will God's grace come. That slave of God will have no titles, because at that stage all titles, all fame, all glory, and all praise will belong to God. All actions will be the actions of God. All behavior and conduct will be the behavior and conduct of God. All wealth, all grace, all qualities will belong to God. Every look, every word, and every sound will belong to God. He will have handed over all his intentions, everything. This slave, this one who has lost himself, will have nothing.

And then God, the One of limitless grace and incomparable wealth, will give everything to him. From then on he will only be explaining and demonstrating the grace and praise of God. He will be one with God. It is only through such a slave that sounds will come which contain the explanations of all three times: the beginning, this world, and the hereafter. That power will explain all the sounds from all times.

My children, if we want to merge with a sheikh who is a slave of God, what must we do? We must have perfect faith in him. We must have a relationship which allows us to merge with him in the same way that he has merged with God. Just as all his desires died within God, our thoughts and desires must die within that slave of God. Just as his heart merged with God, we must place our heart within the heart of that slave and merge with it. We must place our words within his words and our intentions within his intentions. At that stage, the two will become one—one life, one heart, one thought, one intention, one prayer, and one worship. Then we will be in a state where we can see the One.

In that state, how will the sound of God be experienced? Just as the voice of God comes through the slave after his own sound disappears, in the same way, when you reach that state, all the histories connected with God and all the explanations of God will come through you.

If you can merge with the sheikh or *sayyid,* your teacher, then just as your cells and energies merge in your awareness, just as your perception knows and your awareness understands, just as your judgment and intellect know and your subtle wisdom knows and understands, just as your divine analytic wisdom discriminates and analyzes and your divine luminous wisdom reveals things to you—in the same way, all of the thoughts that come to the sheikh will be known by you. All of the sounds and all of the speech that come to him will be known by you. Whatever happens to him will permeate your body. The same awareness, the same thoughts, intentions, prayers, and worship, the same qualities and actions, and the same peace and tranquility and wisdom will come through you, because now the two of you are connected. Even though the bodies may be separate, the two hearts become one, the intentions and prayers become one. Just as all seven states of consciousness (feeling, awareness, intellect, judgment, wisdom, divine analytic wisdom, divine luminous wisdom) merge and operate within you—in the same way, his qualities merge with yours, and your qualities merge with his.

Then, whatever your sheikh is thinking, you will know immediately, and whatever you think, he will know. The two thoughts will become one. Whatever he seeks, you will know and will do that immediately, and whatever you ask, he will know and the reply will come at once. He will know what you are saying inside and will comfort you in the same instant. He will know what you intend and yearn for, and you will know whatever he intends. His intentions will then become your duty and your actions. Thus the service you perform will come directly from the knowledge of God. You will do things knowing what they are. All of your actions will arise from the knowledge of God's thoughts.

This is how you establish a connection to the sheikh, who has a connection to God. Your sheikh must permeate you, in order that your thoughts, intentions, actions, and prayer will all become one with his. That is the true state of *imān,* the state of absolute faith, certitude, and determination. When you establish this state, all these become connected with one another. Just as your own perception and awareness operate within you, his words must fill you. Just as the sheikh has died within God, your heart and all of your intentions must die within the sheikh. You must have a heart of light and the completeness of wisdom. In that state you exist as his body. You and the sheikh merge. The two lights become one, and they both merge with the effulgent light that is God. All three lights merge into one. That is what is called the Triple Flame. You must develop the faith, certitude, and determination needed to establish this state.

This is the way to establish that connection to the sheikh. This is the true connection. A few moments ago I was thinking I needed some air and immediately someone picked up the fan and fanned me. Sometimes I think I need water, and at that very moment some child will bring me water. Or I may think, "Where is this child? I have not seen this child for a long time," and that child will come. In this way, a thought can immediately bring somebody. This is the connection. This is the way every connection is established. If I think, "Where is this child? He has not done this," I will then find him doing it. He will suddenly think, "Oh I forgot!" and he will do it. That is unity. When the teacher thinks about something, his very thought will go and caution the child, and the child will start to do it. Such is that power, that connection. Where there is faith, that thought will go and ring like a telephone and the child will come immediately. This sort of connection is a true connection.

If we are in that correct state, then the connection will be there and those sounds will be heard, but as long as we are not in the right state, the bell will not ring. No matter how many thoughts and intentions you have in your mind, and no matter how much you say, the bell will not ring. Some people come and request, "Look after my baby. Look after my child. Look after my grandchildren." But if no connection has been established, the bell will not ring. Only if there is a connection will the plea be heard.

DR. AJWAD: So there has to be a connection with you, Bawa, is that what it means?

BAWA MUHAIYADDEEN: Only if we have that connection will such a state exist. That is why it is said, "Find a sheikh and learn through him." This is not a thing that can be found in writings or books, in philosophies or religions, or in jungles; it lies far beyond all these things. It is something very subtle within the cage of the body. Only when you understand this subtlety can you establish a connection. Otherwise you will never receive it. You must try to establish a connection in the place which is connected with that Power. You must try to dig a spring and lay it open. Allah has placed His history there within you as a secret, a most subtle, mysterious secret.

QUESTION: How can a disciple overcome the fear of giving up his own learning, his own book, and accept the sheikh's book?

BAWA MUHAIYADDEEN: You have gone swimming, haven't you? When you go to Atlantic City, on the way there you may wear a jacket, shirt, tie, and trousers. But when you get to the beach, you remove them and wear a bathing suit, don't you? To swim in the ocean you have to take off those clothes and put them aside, and you don't put them on again until after you have finished swimming. In the same way, if you want to establish a connection with God, you have to remove all the learning of the world. To merge with God, you must remove all the trappings and cleanse yourself. That is how you can make your heart clean—by bathing, by immersing yourself in the water of His grace. Then when you return to the world, you may once again put on the uniform of the world, the suit and tie, if you like. But while you are bathing in His grace, you must give yourself completely to Him. Do you understand?

Once there was a man who had twelve children and many, many relatives. He was as rich as the lord of a kingdom, but in spite of all his wealth, he had many duties and obligations. He had to educate his twelve children and look after his wife, his relatives, and the many people who came to see him. His many thoughts and worries would not let him sleep. He had to give so much money here and collect so much there. Sometimes he had to deposit money in the bank to gather interest, while at other times he had to withdraw money. Because he was filled with these concerns, he had no peace by day or by night. His whole life was full of worry and difficulty. He was always writing something in this book or that book, working on an account here or an account there.

All of his days went by like this. After a while he began to think, "I have no peace." He went to see several doctors, but still he could not sleep. A few doctors even came to his house, but nothing seemed to help him. And although he took more and more medicine, his worrying only grew worse.

Now, this man had three close friends that he thought might help him. "I have no peace," he complained to them. "What am I to do? I cannot find any peace, no matter what I do. On top of everything else, now my eyes are burning. Is there any salvation for me?"

"You seem to have a great worry in your mind," his friends told him. "If you could find a good sheikh and establish a connection with him, then perhaps you could ask him to help you. You might be able to sleep in peace then."

"Is that so? And where do you find such a sheikh?" he asked.

"We must search until we find a really good one for you," they said.

So his friends brought one sheikh after another, but not one could cure him. The man still had the same worries as before. In fact, they became worse. He thought, "What can I do? I still have no peace. I'm suffering more than ever."

Finally they found someone like me, a fool like me. Why do I call myself a fool? Because I keep saying, "You must give up this, you must give up that, you must drop this. You must give up your thoughts, you must give up your intentions." Little by little, I tell you to give up one thing, then another. At first I may speak gently and then a little more firmly. "You must give up blood ties; you must give up earth, sensual pleasures, and gold; you must give up the desires of your mind."

Now, this sheikh treated the sick man the same way. And after some time passed, the man began to wonder, "What is he trying to tell me? He must be some kind of idiot with a one-track mind. He tells me to give up hunger, give up desire, and give up my food. How can I give up these things?"

"Try giving them up little by little," the sheikh told him. "You will feel comforted after a while. Go slowly, little by little."

The man thought some more about the sheikh's advice. "What he says is very different from what the others said. It's true that since I met him I do feel a certain amount of comfort, but I still have my worries and I still can't sleep." So he told the sheikh, "I can't forget about this thing called love or give up the attachment to my wife and children. That is still difficult."

"Don't be in a hurry. Proceed gradually," the sheikh repeated.

Thus, little by little, the sheikh continued to sharpen the knife for him. Each time the man came to him he sharpened the knife some more and gave it back, saying, "Try cutting this, try cutting a little more." So the man kept slicing, whittling away a little at a time. But still many things remained.

Finally the man decided, "I can't do this if I stay here. I must go and hunt for a secluded place. Only then can I find peace."

"Perfectly true," the sheikh replied. "Why go here and there? Come with me. Come where I am going. Let us go together to the same place."

"Oh yes, I'll get ready and come with you."

"Now make sure you throw everything away. If you need anything, perhaps we can get it there," said the sheikh. "Come along."

And so they started their journey. As they were walking along, the man grew hungry; he was panting from hunger. "What is troubling you?" the sheikh asked.

"I don't know," said the man. "I don't seem to be aware of anything. I feel as if I'm going to faint."

Just then the sheikh saw an old lady and asked her for some food. She told him she had nothing to offer except yesterday's porridge. "Do you have a little something to go with it?" the sheikh asked.

"Well I have two fried chilies," the old woman said.

"Good, we'll take those."

"And I have some old buttermilk, a bit of salt, and a little lemon pickle."

So the sheikh mixed all of these together. Then he plucked two large leaves from a tree and made them into a cup. "Now drink this," he said and poured the mixture into the cup. The man drank it eagerly. The pot was quite full, and so the sheikh kept pouring cup after cup, and the man kept gulping it down.

Finally the man looked up and said, "I am fifty-five years old, and in my entire life I have never tasted anything as delicious as this." He drank so much that his stomach grew quite large and he felt very tired. It was now three o'clock in the afternoon.

"All right, lie down until you get over your fatigue," the sheikh said.

The man slept and slept. He did not wake up until eight o'clock the next morning. "Ah, are you finished sleeping now?" asked the sheikh.

"O swami, O my sheikh, I have never had such a refreshing sleep, not in my entire life. I have never known such comfort!" he exclaimed joyously.

"Is that so?" replied the sheikh. "Do you feel refreshed and well now? All right then, come along. Let's go."

The sheikh then took him along to join the other disciples. He gave them all some work to do and told the man to join the others for prayer and worship.

Twelve years passed in this way. Then one day the man asked, "Oh sheikh, where is my gnānam? I still haven't received wisdom." His problem was that each time he tried to pray, he would start thinking, "I left so much money for my children, so much for my wife, and so much for my mother. I wonder whether they divided the money according to my wishes. I don't know whether they are actually sharing the money and giving to charity, or taking it all for themselves. I can't stop wondering what happened to that money." As soon as he sat down to pray, all these thoughts would come into his mind. He kept wondering whether he should have given more detailed instructions. "My money must be gone by now," was the one thought in his mind whenever he went to pray.

So although he had come a long way, he still had no peace. That old connection was still there. True enough he had given up everything else, but this one worry was still with him, and he was unable to control it. The sheikh had told him, "Cut this away, cut that away. Don't you have the knife? Bring it here." But even after twelve years, he had not been able to erase what had been written indelibly earlier.

And so he finally came to the guru and said, "O sheikh, I still have not attained a state of peace.''

"Did you bring your book of accounts here, your ledger book?'' the sheikh asked. "Why don't you give that book to me? If you want peace, hand it over to me. I will send it to the Accountant, and each one will get whatever he should get. Then you will have peace and tranquility. But as long as you cling to that book you will never have peace. For twelve years now you have been doing the same accounting in your mind, and as long as this old book is inside of you, as long as you are doing your old accounting job, you cannot go on to a new job. You have to hand that book over to me. Until you do, your mind will never know peace, and you will never sleep comfortably.

"Your problem is that these accounts have become energies implanted within your body. They are the energies of maya, or illusion. They are diseases that will finally kill you. As long as you nurture these *shaktis,* or energies, they will continue to devour you from within. Like viruses, they are within your very essence, sucking your blood. So how can you find any tranquility? How can you sleep in peace? Throw this book away. Only then can you know peace and be happy, comfortable, and relaxed.'' This is what the sheikh told him.

"O my sheikh, it is true,'' the man agreed. "I left instructions for each individual to get a certain amount of money, but I keep worrying whether one person may have grabbed another person's share. I can't stop worrying about it. That is why I am so unhappy.''

Then the sheikh told him, "When you started this journey you packed your hunger. For the sake of your hunger, you brought some rice. For the rice, you packed some curries. For the curries, you brought a container of drinking water. For all this, you built a bathroom. Then you acquired bedding and shirts and coats. You also brought along some money for your journey. You packed medicines for your health. Next you built a house to live in. You gathered all this torpor, this fascination. You have gathered together so many things into a huge bundle. Look at how much you have brought! You have enough with you to lead you to your death and your birth. Yet you are searching for medicine that will help you in this world and the next.

"How can you say, 'I want peace,' when you are carrying such a load? If you had dropped this bundle before you came here, then within three months you would have known comfort.

"A pregnant woman will become aware of her pregnancy at about three months. By that time the signs of pregnancy are evident. Day by day the baby grows until finally it is born. Now, if you had given up this burden when you first came, then within three months of your arrival here you would have become aware of a seed of light within your heart. Then, after ten years that light would have been perfected and complete. And at the end of twelve years you would have become a light. You would have disappeared and become a resplendent light.

"But since you held onto this bundle, the seed did not germinate and grow. You have been carrying this big burden around with you instead of trying to nurture the seed properly. Even though you were with the sheikh, you did not make that effort. Now you must take your accounting book and all those burdens and throw them away.

"Look at the way an ant finds what it needs. If there is sugar somewhere, the ant will find it. You do not have to tell the ant where the sugar is; he will find his own way to it. In the same way, if you had left your bundle somewhere, then all your relatives, all your friends, and all your attachments would have found their way to it by themselves and taken what they wanted. They would not have needed your permission or your instruction. So why did you need to worry? You lost the freedom of your life with all that worrying.

"So pluck it out, throw it away, and let each one take what he needs. As long as you are attached to that huge burden, you can never hope to achieve peace. Throw it away. That will put an end to your obligations."

In the same way, we too must perform our duty in every area of life, then drop it and proceed. We must maintain that connection to the One, to our goal. If we can cut each section from our mind and leave it behind, then the path will become very easy. We must think about this. As long as those thoughts and worries are within us, we will not be able to sleep and we will have no peace.

My children, it is all right to continue doing whatever your duty is until the right time comes; but meanwhile, little by little you must keep cutting the burdens away. Cut them gradually with your wisdom, and keep cutting, even if you cannot throw them all away right now. Sometimes I look at one of my children and say, "My child, you don't seem to be cutting or getting anything done. You have only succeeded in dulling the knife. Let me tell you how to use the knife. First of all, it must be sharp, so you can cut very gently. You must realize what needs to be cut and whittle away very subtly a little bit at a time. But instead, you have been trying to cut through rock with it. Then you come and complain, 'The knife is dull, it won't cut. It hurts me when I try.' If you blunt the blade by cutting away at a rock, and after that try to use it on what needs to be cut, then naturally it will only end up hurting you.

"These things are so subtle. You must use the knife when it is sharp and cut very gently. Then it will be easy. But until you realize when the knife should be used and what should be cut, there is no use telling you. Until you realize the nature of the knife as well as your own nature, both you and the knife are in trouble. So for the time being we will just say a little and wait until you yourself understand what the knife is for and how it must be used."

All right, my children. Have you understood the point? No matter what pond or lake or river we go to, and no matter what kind of net we use, all we want is the fish. No matter what book we read, it is the inner meaning, the point of wisdom and truth, that we need. No matter what story we tell it is the point, the meaning, that we must take. That is the important thing, that is the sharpness of the knife.

DAVID FREUDBERG: The children from Boston have a question. One of the children had two accidents. The first happened at about two o'clock in the afternoon, when she was walking along the street. Someone came up and stole her bag from her, and she was very shaken. The next day, again at two o'clock, in a different part of the same town, another person came up behind her and hit her over the head. Again she was upset, and although it didn't shake her faith, still, she was concerned.

BAWA MUHAIYADDEEN: Good. One snatched your bag, the other struck you on the head. This is not a big wonder. After all, you were going only in search of God, in search of that one treasure. If you go in search of that treasure in the right way, you will realize how many people inside of you are beating you up. There are so many dangers within you, so many beatings, so many people grabbing things from you, so many people biting you. Many enemies are right there inside of you.

Compared to the inner enemies, these outer matters are very trivial. If you lost your faith through worrying about these two small things, how can you overcome all the enemies within? Your faith, certitude, and strength must prevail so that you can chase away all the people on the inside. These experiences were just meant to show you what lies waiting inside. That was a tiny pat on your head, that's all.

In the Tamil epics there was a saint named Pattanathar. He was a recluse, a wandering mendicant. He would roam about the streets all day, not caring where he was going. If somebody gave him something to eat he would eat, otherwise he went hungry. But one day he went into a garden, saw some nice cucumbers, and felt a desire to eat them. So he sat down, plucked two or three, and started to eat. Immediately, the guard ran up to him shouting, "Hey, you rogue! You came and stole from my garden!" And he beat the mendicant mercilessly.

After his thrashing, Pattanathar sat down. Soon he said, "All right, now, beat some more and keep on beating. Let the one who ate the cucumber receive the blows. He is the one who asked for that cucumber. He is the one who wanted it. Beat some more! Beat some more! Let him get the beating, let him get thrashed. Go on, beat some more!"

The guard began to wonder, "What is this? The more beating he gets, the more he asks for." Then he beat him some more.

But Pattanathar just kept on shouting, "Let the one who had the desire for the cucumber get the beating. Let the one who ate it receive the blows."

So the guard continued beating until he was too tired to deliver another blow. Pattanathar's body was moaning and groaning from the pain. "Ah, are you groaning?" he said to his body. "You wanted to eat that cucumber and you did. You had that desire, didn't you? All right, now you have to groan. Now you have to accept the punishment. In the future, do not yearn for these things. Do not desire them.''

Then Pattanathar sat down under a tree. "From now on, wherever I go, I will only eat if somebody brings food to me and offers it with a melting heart. Otherwise, I will not eat," he said firmly. "If someone brings me food and does it with good feelings and a melting heart, I will eat that food of love. That will be my only food, not this food of beatings.''

In the same way all things that happen to us are the food of beatings. We must not worry about such things. Whatever comes to us is meant to correct us, to improve us. Any difficulty that befalls us is meant to help us go one step forward. As long as we have absolute certitude in God, then no matter what dangers, difficulties, troubles, or suffering come to us, they will only make us move forward. These things help us to progress, to move forward on the path.

Never forget your goal. So, if you receive a blow on your back, that is a signal for you to go forward some more. It is a sign to progress.

DAVID: This next question has to do with politics. If we can fulfill that obligation to cleanse our lives, to live without ego...

BAWA MUHAIYADDEEN: That certainly needs to be done. Have you seen how a washing machine works? You drop the clothes inside, put in the soap, and fill it with water. The machine removes the dirt, then it fills with water a second time, rinses the clothes, and finally spins the water out. After the clothes are dry, you can wear them. So the washing machine performs its duty properly, doesn't it? It washes away all the dirt and makes you look nice and clean. Does it keep any of the dirt? No, it removes it and makes you happy. Does it keep any of the pleasure you feel? No, it keeps nothing.

If you can function in the same way, it will be good. That is your duty. If a mere bit of machinery can do it, why can't we? We have so much subtle machinery within us. We have to find the appropriate machine for each need that arises and use it to get the job done.

So, get rid of all the dirt the world has put inside you. Attain some peace by throwing out those things. If you put them in the machine and get them washed, you will have peace. All the garbage that the world gave you—bring it here and drop it in the washing machine. Clear yourself of all that garbage, and then you can wear clean new clothing and look beautiful. Everything the world gives you is dirt, so it all must come here to the washing machine. The machine will wash it and return it to you nice and white. Then you can give it back to the world as clean white clothes and say, "This is the way the truth is. This is what it is like." And others can also wear that truth.

Do you know what the washing machine is?

QUESTION: How can we distinguish between the times when the sheikh is leading us through an experience in the world to show our wisdom how to cut something, and the times when the mind is just taking us through something and tricking us? How will that be shown to us inside?

BAWA MUHAIYADDEEN: When you go to bathe in a stream, you jump in and immerse yourself completely. Only after you are in the water do you know whether it is cold or warm. If it is cold you feel the chill, begin to shiver, and say, "Oh, this is too cold." But if it is warm, you realize it and say, "Ah, this is warm!" You examine the experience with your wisdom.

In the same way, you must immerse yourself within the sheikh. With your faith you must go within him and discover the point. Once you know that point, your awareness will increase, and you will know when you are within safe limits. When it is icy, you will freeze and will realize, "This is too much! I must escape!" When it is too hot, you will burn. But as long as the warmth is within limits and bearable, then stay within those limits. As long as you remain within the limits and maintain that balance, it will be good for you. Once you know what is safe, keep that balance.

Like that, use your wisdom to examine the limits that exist within every experience. Then you will be able to tell whether it is your wisdom guiding you or your mind tricking you.

Remember, I have nothing to gain from your coming here. I do not need anything from what you are receiving. If you go to a lake, does the lake want or need anything that you are carrying? No, but the things that the lake has, the water and the fish, are necessary for you. You need what the lake has, but the lake does not need anything you have.

So, wherever you go, if you find things you need, then stay in that place. But if you find that something is desired of you, if you or your possessions are wanted, then escape from that place and run for your life. If you go to a sheikh or teacher and find that he is coveting what you have, make good your escape. But if you want what is in the sheikh, then realize that this is your place, and stay as long as you still need more. Do you understand? Good.

BILL CONNELLY: Bawa, did you ever have the problems that we have? Did you ever have the same kind of thoughts and desires, or live in the same kind of situation? Were you ever in our state?

BAWA MUHAIYADDEEN: Even now I have the same problems, because all of the things you are giving to me are within me.

A bank building is made out of earth, fire, water, air, and ether. That is the body of the bank, its structure. Inside, there is a safe, but the safe does not come with money already inside it. Your money must be deposited in the safe, and later on that same money will come back to you. At one time you may deposit cash and get a receipt in return, at another time you may receive cash in return for a check.

Does the safe keep any of the money for its own use? No, it merely collects and stores whatever you give it and then returns it to you when you ask for it. The safe does not enjoy any benefits from that money. What does it gain? Only the weight of the money and the worry that a thief might come to break it open. You have just one difficulty—how to store your money, but the safe has many, many difficulties. Now, the trouble that you have brought, the amount of money you have, may be very small. But the safe must store not only your money, but all the money that everybody brings. It cannot enjoy that money; it is busy worrying about too many things.

In the same way, it is difficult for the sheikh. If he is a true sheikh, this is how it will be. He will have no peace at all, and he will have to suffer. But if he is a rogue, he will try to appropriate what belongs to you and plot ways to make use of your property.

BILL: What if you take your property to the bank and you don't want it back? What happens to it then?

BAWA MUHAIYADDEEN: If you do not want it back, the money will be passed out to those who desire it, and then there will be fewer rogues coming to trouble you. If you bring the correct things and hand them over to the sheikh, he will accept what you give him; then he will transform it and return it to you as something worthwhile. If you hand over your faith, certitude, and determination, he will accept it and transform it. If you are eligible for that transformation, then what he hands back to you will be a treasure of grace, a wealth of grace. But if you are not qualified to receive that transformation, then he will simply return what you gave. He will return the same thing back to you.

Only a true sheikh can do this.

QUESTIONER: So many experiences in the world create fears. If I remove myself from the world it is easy, but when I return to the world and want to live in it, then there is a conflict.

BAWA MUHAIYADDEEN: Are we looking at the world outside or are we looking at the world within? This is what we must reflect upon. The world is a stage, and our minds are actors on this stage. We are all just actors, and the things that we see outside are merely the scenery drawn on the backdrops. We cannot look at this stage, at these scenes, and say that this is the world. What we see outside is merely the acting of our minds. The true world, the real world, is within us. We take these scenes that we have inside of us and paint them on the outside, and then the person inside comes out to do the acting.

As long as we hold onto the inner world which our mind has made, no matter where we may hide, that same world will emerge and become the outer scenery. That inner world will exist outside. But if we can leave it, if we can escape from it, then that world and all of the acts which go with it will be destroyed. There will be no more fear after that, no fear at all. We will be in heaven.

QUESTION: How do we do that?

BAWA MUHAIYADDEEN: This is what we have been talking about, slicing away little by little, whittling away these acts. These sixty-four arts that we have learned, all our desires and our cravings, all the things that bring joy and sorrow have to be cut away little by little. If we can succeed in doing that, we need not have any more fears. If a man is not afraid of death, then he will not worry about his life. He will not mind if he dies. Then even the deep ocean will come up only to his knees; the ocean will be like a ship for him, and he will float. But a man who is frightened of death could drown in water that is only knee-deep. The very fear will kill him. This is how it is. *Āmīn.*

April 26, 1979

Session 12

*When Bawa Muhaiyaddeen talks, how can we
know what level to tune in on?*
135

Why does there have to be a day of destruction?
137

*A friend is paying us rent: How much involvement
should he have in household decisions?*
137

Where does duty for my family lie?
139

Why should anyone choose to have a child?
140

I was hurtful to my parents. Now I want forgiveness.
142

Session 12

QUESTION: When Bawa talks, how can we know what level to tune in on?

BAWA MUHAIYADDEEN: What level must you tune in on? When you come here, stay on the lowest step first. The one who does is a very clever person. If you can stay on that step, you will learn all the histories—your own history and your Father's history. Then your path will become easy and you will be able to record whatever needs to be recorded. If you stay at a level where you can understand, you will continue to understand more and more, gaining wisdom, and climbing up step by step.

But if you come here and stand on a middle step or on the highest step, you will not understand. Until you climb down to the bottom step, you will not understand anything. If I tell you some point halfway along the path, or tell you something further along than that, you will not understand. Or if I say, "This is the path." or "Stop! Close your mouth and stop!" you still will not understand. Even if I show you a sign, you will not understand. If you do not come in the correct state, you cannot understand what I tell you.

Once there was a man who wanted to escape from the place where he was without being seen by anyone. "I must get out of here," he thought. However, there were people here, people there, people all over the place, and he wondered, "How can I possibly escape?"

Now this man had brought up a monkey as a friend, and he took the monkey along with him. Not realizing that the monkey would copy everything he did, the man crouched behind a bush to hide and said, "Shh!" The monkey immediately jumped onto the branch of a fruit tree and said, "Shh!" Of course, all the people saw him. The man, however, remained hidden behind the shrub.

Hoping to scare the monkey out of the tree, the man threw a

135

stone at him. But instead of coming down, the monkey threw a fruit at the man. He threw another and still another, and in that way revealed the place where the man was hiding.

If you also take a monkey around with you, you will not be able to keep him quiet by signalling to him. A monkey does not understand such signals; he only knows how to copy what he sees or hears. If you scratch him and say, "Shh! Keep quiet!" he will only say, "Shh!" and scratch you back. If you make a face to signal him to stop, he will simply make a face back at you.

Therefore, if we want to learn wisdom or escape from this world without anyone seeing or knowing, we must not take the monkey of the mind along with us. Before even attempting to escape, we must let go of the monkey. We must let go of all the things we have learned in this world, all the things that we think we have learned, all the so-called wisdom of the world, all that we have seen, all our religions, our wars, our discriminations and differences. If we bundle up all these things and try to carry them with us on the path to God, it will be difficult.

So you must climb down to begin with. You were too high up. Test the first step and see whether it is shaky or firm, and as you climb, test each step that way. If it is firm, then keep climbing.

First you have to draw up a plan, a blueprint. But you cannot climb onto that. A blueprint is not a house. And the line that stands for the foundation is not the actual foundation. It is useless to stand on a blueprint and let your mind jump all over it saying, "This is my house, this is my hallway, this is my kitchen."

It is only an idea of a house, and you cannot live in it. It is only a picture drawn with colored ink. The paper might cost a few cents, and the pen and ink might cost a few cents more. But the real house is going to cost you lots of money. And to build it, you have to struggle and work hard. You have to calculate carefully: How should we build this house? What should we do first? How much of a foundation is needed? How deep must the foundation be? How strong must it be? Which materials will be strong enough? How much will it be able to support? You must think of the foundation from every angle. Then you have to consider how to build on that foundation. What materials will you use? Stone or rock or cement? Or would plastic, iron, or wooden planks be better?

You have to analyze every step of the way. And you must start at the bottom, building from the lowermost layer. Make sure it is strong from the very beginning. That sort of building will benefit you later.

Everything you do must be done like this. First you must learn, and then you must try to understand what you have learned. Next you must sift through your knowledge, and choose the right thing. Then you can build. That is the secret. That is wisdom. And that is how you have to learn from a *kāmil sheikh,* a true teacher.

Therefore, seek wisdom to build the house of your life. All the things you have learned from books are merely blueprints. Your mind and your desire think of all the things you have learned from these books, and they build a fortress. But it is not real, it is only built out of the clay of your mind. All your learning is like that. All the things that you learned earlier are merely paper and ink drawings, blueprints for the house of your life, which you have not yet built. To build that house you must struggle and work hard. What materials must you use? A lot of acute intellect, wisdom, and the subtle qualities of God. These are the materials you will need.

If you are willing to do that, then you can learn. But if you set out with your own plan, your own blueprint, then you cannot learn. One matchstick is enough to destroy the paper. Or if a little water falls on it, the ink will wash off. Or if you leave it lying around somewhere, termites might eat it up. Even if you hide it very carefully, a rat might come, tear it to bits, and carry off the scraps to build a house for its babies. If you think, "I must preserve this for posterity," it will be pointless, for paper decays when it reaches a certain age.

Therefore, think hard. There is a big difference between book learning and the learning that comes from true wisdom.

QUESTIONER: I do not understand why there has to be a day of destruction.

BAWA MUHAIYADDEEN: Have you not understood why? The day you understand, there will be no destruction. Anything else?

QUESTION: What is the proper role of a husband and wife toward someone living in their house? I'm speaking of a friend who is paying us rent and plans to stay for about a year. How should he help in the household, and how much should he have a say in the way things are done? Sometimes differences occur over who cooks, who cleans, who does the work in the yard, and who initiates things or makes decisions about the work. Because this person is close to us, he gets involved in our household and in decisions about conducting our household.

BAWA MUHAIYADDEEN: I will tell you something from my experience. If you go to an inn for your honeymoon, the innkeeper gives you only one room in which to enjoy your honeymoon. But if you go back to your own house, you have the freedom of an entire house in which to do as you please.

If you go to a friend's house, you will find the six evils of lust, anger, miserliness, greed, fanaticism, and envy. But if you go to the house of God, who is your true friend, you will find none of these things. God is the good friend, the friend who will save your life. He will even give His life for you. If you go to His house, you will have absolute freedom. The whole house will be yours. That is true freedom.

In your own house you have the freedom of doing what you like, but you risk losing that freedom when you take in worldly friends. Look at the way a fishing line acts when you cast it into the water. It will go on dancing and bobbing this way and that until a fish comes along and takes a bite. The line has its freedom until it is caught by the fish. Some friends are like that. Whatever they have inside of them they will drop onto the other person. That type of friend keeps casting the line of his own thoughts onto others, imposing his own thoughts and ideas on them. Another type of friend will not interfere in your affairs. He will let you do whatever you feel is right and he will look after himself. So when you say 'friend', realize that there are many different types of friends.

Therefore, conduct yourself honorably. You have a guest in your house who is paying rent. Ask your husband to tell him what things need to be done around the house. He should understand that he is free to do whatever he needs to do for himself, but that he should not promote his own ideas. He should keep them to himself. Tell him that it is difficult for you when he interferes in your work and your decisions.

Your husband must explain to him in a kind way, "I have a wife and a child, and we have our own way of running our house. If our way does not suit you, then you can look for another place. You must find a situation that suits your needs. Each of us has his own concept of freedom and independence. You should not come and interfere with our independence." Say it kindly, without any anger.

Of course, whenever his suggestions seem suitable and useful, then you can accept them. When they are not, you can say so. Whatever arises, you must always speak without anger or resentment. Try to extricate yourself from difficulties in that way.

What shall we do now?

FATIMA GESNER: I left home a long time ago, and I call occasionally, maybe once every few months. I called the other night, and after I hung up I felt bad. I did not feel any kind of attachment to my sister and my mother, but I felt an obligation, a duty, to do things for them. I am wondering where my duty for my family lies.

BAWA MUHAIYADDEEN: Duty toward parents is necessary, but now, you in turn have become a parent. The father and mother who gave birth to you are still living. If you had married at the proper time and had a daughter earlier in your life, today you might have been a grandmother. Then your parents could have seen you, your child, and your grandchild. They would have seen three generations. But that state of parenthood has come to you only now. Therefore, conduct your life with your wisdom. If children are under eighteen or twenty, you need to look after them. Do your duty toward them according to their nature and their needs.

Several times I have said that in this country, some people give birth to children and hand them over to the hospital or the church. Or they give them up for adoption, and the child is gone. That child has lost the love of the parents completely. Parental love and attachment can get cut off in many ways.

When I am speaking about these things, I am speaking generally, to everyone. You have to apply what is said to your own situation and the way you were brought up. If you were separated from your parents early, if your attachment toward them is gone, you need not think, "Oh, I heard Bawa say this once. I'd better go back and try to revive my connection to them." That was not the meaning.

You have to consider the situation you are in now and maintain the connection with your child. However, if you become aware of some difficulty or illness that your family is undergoing, then certainly you can go and help them. Do what you can at that time. Do you understand?

FATIMA: My mother belongs to a very strong religion, but she is grateful that I found Bawa. I sent her Bawa's books to read and she writes back with beautiful quotes from them. I have the desire to bring her here, but her health is not too good.

BAWA MUHAIYADDEEN: Give her whatever help you can in that direction.

FATIMA: Should I bring her? She is so engrossed in her religion that I am not sure if I should.

BAWA MUHAIYADDEEN: Even if you do not bring her here, it is your duty to make her realize that there is a God somewhere. But you cannot fashion the ship to carry her to God. Your effort should be just to help her realize that God and truth do exist. That is all you need to do. Help her to understand that. But do not set out with the idea that you might take her to God. If she herself decides, that is another matter.

STEVEN YASSKY: Most married people, out of desire and lust, bear children. And sometimes there seems to be a deep-rooted animal instinct to have children, an impulse which does not manifest itself in the mind clearly. I don't know what the reason is.

What does Bawa say we learn from having children? Before my wife and I bring a child into this world, I want to know the reason for it. Once a child is there, we enjoy it and learn from it, but that can't be the only reason to have a child. Why should anyone choose to have a child?

BAWA MUHAIYADDEEN: Why should lust come first? God

created everything. He created the nine openings in the body, including the opening through which we come into this world. Why do you want to artificially close off that particular opening? It is an open door, a natural entrance, a gate. Why do you want to block it so that you will not have children? Isn't that a fault? Instead, you have to control it.

Think about your own birth. "This is how I grew inside, this is how I was born, and this is how I yelled when I came out. Blood and fluids and odors all came out with me. What a horrible stench!"

If you fully understand your own birth, then you will have no need to bear children or to make love, because you will see that as hell. But if you have not understood it, then you must learn about it in that place. It is through that door that you come out of the womb. Right away you start nursing at your mother's breast. You kick her and bite and tug at the nipple. A connection is formed with your mother, and as you go on sucking at her breast, love develops. Later, after the attachment is gone for the one you called mother, after the thought of her has faded, you fall in love. Then a connection forms with your wife. You see the same thing you saw before, but now, instead of calling it mother, you say, "My wife, my love!" You forget that the one you made love to first was your mother. You forget your own history. You forget that all this happened earlier.

At some earlier time, I might have said to have a child so that you could remember what you have forgotten—so you could learn. By reminding yourself, you could realize what happened earlier. It is no use going against nature and blocking off that entrance to prevent birth. Do not use a net. Realize what happened earlier and teach your mind. When you start to learn about yourself, you will understand your own history and the story of your child. Then you can sing:

> Before I have reached the end of my suffering,
> Before I even found out what happened,
> Before I found out why I came here,
> Why were you born, my child?
> This world is tossing me about and tormenting me.
> My child, why did you come into this world?
> I am being tossed and rolled around in this world.
> My child, why did you come into this hell?

After your child comes, you can sing this song. But if you throw a net across the usual entrance of nature and then say, "I am making love," that is ignorance.

Even animals do not do that. They control themselves. In three or four years' time, a cow will have only five minutes of sex. That state of maya, or illusion, lasts only a few minutes. Then, from the time the calf is born until it is weaned three years later, the cow will not let a bull come near her; she will butt it away. So in all the years of a cow's life, only fifteen times does she change her state into the illusory state of the world. But within fifty years of a man's life, count the number of times that he goes into this hell of maya. How many minutes each day his mind spends there! We have to reflect on this. Goats and cattle and other animals spend much less time on illusion than man does. Is he not worse than the animals? His whole life is spent in that hell. You have to understand this. If you block the entrance and think you are free, you will never realize your story, nor will you understand the story of your child and learn from that. All right, until you realize yourself, think about it and act accordingly.

QUESTION: Bawa, in the daytime it is easy to have such wisdom, but what should we do in the nighttime?

BAWA MUHAIYADDEEN: In the daytime, because there is wisdom, you can go out in the open. But at night, if you think robbers and rogues might come in, you have to be more careful. Do you know what a loincloth is? You have to tie up your loincloth. Tie it up very tight and warn the rogue to be careful.

QUESTIONER: I can see that at times I was very hurtful in the way I acted toward my parents when I was young. Even now as an adult, I look at that, and although I know I cannot go back, sometimes I feel an urge to apologize to them somehow. I want to ask God to forgive me for what I have done, but there is also another part of me that is saying I want them to know I am sorry for the pain I caused them.

BAWA MUHAIYADDEEN: First of all, you should think, "My

God, You created me, and You are protecting me every second of my life. You gave me food, You gave me this body, You gave me speech. You gave me eyes to see, a nose to smell fragrances, and a tongue to know tastes. You gave me arms and legs to do my duty, and You gave me a heart to make me feel happy. You gave me all these things. You gave me a life of freedom. You are a friend to everyone. Your love is greater than the love of anyone else in this world. Of all the wealth I have acquired in this world, You have given me the greatest—the wealth of my soul, the wealth of my wisdom, and the wealth of *īmān,* of perfect faith and certitude. You have given me all these treasures, but I have forgotten Your kingdom and You. I have forgotten Your qualities and actions and have discarded them. I realize now that I have committed many faults toward You. May You forgive me for all that I have done to You.''

We have committed such grievous faults toward the One who has given us so much. If you can first reform yourself in this area, then everything else will become very easy. These are only small twigs and branches that have grown from that one original fault. If you correct that fault, you can correct everything else. Then His qualities and His duties will come into you.

Now bring out the apple box. Let's give the children some fruits.

April 27, 1979

Session 13

How can we escape from being food for hell?
147

What can I do in order to know myself?
149

The discrepancy between my intentions and actions affects my faith. What can I do?
150

Once when I was worried, something just popped inside me and my mind was eased—what was that?
151

Is it wrong to expect happiness?
152

Things I thought I had finished with keep returning to my mind. How can I prevent that?
152

Sometimes one needs to rush, sometimes to go slowly. How can we be consistent?
154

How can we be trusting in the company of many people?
154

Session 13

———⊶⊷———

BAWA MUHAIYADDEEN: What plans are we making to go on pretending to the world that we are something we are not? Our grandfathers, their grandfathers and their grandfathers, and so on, for generations back, all deceived the world. This is the way of the world. The pretense that one generation leaves unfinished is carried on by the next. Whatever work the grandfather fails to accomplish, the father comes to finish. The father comes to fool the grandfather. Then, to fool the father, the mother comes. And then we come along to fool the mother. After that, this world comes to fool us. The world comes to dupe the world. And recently certain spiritual fathers called gurus have come to deceive the world. How shall we set about trying to outwit these gurus who have come to deceive the world? Can you give us any suggestions?

The one-span stomach comes to trick every one of those gurus. To trick the stomach comes hunger, to trick hunger comes food, and to trick food comes hell. If you want to escape from being fooled by hell, what should you do? How can you escape? Suggest a way. Tell us please. Sandra? Sandra says she does not know. If she knew she would escape. Dr. Holler?

DR. STANFORD HOLLER: By trying very fervently to follow what is in your heart.

BAWA MUHAIYADDEEN: You must first know what is inside the heart, the right and the wrong. Everything is inside there. The mind comes to deceive man, and to fool the mind the monkey comes. Desire comes to trick that monkey, and illusion comes to trick desire. The earth comes to deceive illusion, and death comes to confound the earth. Then to outwit death, a succession of rebirths comes. Now what do we need to outwit birth? We must find out.

Everything is within us. Truth is only one, but there is the

147

duality of right and wrong. The right path is good; the wrong path is bad. We must understand them both and then choose the right path. But if you want to go on that good path, you have to ask the way from someone who knows. Don't try to go on your own. Keep asking directions. If you inquire at each point from someone who knows, and then go that way, you will be on the right path. However, if you want to go on the wrong path, you will not need to ask directions. You can just watch other people and start running that way. That will surely be the wrong path.

Do not look at the world and run behind it; do not look at a book and run the way it tells you to. Try looking at yourself and run in that direction. And before you run, try to understand your senses. Do not run after happiness and comfort; understand what sorrow is and what joy is and then walk warily. Do not believe that everything is tasty; before you eat you must know that some things are wrong, and some are bad for you. In everything, you must know the right and the wrong. Don't marvel at the things you see in the world; the world is only a small dot, a small point; look at yourself, understand yourself, and marvel at what you see there.

Do not look at others and ridicule them; look at yourself and ridicule what you see there. Do not be angry at others; be angry at your own ignorance. Do not find fault with others; look at the faults in your own actions and the faults in your life, and understand them. Neither praise nor ridicule another person's meanings and intentions. Your eyes are the sores and wounds of your life; let them see and understand who you are. Your mind is your hell. Your thoughts are the screens and veils in your life that will hide the truth from you. Your desire is your hypnotic fascination with torpor. And the joy you feel when you see something is a disease that will kill you later. Your birth will be the cause of your death.

So realize yourself and look at yourself. Split open your *qalb*, your innermost heart, and look inside. If you understand yourself, then you will discover a way, a plan. And if you know the plan, then the danger of your birth will be dispelled.

Do not close your eyes and meditate; control your eyes and control the millions of animals within your heart and then meditate. Do not close your mouth and meditate; control the many qualities that are deceiving you and then meditate. Do not worship seeking to find joy out of your sorrows; throw away both joy and sorrow and worship God from the place where no joy or sorrow exist. Do not hurt anyone else with bad words or even with your thoughts; all the animals you are bringing up within you will scold you and torment you with the very words and actions you used to hurt others. So cure yourself of that hurt inside of you. Do not become a slave to those animals within you; drive them out. Let them go where they want to go, and you go where you need to go. They must obtain their freedom from you, and you must obtain your freedom from them. At that moment you will obtain the qualities of God and understand the mystery of your birth. You will see the explanation of your own history and understand this world and the hereafter. Then you will have freedom and bliss forever. Reflect on this a little. This is the real freedom in our lives.

Are there any other questions that the children want to ask?

CATHY DIDONA: When I look within to know myself I feel confused and depressed. I want Bawa to tell me personally what I need to do in order to know myself.

BAWA MUHAIYADDEEN: If you set out to build a stone house, first you must go to a rocky mountain and blast apart the rock. To do that you need dynamite. To insert the dynamite into the rock, you have to chisel a small hole. And to make the dynamite explode, you have to light the fuse. You must go through so much trouble, sweating and struggling and working hard, in order to get stone for your house.

Each time you make a hole in the rock, it will cause pain both to the rock and to the mountain. It will also cause pain to the hammer and chisel which are striking the rock. Even the hand that is doing the beating will feel pain; and when the hand hurts, the whole body hurts.

What is the cause of all this pain? Your desire to build a house. Each step brings some kind of suffering, but once they are over and you light the fuse, everything will burst open. After that, you will be able to break the rock very easily, bit by bit. There will no longer be any pain.

In the same way, at any point in your body, there are four hundred trillion, ten thousand spiritual forces, blood-drinking demons, ghosts, vicious beasts, snakes and scorpions, bears, lions, tigers, foxes, monkeys, dogs, donkeys, horses, cows, bulls, goats, pigs, eagles, vultures, and many others—all with great energy and strength. There are many millions of energies at work within you. These *shaktis* and *siddhis,* these elemental miracles and occult powers, have built a huge rocky mountain of mind, desire, and karma, which can only be shattered by wisdom. But as soon as you strike the chisel with the hammer of wisdom, all the parts will feel pain. Mind, desire, and karma will cry out. Then what do you need? You need the strength of faith, certitude, and determination. You must hold on very firmly, for if your *īmān* is stronger than the rock, no pain will be able to afflict your body. That certitude will take away the pain and help you to crack open the rock of mind, desire, and karma. And once you succeed in blasting that, the work will become very easy.

It certainly is hard to split the rock open and it does indeed cause pain, but don't give up and run away. Use your wisdom properly. Be strong, stand firm, and continue to beat and chisel away at the rock.

QUESTIONER: There is a big discrepancy between my intentions and my actions. Sometimes this causes me to lose faith.

BAWA MUHAIYADDEEN: The reason your actions do not match your intentions is your lack of certitude. You are driving down the road, but your eyes are not on the road and your hands are not on the steering wheel. Instead, your foot is pressing harder and harder on the accelerator, and your hands are just lying idle. When you act like this, accidents are bound to happen. Your heart should direct your attention to the correct places, so that your eyes will be watching the road and your hands will be guiding the steering wheel. Then your journey will be a safe one.

But right now your sole focus of attention is on the accelerator. This attitude has been the cause of the accidents in your life. You are not going where you want to go, and yet you keep pressing the gas pedal instead of controlling the steering wheel. That is why your car is racing here and there and everywhere. That is why your life is now in this state.

If you will focus your attention in the world correctly, you can escape. First of all, use your wisdom. Deposit faith, certitude, and determination in your heart and steer your life properly. Place your intellect on the steering wheel and turn it carefully, controlling it with your wisdom. Use your feeling and awareness to control the accelerator and the brake. Your foot will be there to do the work, but all your attention and caution and wisdom will be focused on the road in front of you. Hold that steering wheel of your life properly, and you will succeed at every stage of your journey. Then your life will proceed smoothly.

SARAHAMMA ASCHENBACH: I was very worried about something for a while. Then, just as I was falling asleep, I felt something pop inside me. It was very strange. But then the worrying of my mind was eased, and I slept well and felt better. I was just wondering what that was.

BAWA MUHAIYADDEEN: Since it popped, you have had a little peace. But after two days go by, it will say "Toop!" and come back again. Then you will have a headache and depression and all sorts of things. Think about this. You must play back all the reels of your life and analyze the right and the wrong that you see there. If you analyze it properly, if you see what was wrong in your life and then find out why it went wrong at that time, then you will say, "O my God! Everything I did was wrong. I didn't go on the right path earlier, and I still haven't found it. All this time, all these years, I have been on the wrong path. This is no good for me. I must throw away all those wrong things and follow only what is right."

If you do that, then the pop and the toop will both disappear from your life, and you will learn the wisdom you need to proceed on the right path. Search for that path with certitude; seek what is right for you.

In the East we don't raise cats inside the house, so what does a cat do to survive there? It sneaks into the kitchen and steals food, then it runs over to the kitchen fireplace to defecate, and afterwards it scratches among the ashes to hide its feces. Sometimes there are still some glowing embers, so the cat gets burned and runs away howling. But after a little while it comes back to dig in the same place and gets burned again and runs again. Of course, if there are no more glowing embers, the cat can do its job, cover it up, and go away unhurt. But no matter how often it gets burned, it will keep returning to the same place, because it hasn't the awareness or the intellect to learn from its past experience.

Your cat mind is just like that. You have not learned from the suffering you have undergone in your life. You have not even thought about it. Many different reels and stories have gone by in your life, yet you still are not reflecting upon them. Just as the cat returns to the glowing embers, you are returning again and again to the same state, digging and digging in the same place. When you dig among the glowing embers, they burn you, and you run away. But then you come back again to that very spot. Discard this cat intellect which is born of ignorance and lacks awareness. Understand yourself through wisdom. If you can do that, then all this fatigue and sorrow and suffering will not affect you.

SARAHAMMA: Every time I look for any happiness in my life, I get hurt. So is it wrong to expect happiness?

BAWA MUHAIYADDEEN: You must search for happiness, but not in the way the cat does. It eats meat and drinks milk in the kitchen and immediately wants to defecate in the same place. If it went outside and dug in the sand, that would be much easier. But the cat is impatient and lazy. It likes to take a short cut, and that is the cause for its trouble. Joy for the cat is to return to the same fireplace. You also want to find your joy in the same place. You want to find it fast, you want instant happiness. That is dangerous. Understand first. Analyze and see. Or else just remain quiet. The greatest joy is to be still.

CATHERINE WEINBERG (TOPI):   I have a problem with the old reels which keep coming back again and again, even after I think I've realized what mistakes I've made. Sometimes it won't even be like my own voice speaking. Thoughts will keep coming into my mind—criticisms, judgments—different things that my father and mother taught me as a child. At times I think I have understood what was good and what was bad and that I am finished with it, but it still keeps coming back and coming back.

BAWA MUHAIYADDEEN: You learned arithmetic in school, addition and subtraction, didn't you? After you go to the supermarket, do you think that the money you have spent there is still in your bank account? Do you think those dollars are still there? That kind of calculation is not accurate. Those assets are no longer in your bank.

You spent so much in the supermarket in vain. You have to take stock, to calculate how much of your credit has been wasted. "I spent this much out of my savings, I gave this much to charity, and I spent a lot on my body." Go through your accounts and see how little you still have left in the bank. As those reels play back to you, you will say to yourself, "Look how much I have spent already! And there has been no profit at all from it. I ate and defecated, I slept and woke up. That's my only profit. The rest is gone."

All your past expenditures have been in vain. You must stop purchasing all these wrong things. From now on buy only what is right and hold on to it with certitude. Take the little bit you have left and go on the right path. Strengthen your certitude and follow the path of wisdom.

Instead of going to so many movies, look at your own movies. As you play back the reels that are within you, you will be able to analyze your entire history from the time you were born: what you did, what you thought, what you ate, how you laughed, how you smiled, where you walked, what you sought and accumulated, how you called for your mother, your grandmother, your father and grandfather, your sisters and brothers. All these stories will be seen: your love for earth, gold, and sensual pleasures; your arrogance, karma, and maya; your lust, anger, miserliness, attachment, fanaticism, envy, intoxication, murder, falsehood, and lies; the differences you feel between the I and the you, your bigotry toward castes and religions—you will see all these stories as you play back the reels. You will see the whole world. This is true for every one of us.

These reels play back our own history. If you want to see them, you must first open your wisdom and fit the reels onto the projector of the intellect. Next you have to put up the screen of *thānam, nithānam, avathānam,* and *gnānam* (surrender, balance, concentration, and wisdom). Then when you switch on the light of wisdom in the projector and play back the reels, your history will unfold.

Your own movie will appear on that screen. You will look at all the acting you did and say, "Tut, tut, tut. I cried and I laughed, I praised and ridiculed, I ate and I swallowed. What a wonder all this acting was! My act was certainly something to behold." But then you will feel sad and think, "It seems as if I am the only one witnessing my own acting. No one else wants to look at it. I was the actor, and now I am the audience. I will have to feel the joy or sorrow and do the laughing or crying. No one else is going to look at my reels." Then you will realize that all this false acting was a waste, and you will transform this world from a drama stage to a prayer stage. When you pray on that stage your prayer will be your act, and God will be watching. You and God will be watching at the same time when you pray. In that state you will pray alone.

If you want to propagate the world, you need two people, a male and a female, and if you want to carry the corpse to the cemetery, you need four people. But if you want to pray or meditate, you need only one. For true prayer or meditation there is just one. Only God can pray to God. Once you transform your qualities into God's qualities, you can leave this stage of corpses and change it into a prayer stage. All of us must reflect upon this.

QUESTION: When you have to act at different rates of speed, can you be consistent? Sometimes when you go fast it's hard to act with the same knowledge as when you go slowly. Also, how can you be trusting when you're with a lot of people?

BAWA MUHAIYADDEEN: If the needle on your speedometer is kept at the right point and left there, then the car will maintain one speed. It won't go fast at one time and slow at another. It is because you haven't kept the speedometer needle at the right point that the car is going at different rates. If you get onto a donkey, it pokes along. If you climb onto a horse, it runs fast. If you get onto a monkey, it jumps into a tree. If you climb onto a water buffalo, it lands you in the middle of a pond.

Like that, you are switching from mount to mount, and so you have differences in speed. But if you ride the right mount and hold it steady, then you will be consistent. The mounts that you are bringing up within you are not right. And even when the mount is all right, you are not right. Even when you are all right, your mind is not right. Even when your mind is all right, your heart is not right. Even when your heart is all right, your thoughts are not right. Even when your thoughts happen to be all right, your desire is not at all right. And even when your desire seems right, the control is not right. That is what is wrong. Thank you.

May 1, 1979

Session 14

How can I prevent my arrogance from
blocking my trust in God?

159

How can I overcome anxiety and sorrow
to see God's light?

161

Session 14

QUESTIONER: I have trouble with arrogance and trust. I want to have trust in God, and I want to have trust in the guru, but a wall comes up against it.

BAWA MUHAIYADDEEN: Suppose you are a manager of a company which needs to deliver a million dollars to their branch office three thousand miles away. They wrap it carefully and give it to you because they trust you. It will take you a week by train to reach the other company. During that time, what will you do to safeguard the money? You will either strap it around your stomach or hide it inside your clothes. Your complete attention will be on that parcel at all times. If you should become sleepy, will you just go to sleep? No, you will say to yourself, "They have trusted me with this package, and I must deliver it. I have to be careful not to let the money fall into the hands of thieves, or I will be called a thief. I must not allow that. They have placed their faith in me, so I have to make sure that I hand over this money and maintain my self-respect."

Therefore, if you should feel sleepy, won't you take some water, wash your face, drink some coffee, or walk a little bit? Somehow or other, because of your determination to take that property and hand it over safely, you will do whatever you can to dispel your fatigue and ward off sleep. The entire time, your heart will be beating fast and you will keep thinking, "Is a robber coming? Will some thief take it away from me?" You will be focusing your attention on that every minute.

But once you have delivered the money to the branch office, the burden will be gone. The moment they have taken charge and given you the receipt, your responsibility will be over, and the weight will be gone. Then you will say, "I feel so tired," and the six days of sleep that you missed will come over you all at once. The moment you fall on your bed, you won't know what's happening, and you will snore like a train engine. What became of sleep during those six days? You were able to hold it off, weren't you?

Now, just as that money was placed in your protection, faith in God has also been given to you in trust. If you want to seek the good thing which is God, if you want to go to Him, you must protect the faith you were given. It is the treasure which will liberate your soul. If you want to reach God, you need the same kind of determination you would show to protect the money. If you could focus so much attention and concentration on delivering something that merely belongs to the world, how much more determined you must be to protect the thing that will liberate your soul.

God has given everything to you in trust. He has given you the treasures of His kingdom, the treasures of divine wisdom, and the effulgence of the soul. You have to strengthen your faith and say, "I must keep what He gave me in trust and hand it back to Him." No matter what state you are in—whether you are sick or well or sleepy, in your prayers or whatever else you are doing, you must at all times have the determination to say, "I have to take this and deliver it safely." If someone comes to fight with you, and you become arrogant and argue back, then the other person will find out that you have a treasure and will take it from you. Or if you are talking to a man and you begin drinking with him, he will discover what you have and will steal it. So you must have inner patience, contentment, trust in God, and praise of God known as *sabūr, shakūr, tawakkul,* and *al-hamdu lillāh.* If you want to carry God's property, you must acquire these qualities.

As soon as faith develops within you, your arrogance, your karma, and your maya, or illusion, will all vanish, and you will earn respect and honor. God will know that you have placed your faith in His faith. Then He will place His certitude within your certitude. He will place His patience within your patience. He will place His contentment within your contentment. He will place His trust within your trust. He will place His praise within your praise. He will place His qualities within your qualities. That is the plenitude and the completeness called *Īmān-Islām.* It is the preface to *Īmān-Islām.*

So you must strengthen your faith in this manner. Do you understand? Do it like that. As closely as you would guard a worldly treasure, you must guard this also. Until the moment that you hand over the treasure which belongs to God, you must keep that strength of faith.

QUESTION: How can I overcome anxiety and sorrow to see God's light?

BAWA MUHAIYADDEEN: If you drop what you have within you, if you drop the burden you are carrying and place wisdom within you, there will be no burden. Wisdom is not a heavy weight. But if you remain full of the things you are holding on to and try to place wisdom inside as well, it will be too heavy.

The less wisdom you have, the heavier the burden will be; the more wisdom you have, the lighter the burden will become. As long as you don't have wisdom, you will hoard so many unnecessary things, and they will be heavy. But once you have acquired wisdom, you will realize that all these things are rejects, and you will drop them. They are meant for the trash truck. When you have dropped all of the things that you are holding inside, you will realize how light wisdom is. Wisdom, truth, grace, and God's qualities are very, very light. They are resplendent.

If you use a flashlight to look at something, you will be carrying the weight of the case, the batteries, and the bulb. But the light inside you has no weight at all. Drop your own heavy lamp, and use the resplendent light within. That light is very subtle and very easy. With that you will see what needs to be discarded, and then you can travel light. There will be no weight.

May 18, 1979

Session 15

Can you tell me who Jesus ﷺ is?
165

Why did Jesus ﷺ come?
165

Is Jesus ﷺ with us now?
167

How can we establish a direct connection to God?
167

What man can be righteous before God?
168

Why is man here?
169

Why do some people not love God?
170

Is Jesus ﷺ God?
170

Session 15

QUESTION: Can you tell me who Jesus ⒜ is?

BAWA MUHAIYADDEEN: People say he is the child of Mary ⒜. He is a representative of God, one of the many prophets that God sent down, and he is also a man and the son of Mary ⒜. That is all I can say.

QUESTION: Can you tell me what he came to say? Why was he here?

BAWA MUHAIYADDEEN: Each prophet was sent to convey the commandments of God, the laws of justice: Adam, Noah, Abraham, Ishmael, Moses, David, Jesus, Jonah, Job, Jacob, Idris, Isaac, and Muhammad, may the peace and blessing of God be upon them all. God told each one of them, ''Go! Tell the people that I exist. Tell them that there is one God and that there is a Judgment Day, and that they must live believing in God and in that Day of Inquiry. Tell them that good and evil, truth and falsehood, and heaven and hell do exist and that they must realize the difference between them.

''In the world today man has become a beast. He has transformed himself into satan. Go and instruct him. Tell him about these good things. Help him to change from an animal back into a man. Go! Change him from the form of satan into the form of a man.''

This is the reason each prophet came. They did not come to form different religions and create divisions among people. They did not come to say, ''My religion, your religion, my caste, your caste.'' The various undertakings of different religions have caused them to thrive on racial distinctions and religious bigotry and have led to fighting with others and acts of murder. God did not send His messengers to teach such things. They brought with them only words and actions based on truth. ''Do not tell lies. Love your neighbor as yourself. Realize the hunger of others as you realize your own hunger. At least share what you have with your neighbor.''

These are the actions that God teaches. Now in your experience, how many people have you seen who tell lies?

QUESTIONER: Many.

BAWA MUHAIYADDEEN: Don't any of them profess to follow some religion or doctrine?

Everyone will have to answer for himself on Judgment Day. If a person commits a fault, no matter who it is—your father, your mother, your husband, your wife, or even your own child—the day that each goes to his judgment, the good and evil that he has done will go with him. The judgment will take place between that person and God. The good and evil that each one does is his own story. It cannot be shared among others. When you are going to your judgment, you cannot say, "I will take some good from my mother, a little bit from my brother, and a little from my sister. In that way I can fill up my box." You cannot do that. Each one carries his own tape recording of whatever he has done. There are pictures and records of everything. The records of his entire life go with him, and his judgment is based upon them. He will reap the benefits of what he has done.

God is watching every breath, every thought, every step we take. He has a very keen ear, a very keen eye, and a sharp sense of smell. His speech is comforting and His heart is clear. He is able to see everything. He can look at you and see what you are doing. There is no need for a lawyer to speak for you or argue your case on Judgment Day, because everything is recorded. God is the lawyer. He is also the witness, the One who knows everything. He is the One who gives the judgment. Can anyone else judge you? Can anyone else forgive you for what you have done? No, only God can forgive you.

You must have the feeling in your heart that God is always with you, watching you every moment. Within each life God exists as a very secret part which gives power and light to that life. This secret part is a light that watches and records every thought, every intention, every word, and every action. Everything it records will go with you on Judgment Day.

Because that part is within us in our every thought and intention, we must realize what is right and what is wrong at every moment, and when we do something wrong, we must immediately ask to be forgiven. Not only must we ask for forgiveness, we must also be sure we do not repeat that same fault. Not doing it again is asking for forgiveness and being forgiven.

Now, you are going to school to study nursing aren't you? You are learning from a book, but the book itself cannot do the work of nursing for you. It cannot come along with you and say, "Look at this, look at that. Do this, do that." It can only help to point the way. It is what you take from that book which will serve you as a nurse.

In the same way, the prophets simply came and conveyed the commands of God. They gave you His words. But they won't come along with you. It is not possible for them to come and forgive you. It is up to you to understand those words and do what they say. Only that will help you. You can try raising your arms and think that Jesus (ﷺ) or someone else will come and do this or that and save you. But think about it a little and see if it will really work.

QUESTION: Is Jesus (ﷺ) here in his spirit with us now?

BAWA MUHAIYADDEEN: God is everywhere. Jesus (ﷺ) may also be here, as well as all the representatives of God, His messengers, the eternal prophets. But the Supreme Power is God. Without His word, without His law, without His permission, the prophets cannot do anything. No one can do anything without that. The prophets follow His orders. God commands them, "Go and do this," and they do it, "Go and say this," and they say it.

If we can imbibe the words that they brought from God and establish a direct connection with that Supreme Power, it will be good. We must try hard to achieve that kind of connection.

QUESTION: How can we do that?

BAWA MUHAIYADDEEN: It can be done. If you place a seed in the earth you have to water it, fertilize it, and protect it. You must care for it until the tree grows and bears fruit and the fruit ripens. If you do that, you will have fruit to eat.

In the same way, if you want to make the truth grow within you, first you must plant the seed of faith inside. Then you have to nourish it with good intentions, good thoughts, and good duties toward God. You must love other lives as your own life, treat the hunger of others as your own hunger, treat the sorrows and joys of others as your own, and treat the illnesses of others as you would your own. You cannot do this with words alone, it must permeate your actions. Those duties and actions are the fertilizer which must be placed on the seed of faith in God. Then that seed of faith will grow and flower and bear fruits that will ripen. Do it that way. That is the only way.

Do not set out to correct the world; correct yourself.

Do not preach to the world; preach to yourself.

Do not find faults in others; look at your own faults.

Do not laugh at what the world is doing; look at yourself and laugh at what you are doing.

Do not go around praising the world; look at yourself, examine your own state, and see what deserves praise and what deserves ridicule.

Do not think that by examining the world you can reach the opposite shore; study yourself if you want to reach that snore.

Do not set out to study and cure the opinions of the world; cure your own opinions first.

Do not try to make the world clear; if each one will make himself clear, the world will become clear automatically.

Do it this way and it will give you the victory of your life.

QUESTION: May I ask a question about something that was said earlier?

BAWA MUHAIYADDEEN: If there are questions, ask them and finish them off. If you came to ask questions, finish asking them. If you came to realize things, study the things you need to realize. If you came to learn, sit silently, listen, and learn. But as long as there are questions, ask.

QUESTION: If you go before God, when the time comes to be judged, what is righteous before God? Considering a man's actions, who can be righteous before God?

BAWA MUHAIYADDEEN: Right. In the presence of God, what man can be righteous?

Look at what happens if you throw a piece of wood into the fire. You can touch the part that is not burning, but the part that is burning cannot be touched. It has become fire.

When a man goes into the presence of God, if he puts only his head in, that part becomes like the burning wood. It cannot be touched. But the parts that remain outside—the mind, desire, satan, lust, anger, miserliness, ignorance, conceit, vanity, the I, and the arrogance of the mind—all these can be touched. These parts that do not go into the presence of God remain as wood. One part is thinking of God, but the other parts are still outside. The mind, desire, arrogance, karma, illusion, religious bigotry, racial bigotry, the desire for earth, sensual pleasures, and gold, and many different intentions and thoughts are still outside the fire. Only that one portion is saying, "O God," while the others remain cold. Anyone can grab on to those cold parts and try to pull the man out. Satan can pull him, desire can pull him, wealth can pull him, jobs can pull him—all these can pull the man out so he is no longer with God. But if everything has gone in, then the fire has consumed him and there is nothing left to touch. He has become fire, so no one can touch him.

This is the way it is. If every part of you goes into the presence of God, you no longer exist. There is nothing left, no man, only God. You cannot be touched. There is no I. There is no *my* property or *my* city. Nothing can be called mine; everything is His. The story is finished. There are no more questions to ask of Him. There is nothing further to study or to say.

But as long as you remain in a state where part is in and part is out, you can always be pulled out. Only when every part of you has gone into His presence and become one with Him are you clear. Then you cannot be pulled out.

QUESTION: Why is man here? Why are we on earth the way we are, if we were meant to be with God?

BAWA MUHAIYADDEEN: That is a very good question, a very good question. You want to know why we came here?

If you were there, would you know about God? There it is a great mystery, but here in this world His story is revealed. Here you can see His power, His qualities, His actions, His artistry, His medical work, His scientific work, and His work of divine wisdom. Here He manifested the sun, the moon, and the stars. Here He created mountains, oceans, valleys, flowers, fruits, and birds. All things that move and display their beauty and fragrance are His work. We see His story in the falling leaves and in the blossoming flowers. The creeping ant, the birds that fly, the heavenly bodies, and all things that move proclaim His presence, His power, and the artistry of His creation. They point out how a living man is going to die and how a dying man will live on. The world of the Mechanic can be seen in every little thing.

This world is a school, and we came here to learn His story by studying His actions, His justice, and His ways. We have to study each thing we see, and as we learn from these examples we will exclaim, "My God!" Our faith will become strong, and from that faith will come the firm conviction that He is there, existing as a great power. In everything we see, in every bit of His artistry, even in the grass and the weeds, we can begin to understand His power. Each thing tells a part of the story of God. He sent us here, saying, "Go, and understand all of My creations. If you understand the stories that they contain, you will understand Me and accept Me."

QUESTION: Why do some people not love God?

BAWA MUHAIYADDEEN: Why should you worry about that? It is all right. God will look after that. He does not suffer because of that. He is not worried because some people do not love Him, so there is no need for you to worry. If you love God, look after your own needs. If you need water, take it and drink. If another man does not need water, do not try to give him water. He will not want it.

Have you anything more inside of you to ask?

QUESTIONER: Well, I have loved Jesus (ﷺ), and I have followed Jesus (ﷺ). So I came to ask you about him.

BAWA MUHAIYADDEEN: You trusted the fruit and did not trust the tree. It is only if you get hold of the tree that you can eat its fruit, is it not? If you can do that, you will get all the fruit you want. Get hold of God. The taste is with Him. The taste is not in the flower, the taste is in God. He also has the fruits. Just because a horse goes on a journey, do not put your trust in that horse. Trust in God.

QUESTION: Then Jesus (ﷺ) is not God?

BAWA MUHAIYADDEEN: There is only one God. What is called God is alone. We cannot say that Jesus (ﷺ) is God. Nothing that appears is God. The sun, the moon, the stars are not God. Anything that was created has a limit and must perish sometime. Anything that appeared must disappear. God alone never appeared and will never disappear. God was never born and will never die, but exists forever as a mystery, a power dwelling within all lives. That power has no form or shape, no wife, no children, no birth, no death, no desire, no mind, no hunger, no illness, no sleeping, no waking, no joy, no sorrow, no anger, no impatience, no sin, no evils, no infatuations or torpor, no selfishness, no discriminations, and no hatred for others. There is nothing equal to God, nothing comparable, nothing deserving that high title. Nothing but He can possess His power. There is only one God. He is the only king for His kingdom, the kingdom of justice and perfect purity.

But for hell there are many gods. There are dog gods, cat gods, elephant gods, satan gods, sun gods, moon gods, snake gods, rat gods, fish gods, vulture gods, eagle gods, lion gods, tiger gods, bull gods, cow gods, horse gods, buffalo gods—so many gods. They are the gods of hell. God is not like that. What is called God is One.

The prophets, the teachers, the saints, the *qutbs,* the angels, and the heavenly beings came to redirect us and show us the right path. We should follow them. They will lead us to the path of truth, to God.

Come, sit down and learn. Sit with determination. Don't waste your time. If you want wisdom, then come, sit down with the intention of learning, and learn.

May 24, 1979

Session 16

*How can I balance my spiritual life
with my physical needs?*
175

Could I have a name to guide my qualities?
175

Please speak about religious indifference.
176

Should we expect any more prophets?
182

I've studied singing. Should I continue?
184

*How can we transform our thoughts
into thoughts of God?*
186

Who is the Messiah and has he come yet?
186

Session 16

BAWA MUHAIYADDEEN: My love to you, my children. May God protect you all. My children, would you like to ask any questions?

QUESTIONER: I would like to learn how to balance my spiritual life with my physical needs.

BAWA MUHAIYADDEEN: Now, a balance is built with a scale on each side. To use it you must put lead weights on one pan and the things that you want to weigh on the other. But before you put anything on either side, what must you do? You must be sure that the two pans are in perfect balance. Then you can put the weights on one side and your goods on the other and measure out the exact amount you want. This way you will not be short-changed. But if the pans were not properly balanced initially, if one pan was high and the other low, then you may end up with less or even more than the scale indicates.

In the same way, the mind and the body have to be in perfect balance. Those two pans must be under one control. Then you will not be short-changed in your spiritual advancement, your prayers, the pleasures in your life, your happiness, and whatever good things you want. But if these two pans are not properly balanced, if the mind is out of balance, then you cannot measure anything accurately. Therefore, the first step is to balance the two pans, your mind and your body, correctly.

Any other questions?

LEO PILON: I would like to ask Bawa if he would give me a name. Maybe that name would give me some insight as to what qualities I should try to perform.

BAWA MUHAIYADDEEN: Isaac. He was a prophet. You need to develop the qualities of the Prophet Isaac (≈). If you have a name with no meaning, your qualities will grow in the same meaningless way. That is why God declared that His beautiful names are very good for man. Each one of His names has a beautiful meaning corresponding to His beautiful qualities. There are specific actions, duties, and qualities of God that are appropriate for each name. That is why we give people these names, so they will strive to attain the corresponding qualities. Otherwise what good is a name? Names are only given so that you may imbibe those qualities and perform those duties. If you give the names of lions, tigers, and bears, then you will follow the qualities of those animals. To live as human beings, we need human qualities and human names.

May God grant you those good qualities, the qualities of Isaac (≈), his actions, and his conduct. *Āmīn.* May God grant you those qualities.

DAVID FREUDBERG: Bawangal, the problem of my religion versus your religion seems to come up a lot and I was wondering if you could speak some more about that.

BAWA MUHAIYADDEEN: Good. It is difficult for us to solve these problems. True human beings won't fight with each other over such issues. But if people have the qualities of animals, then they will continue to quarrel and fight. And when animals fight, how can we talk to them about wisdom or advise them?

God doesn't say the things that these people say. He sent down 124,000 vice-regents, prophets, saints, and lights of God, all with the same message—that there is but one God. He is a treasure which has no form, no shape, no color, no religion, no race, no differences. He has transcended religions and philosophies. God exists in a state beyond all such things.

God is the life which exists in all lives, the power within all lives. Within water His power exists as that which cools the body and quenches the thirst. Within fire His power exists as the heat that brings comfort to His creations. Within earth His power is the cooling force for the seeds that are planted there. And within air He is the coolness which comforts and creates peace in all the lives He created. Whatever coolness or warmth each creation needs from the sun or the moon or the sky, He gives according to the needs of that particular creation. He is the fragrance in the flower, He is the taste in the fruit, the shade of the tree, and the light within the gem. Within man, He is wisdom.

God has given His three thousand divine qualities and attributes to man. He has endowed him with His peacefulness, His equality, His justice, and His laws of justice; with His surrender, concentration, balance, and *gnānam,* or grace-awakened wisdom; with His four qualities of shyness, modesty, reserve, and fear of wrongdoing; and with the seven levels of wisdom: feeling, awareness, intellect, judgment, subtle wisdom, divine analytic wisdom, and divine luminous wisdom.

God's power is found in all lives. He has endowed them with His good thoughts and good intentions. Even the shine on the leaves is an aspect of His power. He is that magnetism in the shrubs and the grass that makes them grow. That power is God. He can be seen in all places. At every point where you focus your wisdom, God can be seen. He is—my God! You will find Him in water, in food, in the taste of a fruit, and in the sun and the moon. Wherever you focus your wisdom you will see God there, and you will say, "O my God, this is Your wonder!" In every place that your wisdom resplends you will see God, but wherever your wisdom does not resplend, you will not be able to see God.

That absolute power that is God exists in a state of resplendent purity. God sees all, He knows all, He protects all, He feeds all, He listens to all, and He performs His duty toward all. He carries and sustains all. That is—my God!

God is looking at everyone. But man is not aware of Him, man is not looking at Him. The world and God's creations have not seen Him. Those who depend on histories find that He has none, because He is God. He has no history, no form, no house, no garden, no wealth, and no maya, or illusion. Therefore no one has seen Him.

But if a man becomes a true man, if he realizes the man within him and becomes aware of the qualities, actions, conduct, and love that exist in that man within, if he comes to that state of peace and equality and begins to understand the state of man's true wisdom, and if that wisdom grows within him—then, he will see God. He will relish the taste of God and see the light of God. When he sees that light, he will reach perfection, peacefulness, and equality. He will see all of God's energies, His miracles, His cells, and all of His creations. He will see God within all lives and recognize His power in everything.

If a man develops patience, tolerance, peacefulness, and the inner patience, contentment, trust in God, and praise of God known as *sabūr, shakūr, tawakkul,* and *al-hamdu lillāh;* if he develops the four higher levels of consciousness: judgment, subtle wisdom, divine analytic wisdom, and divine luminous wisdom; if he develops virtues and good conduct and the qualities of compassion, love, and justice; if he realizes that all lives are his life and all suffering is his suffering, all health is his health, all hunger is his hunger and all difficulties are his own difficulties, if he can establish that state and those qualities—at that point of realization he will be transformed. He will be reborn from this physical state into another state.

But one who fails to realize his inner self and change his state will not see God. He will continue to exist as the earth, fire, water, air, ether, mind, and desire of this body. Unless man changes and is reborn within, he will never see the kingdom of God. Unless he loses his arrogance, karma, and illusion and casts off the three sons of illusion known as *tārahan, singhan* and *sūran,* and unless he gets rid of his lust, hatred, selfishness, miserliness, attachment, fanaticism, envy, intoxicants, sex, theft, murder, falsehood, and earth, fire, water, air, ether, and desire, he will never see the kingdom of God. He has to change from these twenty-four qualities and actions, these twenty-four aspects that make up his form. When his qualities and his form change, he will be reborn in the qualities and actions of God, reborn in His conduct, His behavior, His beauty, His peacefulness, His equality, His patience, His compassion, and in His selfless duties and actions. Only when man changes and is reborn in those divine gracious qualities will he become an heir to the kingdom of God. Then he will obtain the kingdom of God, and he will see God. But if he does not change his present state, he will never see God and His kingdom.

Religions must understand this. When Jesus (ᷡ) said that unless man is born again he will never see the kingdom of God, he did not mean that a man's body must die and then be reborn. That is not the correct interpretation. If he dies and is reborn in another body, he will only end up in hell. Jesus ⊚ meant that before a man's physical body dies, his qualities must die and he must be reborn in the qualities of God. His selfishness, his pride, his vanity, and his arrogance must change. The differences of the you and the I must change. The fighting and battles and wars must change. The duality that causes one animal to kill and eat another animal must change. When all of those qualities change, he will be born as man and transformed into the qualities of God. Then he will show the compassion of God for all lives, and he will never kill any life. In that state he will see God and enter the kingdom of God.

So we have to change now. We have to change our qualities and be reborn in the qualities of God. Only then can we see God. Religious fanaticism is arrogance, and those who have this fanaticism are like elephants. An elephant, unlike a man, doesn't need a path to travel through the jungle, because wherever he goes he forges his own path by uprooting or bending down all the trees in his way. It is only man who needs a path to walk through the jungle. And only man needs a path to travel to God. In order to show that connecting path between God and man to those who have come to this world so that they can return to Him, God sent 124,000 messengers. They came to establish that there is one God, and that He alone is our Father. All the prophets who came said, "God commanded me to convey this message to you: Pray to Him and worship only Him." No prophet ever declared that he himself should be worshiped or that he had come to establish a particular religion. What they all said was that there is only one God, our Father, who is perfect purity. Trust in Him. Have faith in Him alone. The saints, the *qutbs,* the vice-regents, and the pure ones who came here brought the same message to mankind.

Those who came to convey God's commands were many. But from that group, twenty-five prophets were specially selected, and from those twenty-five, eight notable ones were chosen: Adam, Noah, Abraham, Ishmael, Moses, David, Jesus, and Muhammad, may the peace and blessing of God be upon them all. What these eight brought with them was the explanation of God. They explained His qualities and actions and showed man the way to reach God, the way to see God. They brought God's voice and God's knowledge with them. It was God's resonance and His words that came to the prophets, and they transmitted that to mankind.

This history of the prophets is not as you see it on television, nor is it what you read in books. God's voice, His sound, His words, are all in the form of light. All of God's words came in that way, as light. You cannot make light into a material form. Light can only be absorbed by another light. For example, if a car with a twelve volt battery approaches another car with a six volt battery, the light coming from the first car's headlights will absorb the light coming from those of the second car. And the driver of that car will be blinded by the dazzling light from the first car.

The words of God are light. In the heart of man there is a light which can draw in that light of God. It can attract His light, His power, His words. We must draw that light into our hearts. Only then will we have any understanding of the words of God.

That light has no form and will not be found as anything that has form. You can never produce the original light by reading books or watching television shows and dramas. There is no light in those things. That is only dancing and acting, just makeup that says, ''I am high. You are low. My religion is great. Your religion is lesser.'' That is all book knowledge and makeup. We can never reach God with that makeup. It has no light. Only if the religions have light within can they draw in His light.

When the words came from God to the prophets, they came in the form of divine light. When the words came from the prophets to the people, they came in the form of power. From that power came wisdom. And when that wisdom comes to man and begins to resplend, he will be able to understand the meanings of the words that were told to him. That wisdom then becomes the power of God. And when the explanation within that power is understood, he will say, ''My God! My God!'' Whatever he tastes he will say, ''My God, what a wonderful taste! This is a great wonder. O my God!''

There are four kingdoms: the kingdom of animals, the kingdom of hell, the kingdom of the souls, and the kingdom of God. This world is the kingdom of animals. The kingdom of hell, which is the kingdom of satan, is where the spirits and ghosts and demons exist. The kingdom of the soul is where the souls dwell. God is in the kingdom of God.

In this kingdom of animals, it is very difficult to find a true man. The prophets came to make man into a true man, so that he would be able to control all these animals. Here, there are not only four-legged animals, but also many two-legged animals. There are monkeys, donkeys, lions, tigers, bears, elephants, snakes, chickens, and rats. God sent the prophets to change the animal kingdom into a human kingdom, to make these animals into men. They came to change the animal qualities, the satanic qualities, and the qualities of demons, ghosts, and vampires into human qualities.

They came to warn us that there is a Day of Judgment, on which there will be an inquiry. That is why the prophets came to earth. No prophet ever claimed that he was God or said, "This is my special religion." Neither Moses⊙ nor Abraham⊙ said this, nor did Jesus⊙ or Muhammad⊙ or any other prophet.

This is what God commanded them to say: "We are all the children of Adam⊙, the human race, the family of Abraham⊙, and the followers of Muhammad⊙. These four sections are one. All are the creations of God, and the whole world is made up of this one family. Our Father is the one God who alone is worthy of worship. We should worship nothing else." This is what God told them. This is how it is.

If those with animal qualities attain wisdom, they will realize this and become men. We must not get involved in the fights of elephants, donkeys, tigers, or monkeys. They only beat their chest with pride and vanity, shouting, "I am big. I am great!" We should not be involved in that. We should quietly walk away from them. Let them keep their disease of fecal arrogance. They have to clear themselves, but if they cannot, then what can we do? We can only say, "Thank you very much. If you want to listen, you can listen." Otherwise we should bid them goodbye. If you ask a man what he wants and he says, "I like my religion," then say, "Okay, fine, keep it." But if somebody says that there is one God, then say, "Very good." Understand and accept that person.

Once you find peace within yourself, you can find peace in the world. If you have equality within yourself, you will see equality in all lives. If you have purity in yourself, you will see purity in all lives. If you have love in yourself, you will see love in all lives. Whatever is in your heart is what you will see in the faces of others. When you look at them, you will see only your own reflection. Whatever fault you see in them really lies within you. When you look at others, you only see your own reflection, not what is truly there. So correct yourself and then you will see all lives as one.

This is what Jesus☺ and Moses☺ and Muhammad☺ told us.

QUESTION: If Muhammad☺ is the last prophet, are we to expect no more?

BAWA MUHAIYADDEEN: No more. There will be no other prophet after Muhammad☺. So if another prophet comes, it will have to be a prophet that has already been here. They say that a prophet who left this world will come back again, and the world accepts that. All four religions say that, but only when we believe in God will any prophets come to us. We have sent God away, we have asked Him to go away. Why should prophets come to a place where God will not come? We do not have the qualities or actions of God. We do not have trust or faith in God. We do not have the compassion of God. We do not have the fervor of firm determination and certitude in God.

Such a state does not exist in this kingdom of animals, this kingdom where one life kills another life. Here we find only arrogance. Here we find the religions of Hinduism, Zoroastrianism, Christianity, and Islam (*Zābur, Jabrāt, Injīl,* and *Furqān*). We travel from the north, south, east, and west along these four main roads or their many offshoots, saying: I am Catholic. I am Protestant. I am a Muslim. I am a Jehovah's witness. I am Shiite. I am a Sufi. I am Hanīfī. I am Hanbalī. I am Mālikī.

Now, in every city there are the main roads that lead to the city hall, and there are also many side roads leading to the supermarket. But there is no use in fighting over which one to take, because whether we go straight down the main roads, or go in circles on the winding side roads they all will eventually end up either at the supermarket or at the city hall. City hall is the world. Here you celebrate birthdays and build memorials for death days. You get your birth and death certificates and then go back home, but after that you have to return to the world again. Finally you end up in the kingdom of hell. All you have done is to travel from the kingdom of animals to the kingdom of hell.

The four main roads will take you to the city hall, and the side roads will take you to the supermarket, but there is no road that will take you from the city hall or supermarket to the kingdom of God. If you want to go to God, you have to open your own road. All other roads must be left behind; they will only take you as far as the city hall. There are no roads beyond that and no people beyond that. Nothing at all exists beyond that. So, if you want to go beyond, if you want to reach God, you have to forge your own way and travel alone along that very tiny, pointed path. You have to cast off everything and travel free. You must cut a path with the knife of wisdom and walk with the legs of perfect faith, using the staff of determination and always remembering the four states of surrender, concentration, balance, and *gnānam*. The path is very, very slippery, and each time you climb up one step, you may slip back down four steps. So you must walk with the light of *gnānam* and hold fast to the staff of faith and certitude, bearing the sword and axe of *īmān*. With that help, you can travel beyond the city hall.

To go beyond is difficult. No race or religion, no arrogance, no karma or maya exist there. There, only God meets God. This is a faultless path that gives you absolute freedom, but to travel it, you have to leave everything behind and say, "Give it all to somebody else. I am going. I don't want any of these things." And then you can go. While you are still traveling along the main roads, you can call upon your wife, your relatives, your wealth, your religion, or your race to help you, but if you want to go on to God, you have to leave behind all of these things. Only if you travel free and unburdened can you escape. It is very rare to find even one in ten million following that true path. It is even rarer to find one in a hundred thousand, and almost impossible to find one in a thousand. That is why the prophets, the angels, the pure ones, the lights and saints and *qutbs* had to come—to try to show mankind this path. They did not come to this world to do business. Try to understand that.

Let whoever has that knowledge escape and go along this path which points to God alone. Let the ones who want to fight keep on fighting. Let the man who wants to eat the other man keep on eating. If animals want to devour other animals, let them. Let the monkeys that want to smile at other monkeys keep on smiling. If a snake wants to swallow another snake, let it. If a fish wants to devour another fish, let it. If the earth wants to eat earth, let it eat earth. What can you do about that? You should simply say, "O my teacher, it all happened just as you predicted." Or, "O my God, what You said is true. Everything You said is true. Now I realize that animals eat animals in this animal kingdom. Earth devours earth." And then say goodbye and go off along your path. You can also say "O God, I have no more problems. I have finished my journey here, and I am coming back to You." Then go along with God. Say goodbye to the earth with a "Thank you," and go your way.

JESSICA BORASKI: I studied classical singing for three years. Could Bawa advise me as to whether I should continue it?

BAWA MUHAIYADDEEN: What advice can I give you? That is your job, isn't it? If you studied that to earn a living, you have to do that job. But if you don't like it, then you need to study something else and get a job based on whatever you study. We dance, we sing, we become slaves to one another. We run, we jump—all for the one-span stomach.

[Bawa begins to sing:]
    Dancing and singing and becoming slaves to one another,
    Searching and running, O Golden One!
    All for the sake of the one-span stomach.

We dance, we sing, we become slaves to one another, we search, we leave this country and go to another country, we go from one city to another and we run about for the sake of the one-span stomach.

    One for meditation,
    Two for propagation,
    Four to carry the corpse.
    This is the way of the world.

If you want to meditate on God, only God can meditate on God. Only God's qualities and actions can meditate on God. God's equality and tranquility and peace can meditate on God. God's power and His conduct can meditate on God. There is only one for meditation. God must meditate on God.

But if you want to enlarge the population of this world, you need two people, a woman and a man. And in order to carry a corpse to the cemetery, you need at least four people. This is the way of the world.

> In the fortress of races and religions,
> In the marketplace of arrogance,
> There are crowds and multitudes of people.
> But when the Angel of Death comes,
> They quickly run away.

In the fortress of religions and races they say, "My race, your race. My religion, your religion." There are so many people in that fortress. Those who have the force and arrogance of the I flock to the marketplace. There are millions and billions and trillions of people in this marketplace. But when the Angel of Death comes, all of them take to their heels and run. They all run away.

> In this world there are millions upon millions of creations.
> But of them all, the human birth is the most exalted.

Out of all those millions of forms that exist on this earth, the human form, the human birth, is the most noble birth. The one who understands and realizes the truth is a *gnāni,* a true wise man, a divine human being. One who does not understand this is not wise.

> In the fortress of races and religions,
> In the marketplace of arrogance,
> Man's whole life is trouble and suffering.
> Beg to find God's truth and reach the shore.

When you look at the people in this fortress of races and religions, their whole life is a life which is staggering, or rocking. But you must try to realize God. First you must realize yourself. Once you have understood your state, you must realize God, and in that clarity you must try to reach the shore. Beg Him to help you come to the shore. If you do not reach this state, then what is the purpose of life? What is the use of all this dancing and running? It is only for the sake of the one-span stomach.

> Do not roll on the earth
> With countless thoughts—O Golden One!

In your mind you keep on thinking millions upon millions of thoughts, and you keep rolling on the earth. Do not roll on the earth. Do not keep on thinking millions of thoughts. If you go on thinking and rolling, your human state will be completely wasted and you will realize nothing. This is the state of absolute craziness. Try to escape from this corpse and find a way to reach the shore. Then you can attain a state of peace.

Now, this is a song about the one-span stomach. All that you have to learn is in this song. The entire story of our life, from birth to death, is in this song. The secret of birth, the secret of life, the secret of the world, and the secret of death are all contained in this song. So, do what you like.

What shall we do now?

CLAIRE BECKMANN: As our thoughts arise, how can we transform them into thoughts of God?

BAWA MUHAIYADDEEN: Is that your question? If you don't keep your hands on the steering wheel when you are driving, the car will go its own way. Will you just let it go? Will you follow the direction the car goes? No, you will turn the steering wheel until the four wheels are straightened out, and then the car will run straight. After that, you will continue on your way, driving very cautiously.

Like that, when your mind goes astray, you have to straighten it out. When your thoughts drag you off in some direction, you have to use your wisdom to steer them around. Once you turn your thoughts, you will not have any accidents. The Mechanic has installed the power steering correctly, but it is up to you to steer yourself in the right direction. You might find slopes on one side, stones on another side, and even jungle along the way. There might be many sharp curves in the road. But if you hold on to the steering wheel of wisdom, you can avoid accidents. Your eyes, your thoughts, your concentration, your mind—everything must be right. Then you can drive your vehicle.

Would anyone like to ask anything else?

FRAN COHEN: I would like to know from Bawa who the Messiah is. Or has the Messiah come?

BAWA MUHAIYADDEEN: He has already come. God came a

long, long time ago and gave you all the things He had to give you. He gave you the sun, the moon, and the stars. He gave you wisdom and He gave you His wealth. He gave the world to you. He gave hell to you. He gave your soul to you.

God has given everything to you. So what are you still waiting for? Do not look for someone else to come and redeem you. You have to find your own liberation. Look at yourself. Only when you do that can you redeem yourself. God has already given you everything He has.

Do not be like the parrot who sat on a cotton plant, and, admiring the cotton bolls, he said, ''These are very beautiful fruits!'' Because they looked like fruits to him, he sat there and repeated over and over again, ''Let it ripen. Let it ripen. Let it ripen.'' The parrot would not go away from the plant to search for food. Instead, he sat there watching and waiting. He kept saying, ''It will ripen today. It will ripen tomorrow. It will ripen the day after. It might ripen the next day.'' The parrot waited and waited. Finally, the boll burst open and all that came out was cotton. So the parrot got nothing to eat.

What will happen if we keep saying, ''Somebody's coming. The Messiah's coming. The Messiah's coming. He will come. He will come soon. He will come and show us the way''? Do you know who will finally come to show you the way? The Angel of Death. And then it will be too late. So, do not be like the parrot waiting for the fruit to ripen. Before the Angel of Death comes and catches us, we must try to liberate ourselves, to redeem ourselves.

If you commit a sin, or if you hurt or scold someone, something comes and warns you from within. When you think about it for a while, your heart starts to palpitate. It races and shakes, and then your mind also begins to work on you. That thing which warns you from within rises up immediately and says, ''I scolded him. That was a mistake. Now God will find fault with me for scolding him unnecessarily.'' That thing keeps saying, ''What you did is wrong. You beat him, you scolded him. He did not harm you, and yet you scolded him and he is crying. You will be questioned about this on the Day of Judgment. So go and say that you are sorry and ask for his forgiveness.'' This thing within you keeps warning you to do that. Who is it that warns you? It is God who warns you from within.

God is living within you.

Therefore, do not wait for someone to come and save you, because God is already there within you, warning you. He is the One who showed you, the One who made you aware of your error and warned you. The judgment is also within you. Everything is within you. You do not have to look for someone else to come. You must look within yourself. You must realize yourself. That is the way. If instead, you watch and wait like a parrot, saying, ''Somebody said this. A Messiah is coming,'' then the Angel of Death will come and take you away. He is the only one still to come.

Just as the ripened cotton boll bursts and releases the cotton, when something bursts within you, the Angel of Death will come and visit you. Do not let yourself be deceived.

The earth is deceiving the world, the mind is deceiving the earth, maya is deceiving the mind, desire is deceiving maya, the *nafs* (base desires) are deceiving desire, hunger is deceiving the *nafs,* the visions of the eyes are deceiving hunger, the monkey of the mind is deceiving the physical visions, our qualities and our thoughts are deceiving the monkey mind, time is deceiving our thoughts, religions are deceiving time, races are deceiving religions, ignorance is deceiving the races, arrogance is deceiving our ignorance, karma is deceiving our arrogance, hell is deceiving our karma, and many rebirths are deceiving hell. All these different births, these births of cats and dogs and worms and insects, are deceiving our birth. And finally the Angel of Death is going to deceive this state. Then the Day of Judgment will come. We do not know what is going to happen to us then.

Each one is trying to live by deceiving the other. If we can reflect upon this, it will be good. The world deceives us, the body deceives us, mind and desire deceive us, happiness and sadness deceive us. We must try to liberate ourselves from all of these deceptions.

All right, go and eat your lunch now.

May 25, 1979

Session 17

My grandmother is ill. What shall I tell her?
191

Who is the true guru?
192

What is the Trinity?
194

Who is Jesus ﷺ ?
198

Session 17

————— ·~⌒~· —————

LARRY DIDONA: My grandmother is very ill. Has Bawa anything to tell her?

BAWA MUHAIYADDEEN: May God give us His grace. *Āmīn.* Even if our father and mother forgets us, there is a mysterious Treasure that never forgets. If we have health and wealth, our relatives will embrace us. If we have wealth, religions will embrace us. If we hold titles and positions, everybody will accept and praise us, even kings.

But if all of these things leave us and we have nothing, then the world will abandon us. Kings and political friends will desert us, religions will renounce us, and our relatives will forsake us. If we have an illness that becomes too severe, even the doctor will quit on us. When we have no wealth, no health, and no property, everybody will cast us off. When we are in that state, God alone will hold on to us. Whether we have wealth or no wealth, whether we have strength or no strength, whether we are sick or well, under any conditions, God will never separate Himself from us. He will always live with us. God, His truth, His compassion, and His justice will always remain with us. That God who is eternal will always live with us, both in our happiness and our sadness.

So tell your grandmother, "The first thing we must do is to accept the fact that God is always with us. He stays with us, even if everybody else leaves us. He is the One who will never turn aside. He will always share our sorrows and joys. God is within us and we are within God. Have trust in Him, have faith in Him, and let His truth be in you. Whatever disease may come, whatever sufferings and sorrows may afflict us, we must surrender all of them to God. To surrender to God and live in that state until the last day of our lives will be our exaltedness.

"God is the medicine for our souls and the excellence of our lives. Whatever may come to us, we must have patience, tolerance, and peacefulness. We must make those qualities our food and make the essence of those qualities our wisdom. With that wisdom, we must find a way to trust Him and meet Him and live with Him. This is the only duty we have to perform now. If we can do this, it will be very good. Then we will know peace."

Tell her that. May God protect her. May God take away all her sorrows and suffering and grant her His grace. We will also pray to God, asking for her comfort and health. Tell her that.

QUESTION: My friend would like to know who is the true guru? She is struggling with surrender to the guru.

BAWA MUHAIYADDEEN: The true guru is God. He is the true teacher. In the world you will find many false gurus. They indulge in falsehood and do a lot of business, selfish business, guru business. They do the business of arrogance, the business of anger, the business of religions, races, doctrines, and philosophies. Because these gurus have selfishness within them, they conduct business for selfish purposes. They are involved in self-business, yet they still call themselves gurus. God alone does not have any of this self-business. He alone is a true guru. You have to learn to whom you should surrender.

Observe the ants and all the creeping insects, the sun, the moon, and the stars, the birds, the four-legged animals, the trees, the shrubs, the fruits, and the flowers. They are all creations of God, the works of His engineering, His works of art, His miracles. They reveal His story. They all have souls. They all can move and taste and grow and flower and bear fruit. They are all teachers, or gurus. If you understand that, you will see gurus everywhere. When you taste a fruit you will say, "My God, what a wonder!" When you see the color in a flower and smell its fragrance, you will say, "O my God, what a beautiful flower! What a lovely fragrance." And you will praise God. His secret, His truth, exists in every seed. When you see the potential in a seed you will say, "O my God, what a great wonder it is that within a tiny seed a huge tree exists! Within this tiny point is such a great thing.'' When you look at the sun and see how much light it gives, you will say, ''O my God, how wondrous is Your creation!'' And when you look at the moon, you will say, ''The moon appears small, yet it lights up the night from north to south and east to west. What a wonder it is, O my God.'' When you see how fast a tiny ant crawls, you will think of God. When you see how one ant comes to carry away another ant that is dead, you will say, ''My God, what unity the ants have! Look how they walk in lines.'' When you see how many ants crowd together in such a little room inside the earth, you will exclaim, ''How much tolerance they have!'' When you observe how they can find the smallest crumb of sugar to carry off, you will say, ''What a keen sense of smell they have! What a wonder! All this is Your beauty, my God.''

In everything that you see and even in the things that cannot be seen, truth can be found. You can realize that truth through your wisdom. Observe the trees and shrubs and grass performing their duties without any selfishness. The sun and the moon also perform their duties without selfishness. All of God's creations except man do their work without selfishness. Reflect upon this.

Everything you see in the world is a guru. Study nature, study God's creations, and as you understand each thing, you will realize how many different miracles God has performed. You will understand how the qualities and actions of God are at work in the world. You will see the praise of God in the world, and you will realize His peacefulness. You will see the compassion of God and understand the duties He performs here, nourishing each one of His creations and treating all lives like His own life. In the rains and the oceans and the forests and the rocks you will see and understand God's power at work. Each one of these creations will be a guru to you. And if you know what truth is and surrender to it, then truth will be your guru. But first you must try to understand what truth is. If you come to understand that reality, you too can become a guru.

You must have faith and trust in God, and you must understand His story. Try to understand with your wisdom and even though you are only a man, perform your duty in the way He performs His duty, without any selfishness. That will free you from your selfishness, your torpor, your doubts, your anger, your impatience, your hastiness, and many other evil qualities.

If you can find one among men who teaches such wisdom, he will be an excellent guru, a perfect guru who will give you divine wisdom and protect you. He will not have any selfish business; he will have the actions of God and the compassion of God. If all of God's qualities are complete within him, if he knows right from wrong, if his wisdom is perfect, and if he makes use of it himself and then teaches you how to use it, then he is among mankind a most excellent guru.

Such a guru will be with you in everything you do. As you cross the ocean, he will be the boat and you the traveler. When you cross the desert, he will be the camel and you the rider. When you climb a rocky mountain, he will be your pole, and you must hold on tight. On your journey he will be the umbrella which will protect you from the rain and the sun. You must hold onto that umbrella and receive comfort from him. Whatever journey you undertake, he will be a helper to you. That is the perfect guru.

Give your friend that understanding. Ask her to surrender to Allah, to God. And if she can also find a perfect guru within mankind, then she can ask him to lead the way.

QUESTION: We have another question. My friend also asked if she was really Bawa's child, and how could he still care for her and love her?

BAWA MUHAIYADDEEN: God accepts each person as His own child. We are all His children. If we satisfy our needs and become content, then we will be His true children. God has no needs. He has that quality of creating, protecting, and nourishing, and in that state He is complete. He performs His duty perfectly.

That child is my child. She is my child. If she has any doubts about it, then when she gets rid of those doubts, she will become my child as far as I am concerned.

QUESTIONER: In the story that God has written, I believe in the Trinity. I believe that Jesus ☼ is the savior and that the Virgin Mary is the mother of God.

BAWA MUHAIYADDEEN: Do you have that faith?

QUESTIONER: Yes, I do.

BAWA MUHAIYADDEEN: We have to reflect on this with wisdom.

Every one of God's creations is His child to Him. The sun, the moon, the stars, and every one of God's creations are His children. They are all His. How can we say that only Jesus ⊛ is His child? If we say that only Jesus ⊛ is the son of God, then who are you? Did Jesus ⊛ create you or did God create you?

QUESTIONER: God created us.

BAWA MUHAIYADDEEN: God is our Father. He is the One who created us. God has no form, no shape, no color, no differences, no race, and no religion. He is not like the sun or the moon. He has no equal and no comparison. He has no country, no place, and no name. He has neither beginning nor end. God transcends beginning and end. He is the grace that lives and exists in all lives. He is the power that intermingles with His entire creation and controls all energies and all forces. That is what we call God. God is the One that mind and desire have never seen. He is the one natural treasure, a treasure that will never, never be destroyed. That treasure is the wisdom within wisdom. It is the justice found within justice and the truth within truth. God is the One who dwells in our good thoughts, our good qualities, and our good actions. He is a treasure that resplends everywhere.

We must try to know who God is and to understand Him. We must relinquish the beliefs that we are holding onto. They have imprisoned us in one way or another. We are all in jail. We must open ourselves and analyze what we find with our wisdom. We must open our hearts and look within. Only then can we perceive His beauty and realize His radiance.

Since Jesus ⊛ came into this world, one thousand nine hundred and seventy-nine years have passed. But creation began two hundred million years ago. The world has been here for countless ages, and in that time 124,000 prophets, like Jesus ⊛, have come to this world as God's vice-regents and messengers, as lights and *qutbs,* as the pure ones that come from God. Throughout these two hundred million years, they have come from the east and north and west and south. They all were the messengers of God's kingdom. What do you think happened to those who were born before

Jesus (☺)? Have they all gone to hell?

QUESTIONER: No.

BAWA MUHAIYADDEEN: Could they have attained heaven?

QUESTIONER: Yes.

BAWA MUHAIYADDEEN: There is a kingdom of God and a kingdom of hell. Both before and after the time of Jesus (☺), whoever accepted and performed the duty of God perfectly reached the kingdom of God. But whoever failed to perform the duty of God received only the kingdom of hell, the kingdom of satan. This is the truth.

All of us have burdens that we carry, separations that we have created. Each one of us has built his own jail. We have put up a gate and then locked ourselves in. The four religions are the four gates: *Zabūr, Jabrāt, Injīl,* and *Furqān* (Hinduism, Zoroastrianism, Christianity, and Islam). Each religion says, "My religion. My doctrine. My faith. My God. I am going to heaven, not you." These claims are made by scriptures and religions; they are the words of self-business, or selfishness. But it is not what the prophets said.

The prophets are not God. They are His messengers, who came to tell the people, "There is only one God. Accept this truth and take on the qualities of that one God." They tried to reclaim us from the world of hell and bring us back to the world of God. They came from the kingdom of God and taught us the laws and justice of God. They preached His commandments and acted with His qualities of peacefulness and tranquility. They taught us to act with compassion and patience and to love our neighbors as we love ourselves. They showed us how God treats all lives as His own life. They taught us that the same suffering others feel may come to us one day, so we must learn to see their suffering as our own. The prophets tried to make us understand these things.

God sent 124,000 messengers to earth. One of them was the son of Mary (☺). They were all given the same message to proclaim; therefore, we cannot say that the only gate that opens to heaven is the one which we are standing behind. That gate is really our jail. If we could only escape from it, we could realize that religions are merely laws of the world, laws that were filed in the city hall. The four religions are like four paths that lead to city hall.

Many roads lead to the world, but each one of us came here by one particular path. We can come from any of the four directions—east, west, north, or south. Once we are here, we go to city hall to get various licenses. They can issue birth or death certificates, but they cannot tell a person when to come to this world or when to leave it. Only God can give that permission. City hall can only say, "This child has been born. This man has died. Make a note of it." So, although city hall can give you some documents, it cannot prevent you from returning to the same place you came from.

Everybody comes to the marketplace of the world. People from different parts of the city, from towns, from the jungle, and from the seaside—all come to buy whatever they want.

> Everyone comes to the marketplace,
> But when the sun sets, they return home.

They can't live in the marketplace. Is this place going to be our permanent home? No, the world is not ours forever. We are not going to stay here permanently, are we? We have only come here to this marketplace to buy the good and the bad, to buy happiness and sorrow. Each one buys what he wants, but when the sun sets he will leave this world and go back to his own home.

> If you have good wisdom, believe this,
> O people living in the world.

If you have awareness and true wisdom, then try to understand with faith what the purpose of our existence is, what this entire life means.

> We all come to the marketplace,
> But when the sun sets, see how we go back
>   to our homes.
> If you have good wisdom, believe this,
> O people of the world.
> Look, the body is a two-legged house,
> But does this house really belong to us?
> Above us is heaven, the house of salvation.

Look at your body. It is useless. You are living in this house, but your salvation lies elsewhere. With your intelligence and with your wisdom, try to understand where the house of your salvation is, and find out how to reach that house.

We must reflect upon this. Only when we escape from this city hall and go beyond these laws that rule us, only when we leave behind the four gates that imprison us—can we find our path to salvation. There is no ready-built road, no map, no story to tell us how to get there. With our own wisdom we must open the gate, break out of our jail, and then find our own path. This is the only way we can attain the state that will allow us to pass through into the wide-open space where the secrets will finally be understood.

If we remain in a cell within the prison walls, we will never be able to understand what peace is, what equality is, what justice is, and what the laws of justice are. But if we go to that wide-open space, we will understand the purpose and meaning of all lives. We will understand the actions and the duty of God. Then we can go behind Him and follow Him. To understand all this, we must open up our own path.

QUESTIONER: I read Bawa's most recent book, in which he says that Jesus ㉧ would return to this earth, to this dream. My belief is that Jesus ㉧ is the savior of this particular dream that we are in. This is a dream.

BAWA MUHAIYADDEEN: Those who lived before Jesus ㉧ left their dreams behind and opened the gates of salvation. Now they are living in the kingdom of salvation. Do you know who Jesus ㉧ is? Jesus ㉧ is the soul of man.

Lā ilāha ill-Allāhu wa innī Ādam Safīyullāh: There is no God but God, and Adam ㉧ is the Chosen of God and the father of mankind. There is another prophet to come.

Lā ilāha ill-Allāhu wa innī Nūhun-Najīyullāh: There is no God but God, and Noah ㉧ is the Saved of God, the one who showed equality to all animals and birds. He made all animals understand the miracles of God and made them accept God. There is another prophet to come.

Lā ilāha ill-Allāhu wa innī Ibrāhīm Khalīlullāh: There is no God but God, and Abraham ㉧ is the Friend of God, the one who showed us the meaning of unity: that there is only one God and all people belong to the one family of mankind. There is another prophet to come.

Lā ilāha ill-Allāhu wa innī Ismā'īl Dhabīhullāh: There is no God but God, and Ishmael ⊛ is the Sacrifice of God. He proclaimed that there is one God and demonstrated how to be firm in one's faith. No matter what state we are in, whether affected by sorrow or happiness, in the face of both birth and death, we must believe in that one God. That is why Prophet Ishmael ⊛ came. There is another prophet to come.

Lā ilāha ill-Allāhu wa innī Mūsā Khalīmullāh: There is no God but God, and Moses ⊛ is the Word of God, the one who came to unite mankind and to explain the limitless powers of God. He taught the people that God has no equal and no form or shape; He exists as a resplendent light. Moses ⊛ came as a leader to all mankind. There is another prophet to come.

Lā ilāha ill-Allāhu wa innī Dāwūd Khalīfatullāh: There is no God but God, and David ⊛ is the Caliph of God. He came to explain God's law and His justice and to teach mankind to live in a state of unity. There is another prophet to come.

Lā ilāha ill-Allāhu wa innī 'Īsā Rūhullāh: There is no God but God, and Jesus ⊛ is the Soul of God and the soul within every one of God's creations. He is the life within you, the soul. Accept him. There is another prophet to come.

Lā ilāha ill-Allāhu Muhammadur-Rasūlullāh: There is no God but God. Muhammad ⊛ is the Messenger of God. No more prophets are to come after him. He is the one who explained all the stories from the time of creation, the story of God, the story of man, and the story of good and evil. He explained the laws that the previous prophets had brought and showed evidence for the truth of those laws. He gave mankind an understanding of the prophets, the saints, the lights of God, and all the vice-regents of God. He spoke of the completeness of God and told man that he must realize himself before he can realize God, who has no form or shape. He showed man how to open up the true path through patience and tolerance, through *tawakkul,* or absolute trust in God, through the inner patience and contentment known as *sabūr* and *shakūr,* and through giving all praise to God, saying, *"Al-hamdu lillāh."*

All the prophets came to give the laws of God to man. Jesus ⊛ came as the soul, Muhammad ⊛ came as the Final Prophet, the *Rasūl.* The saints, the lights of God, the *qutbs,* and all the souls proclaim him as that one light which came forth in the beginning and then manifested as the Final Prophet. We need wisdom to understand what life is, what the soul is, what truth is, and to understand what God is, what worship is, and what unity is. We need wisdom to understand that we are one family and that we are with God all the time, united eternally with Him. With our wisdom we must try to understand the various sections within the body common to all mankind and to realize that everyone is equal. We all belong to one family. If we understand this equality, we will know peace.

QUESTIONER: Although I do believe in the saints and the angels, when I found the words of Jesus ⊛, they showed me that I must love God first and love my neighbor as myself.

BAWA MUHAIYADDEEN: There are six kinds of souls: the soul which belongs to earth, the souls which belong to fire, water, and air, and the soul of ether, or illusion. The sixth soul is the human soul, which is a light soul, a ray of light. All of these are part of the body. But just because you have a life, a soul, it does not mean that you can see God with that soul. That same soul exists in all lives. Everybody has a soul, don't they? Jinns and fairies have souls, and both the higher and lower angels have souls. Even satan has a soul. But not all of them can see God. Only if you have wisdom and truth can you see God. Only when that wisdom and truth dawn in you can you see God.

Now you have life, but death will follow. However, if you have wisdom, you can transcend death. If truth is within you, there will be no death. There is no point in just having life. That is not enough. You need the *Nūr,* the light of wisdom. Only then can you benefit and grow. Then there will be no death.

Āmīn.

May 26, 1979

Session 18

*What is the correct way to act
when seeking employment?*
203

Can determination be nurtured?
204

What wisdom will make our faith grow firm?
205

*How can I cut the excessive attachment
to my mother?*
206

*My mother only believes in this world.
What shall I tell her?*
208

How does the disciple see his teacher within?
209

How can we cut attachment to things that are wrong?
211

How much of our lives are predestined?
211

Is it true that no two snowflakes are alike?
212

Session 18

QUESTION: What is the correct way to act when seeking employment in the world?

BAWA MUHAIYADDEEN: When you look for a job you must take with you absolute faith and trust in God. You should not take any arrogance, pride, anger, or the thought that you know everything. What good will that do you? You must avoid such qualities. They are thieves that will steal your wisdom and leave you bare. Once your wisdom is stolen, you will never know peace in your life. If hastiness overtakes you, or if you get angry, whether it be in your job or in any other area of your life, you will not live peacefully. Anger is the guru that leads you to hell.

If you have any of these qualities, you will not be able to do your job well or conduct your worldly life correctly. With your wisdom you must keep all these thieves, these enemies to your life, under control. Prevent them from stealing your wisdom and your faith and trust in God. Take these treasures with you wherever you go and protect them carefully. Leave everything else behind. It is only extra baggage, which could get lost or sent to the wrong place. If the porters do not feel like loading it, they will simply tell you, "It seems to be misplaced. It will show up later." They might even tell you that it is lost. Of course, if you have insured it, you will get back part of its worth, but if it isn't insured, you will lose everything. That is what happens to excess baggage. So carry only what is essential for your life. Carry God and faith in God. Carry wisdom and patience. Otherwise life will be very difficult.

Do not go for an interview with the idea that since you have a college degree you will certainly get the job. You have to be prepared to answer all questions with clear, short explanations. And remember, you are going to be working under somebody else; therefore, when you speak, you have to be humble and respectful. If you act superior or show anger or arrogance, you will not get the position. You will simply get a "Thank you. We'll let you know. Come back later." This is an indication that you have lost the job. After a while you will realize that it was your own qualities which caused the problem.

So, it is good to understand these things before you go for an interview. If someone goes fishing and says, "I am the ocean. I am the fish. I know all about this. I can do it," he could be swallowed by a whale or dragged under by a current or a whirlpool. Only the fish knows how to travel through the ocean. It knows what paths to take in order to avoid currents which we are unaware of, forces that would toss us about and wash us away.

No matter how much we think we know, no matter what education or experience we have had, we should never boast or show off. One who is learned should act as if he is not learned. One who has understood should behave as if he has not understood. If you conduct your life in a subdued way like that, it will be very good. It will exalt you. Both your job and your life will be exalted, and there will be peacefulness within your mind. Your wisdom will grow, and your experience will greatly increase. Do you understand? If you can act this way, it will be good.

QUESTION: Can determination be nurtured?

BAWA MUHAIYADDEEN: If you have faith, determination will follow. It can grow from that faith. If the foundation is good, the building can be erected upon it, but if the foundation is faulty, it cannot. Unless you have faith, you cannot have determination.

Now if you wear a pair of slippers that don't fit, you cannot walk fast. If the slippers are too tight, you will hobble along, and if the slippers are too loose, you will shuffle and drag your feet. The slippers should fit. Otherwise, it will be difficult to go on a journey.

Similarly, if you have the right kind of faith, you can go forward. But if you have blind faith, it is like wearing a tight slipper. And if you place your faith in the world, that also is foolish. You cannot walk with that either. Your faith must fit just right, or your determination cannot grow. It must be true faith. If you can correctly focus that faith upon God, you can continue your journey successful-ly, and your peacefulness will grow. If you have that kind of faith, then determination will follow.

DANA HAYNE: What's the wisdom that will make our faith grow if it is not already firm?

BAWA MUHAIYADDEEN: If your faith is not firm, it is like a cow without teeth trying to eat grass. It cannot grab hold of the grass. You need faith in your life for everything you do. To make a successful marriage you must start out with the faith that you want to live with that husband. To correctly raise a baby, you need the faith that you really want to raise that baby. To produce milk for the baby, you must have the faith and awareness that you want to feed it. Even to go to the bathroom you need to have the faith that you really want to go. To complete anything satisfactorily, you must start out with faith. In every single section of your life, faith is required. First you must have the awareness that something needs to be done and then the faith that you really want to do it.

Just as chewing brings out the taste of what you eat, faith brings out the taste of everything in life. Just as laughter reveals your lovely white teeth, faith reveals your happiness. Your heart blooms and then joyfully displays its beauty on your face. As soon as these flowers of faith and certitude bloom, the fragrance of God will permeate your heart. Such natural beauty and fragrance is pleasing to God. It cannot be accomplished with makeup. Painting your face will not attract the fragrance of God. Even if you cover your entire face with makeup, a man of wisdom will be aware of the places you have not covered, and he will run away from you.

You have to receive the natural beauty of faith and certitude. That is what God wants to see. The moment you create conditions in your heart that God likes, that will make your certitude and determination grow. When the beauty comes, certitude will also come. But until that state comes to you, your faith will be like a toothless cow that is unable to chew grass, so it eats dung instead. In the same way, if you have no faith in God, you will have to be satisfied with chewing on the discarded and rejected things of hell.

You will eat the world and say, "Oh this is lovely." That is what happens when you do not have faith or certitude.

QUESTIONER: My mother has a power over me which I know is due to my attachments to her, and I want to know how can I cut this attachment without hurting her. I feel like I have to cut it to save my life.

BAWA MUHAIYADDEEN: That is very good indeed. These blood attachments, or blood ties, cling to the body. The connection is one of desire, it comes from arrogance, karma, and maya. It is not only directed toward the mother, it is present in everything. Cows and goats have this kind of attachment. Even birds have it. Everybody has it. The earth has an attachment to the seed, and the seed is attached to earth. Water has an attachment to the fish, and the fish has an attachment to water. The body has an attachment to air and air to the body. Fire also is like that, and so is maya. Death has an attachment to the body, while birth has an attachment to mind and desire.

My child, that is the way things are. Everything has an attachment. Anything that is attractive to our eyes contains some kind of attachment. The attachment we have to sounds and to all the various arts and sexual arts catches us and holds on to us. The whole world, in fact, is attachment. If we look, we will see that everything in the world is entangled like stringhoppers (an Eastern dish of entwined string-like noodles). No one has extricated himself from these entanglements, because they are so difficult to get rid of. We should reflect upon this.

A man with wisdom will have only one attachment, the attachment to God. That is an attachment to something which has no end and is without equal, without comparison. That attachment is to the power that lives forever, to God. It is the only true attachment, the only one that is perfect and complete. It is the plenitude of life. One who has that attachment will perform his duty equally to all, without any sense of selfishness. He will see that all lives are as precious as his own life and feel the hunger of others as his own hunger and the joy and suffering of others as his own joy and suffering. He will treat every life as his own life and everyone's duty as his own. That is true duty.

There are four hundred trillion, ten thousand different attachments. You can control all of them and keep each one in its place by using God's beautiful qualities of peace and tranquility. If a bird asks for fruit, give it fruit. If a cow asks for grass, give it grass. If a horse asks for hay, give it some hay. If a donkey needs a wall to rub its back on, lead it to a wall. If a snake asks for a rat, show it a rat hole. If a fish is searching for water, direct it to the water. If a vulture wants food, show it where there is a dead carcass. If an eagle asks for fish, send it to the seashore.

In this way, direct each one according to what his mind is calling for. Teach wisdom and intelligence to each attachment, according to its own level of understanding. Try to release yourself from all these, and then, holding on to God alone, live in a state of non-attachment. You must try to release yourself slowly, without any pain, just as stringhoppers must be untangled slowly, in order not to break the threads. When you are all tied up by thousands of different threads, first you need to hunt for the right knot, loosen it, and slowly unwind the skein. You may have seen the kind of string sack that is knit in such a way that if you get hold of just one end of thread and pull, the whole sack will unravel. But it has to be the right thread. Like that, if you can use your wisdom to find the right knot, you can start pulling the thread out from one end so that the whole sack falls apart. Then what is inside will be seen clearly. That is the way to do this, my child.

Tell your mother little by little, ''Mother, I have love for you and you have a lot of love for me. That is good, no doubt. That is the way blood ties and attachments are. A father also might have a lot of love for his child, and the child for the father. These loves and attachments do exist, but they don't last forever. Those we loved and were attached to in the past have left us one by one. All our forefathers, one after another, have gone on. Even now, some whom we love are in the process of leaving. Those that we are clinging to now will also leave one day. None of them will stay with us forever.

''Mother, you and I feel attachment for each other. If I have a child, that will be another attachment for me and the attachment of a grandchild for you. But in the end, all these attachments only make us cry. If we hold on to them too strongly, one day you will have to grieve when you leave me, and I too will feel sorrow. Every attachment we develop is going to make us sad at one time or another. Even when we are about to die, we will carry that grief with us. Even at that time we will be saying, 'Oh, I'm leaving my child. I'm giving up my house and all my belongings. I'm leaving my mother. I'm giving up my husband and going away.' We will weep as we leave, thinking of all these attachments. This is what attachment does to us. We should not hold on so strongly to those who are going to leave us some day anyway. We should not feel excessive attachment for them. We have to keep it in moderation.

"But there is One who will never leave us, One who will never perish. God will never leave us, not in the kingdom of heaven, nor in the kingdom of hell, nor in this world. And since judgment is in His hands, He is the only attachment we must have. If we hold on to only that one attachment, then we will have joy throughout our lives and even at the time of death. On Judgment Day we will know that joy, because we will be with Him.

"Mother, we should not hold on so strongly to these other attachments. Of course, I have a duty to you and you have a duty to me. This is the duty that goes with love. But while we go on with our duty, the heart must have only one attachment."

This is what you must tell her. Give her this advice slowly, little by little.

QUESTIONER: My mother just believes in this world, so when I tell her anything like that she says this world is all there is, so we have to hold on very tight. She really clamps down.

BAWA MUHAIYADDEEN: You can say to her, "All the people who held on to the world so strongly earlier—are they here now? Are they still in the world? Where is the house they built and the property they accumulated?" Tell her, "It is no use holding on to this world. All those who tried to, have now gone on to another world somewhere else, haven't they?

"At any moment, the very water that we drink could get caught in our throat, and we too might leave. And no matter how well we look after this heart, if it stops once, we will have to leave. Or if one foot slips and we fall, we could die. Or if a car runs into us as we are walking along the road, we could go immediately. Every day, the things that we are clinging to can bring about accidents. Our whole life is a series of accidents. You don't know what might happen at any given time. Every moment is uncertain.

"That is the state of our life. All the things we are attached to are as fleeting as the bubbles that come out of the mouth of a fish and burst when they hit the surface. We are running our lives like that. We open our mouths and the attachments bubble out. But before long they burst.

"So, my mother, place your attachment on God. I am here today, but if something happens to me tomorrow or the day after, you will feel sad, and if something happens to you, I will be sorrowful throughout my life. That is the end result of any attachment. So, let us do whatever we have to do, but our one unshakable attachment should be to God."

Tell her little by little. Talk to her about God and about other things too. As soon as that feeling and that awareness come to her, she will begin to acknowledge it on her own. Tell her a little at a time, not all at once. Go slowly.

QUESTIONER: I guess I get so shaky . . .

BAWA MUHAIYADDEEN: Even if the hole in your dress is very big, you only need a tiny needle to darn it. And to go through the narrow eye of that needle, you must have a very slender thread. You can mend it if you go slowly, little by little, no matter how big the hole is. Attachment is like that. It's a big hole, so we have to darn it slowly, little by little. Don't feel sad about this. Just go about it a little at a time.

JIM SCHARDT: In what way, how and where, does the disciple begin to see his sheikh within? In the course of learning from a teacher, it seems that the disciple will try to learn how to pray. At some point while he's trying to learn how to pray, he may see his teacher within or think he sees him. If he is seeing his sheikh, and if he is learning a little bit of wisdom in his life, and if this grows, how and where does this occur?

BAWA MUHAIYADDEEN: Do you see hunger? Have you ever seen hunger coming on?

JIM: I can feel it.

BAWA MUHAIYADDEEN: Right, it is a feeling. This is how you will know the sheikh, in your feeling. If you come to the right state, you will experience the sheikh in the same way. You won't see him, but you will be going behind him. If you have accepted the sheikh and surrendered to him, you can come to that state and know him within your body and your wisdom.

Look at this thing called hunger. You can't see it, but within your perception and awareness, you can feel it plucking at you. And when you give it the right kind of food, the hunger keeps quiet, doesn't it? In the same way, if you imbibe your sheikh in the right manner, that will stop the hunger of your karma, the hunger of your avarice, and the hunger of all your desires and attachments.

If you drop a bee into the fire, what will happen? It will burn up. The flames will consume it. Where is the bee then? The bee has merged with the fire and the fire has merged with the bee. The bee and the fire are one. There is no difference between them any more.

In the same way, if you become a true disciple or devotee, and if you serve the sheikh in the correct way, if you truly surrender and immerse yourself within the sheikh, then the you will be dead and gone. Only the fire will remain, and if someone tries to touch you at that time, his hand will burn. But as long as you stay outside the fire, there will be two. As long as you have qualities that the sheikh doesn't have, you and he will be two separate beings. Only on tne day that the you dies will you become the sheikh. Then right and wrong, good and bad, truth and falsehood will be understood directly. And when you see something that is right, you will always recognize it as right. When you are in that state, at that level of wisdom, all things will be explained. That will be the correct food to appease your hunger. That level of wisdom will know. There will be no room for wrong; you will be filled with right. But as long as you do not attain such a state, you will not have this inner awareness.

MARGOT WEENING: How can we cut the attachment to things that our wisdom tells us are wrong, things that affect our whole state? What about when you can see what is right and what is wrong, but you still have an attachment to the things that your wisdom tells you are wrong?

BAWA MUHAIYADDEEN: You are attached to food, but if there is no salt in it, will you eat it anyway? It only needs a tiny pinch of salt, yet without it, there is no taste. You would put that food aside wouldn't you? So why don't you do the same with these other things?

Whenever you can see the difference between right and wrong, it is only your attachment that makes you choose the wrong. Your wisdom tells you it is wrong. It is not tasty. So, just as you would reject food without salt, try to reject that too. You must say, "Ecch! It has no taste!" and push it away. Do it like that.

CATHERINE WEINBERG (TOPI):   I would like to know how much of our lives are predestined and how much we are responsible for?

BAWA MUHAIYADDEEN: God has already taught you everything. It is all written within you. Before you came here, He told you, "I'm sending you to a school called the world. It is a temporary place. You have to go there for a little while in order to learn about My history, your own history, and the history of many others. You have to know who created everything, who is responsible for everything, who is the Guardian in charge of you, and what is your true property. Once you have learned and understood all these histories, you will realize who you are and who is the One you need, the true One, the One who will live forever.

"After you have studied about these things and many others, you must pass an examination. Then you can bring what belongs to you and come back here. If you do this, you will receive a kingdom that you can rule forever. But first, go to school and learn. Then come back."

God told you this and then sent you here. Now it is your job to discover Him, to know yourself, and to find out what is your true wealth. That is why you have come here. So make your wisdom into a pair of scissors and edit your reels properly, cutting out what is wrong. He has given you everything, but you must cut away all the pictures you have been taking with your own camera and keep only the good reels, those that pertain to your Guardian. Splice them together and cut away everything else. Then His kingdom will be yours.

ANNE HOCHBERG: I have a question that I have had for a long time, since I was little. I hope it is not a silly one. I read in a book that every snowflake is different, no two flakes are alike. And it was a wonder to me, that out of all the snow that falls every year all over the world, is it really possible that there could be no two snowflakes alike?

BAWA MUHAIYADDEEN: As the separate flakes fall, some look large, others look very large, and some are as small as atoms. Some flakes appear to be pure white, others look dirty gray, and some resemble the color of earth. While they are falling, we see different shapes and sizes and colors, but once they have covered the ground, they form a solid blanket of white. Can we still distinguish individual flakes? No, all that we saw as separate earlier has become one complete beauty.

The dog, the fox, the cat, the rat, and man are also like that. All the creations of God fall separately, without being connected to one another. God has told us, "This is the way I made My creations; I placed every quality and every action within them in different ways. Through My resplendent rays of grace I created six kinds of lives: earth lives, fire lives, water lives, air lives, ether lives, and the light life which is man. You have to analyze each one and understand them with your wisdom.

At first you will see My creations as different because you will be looking at each one individually, separately. But later, when you have realized yourself and come to the realm of God's grace, you will look with wisdom at all the lives, and what seemed separate before will be seen as one, like the white blanket of snow. All that you will see is perfect purity and beauty. Then you will realize that everything everywhere is joined together as one. If you look at them while you are in that state, you will see that they are all the same. They are your own life. The sun that you see outside is your own life. The moon that you see outside is also your life. You see the earth outside, and it is also within you. You see the sky outside; that is the maya, or illusion, which you have within you. All the things that you see outside as forms are there within you. All six lives are joined together within you: earth life, fire life, water life, air life, ether life, and the light life, which is the life of man. You must realize that all these forms and colors are not separate; they exist within you as one life.

God created snow as an example to show you the unity in everything. Falling snowflakes may appear to be separate, but do not think of them that way. When your wisdom dawns and understanding comes, you will look at creation in its totality and see everything as equal, as one. In that state you will know only one point, nothing else. Only the power and the grace of God will exist. The things that you saw earlier will not be there. You will see all lives as your own and trust them as you do your own life. You will realize that you are the six kinds of lives.

But if you still have a connection to your karma, if you hold on to illusion and to your thoughts, if you cling to your arrogance, and to such qualities as anger, hatred, and hastiness, then you will see only differences. You must dispel the five heinous sins which came with your birth: intoxication, craving, theft, murder, and falsehood; you must cast out the six evils of lust, anger, miserliness, attachment, bigotry, and envy; arrogance, karma, and maya; *tārahan, singhan,* and *sūran,* which represent the qualities of the elephant, the force of the lion, and the visions of the illusory mind. These are the things that make you focus upon differences.

God has said, "You were created out of water as a form. I placed a ray within that form, and that ray is purity." But as long as you continue to look at the differences you sought earlier, then the water that you were created from will freeze into ice. Do not think that ice is strong or permanent just because it is hard. It does not remain long in that state. After a while, it begins to melt. You've seen that, haven't you? It changes into water, and the water flows away. Then there is nothing left. Like that, you took form in water and in the end you will flow back again as water. Finally, nothing will be left to be seen. Your whole life will be wasted, like a block of melting ice.

God created snow as an example to show you the unity in things. Your body and beauty will melt away, your color will melt away, even your mind and your desire will melt away. Everything that is illusory will melt and there will be nothing left. Your life will be finished and wasted.

If you reflect upon this, if you reflect on each thing in life with your wisdom, then you will see only purity, filling everything, and you will know that one true state. That is a state of beauty, which you will not be able to see again, once the time for it passes. In your life there is a time of youthful maturity which shows off your beauty. At that age you are attractive to everybody. There is also a state of youthful maturity in the realm of wisdom and of devotion to God. That state comes to you when all your differences leave you. That is a state of perfect purity. That is maturity within maturity. In that state you see no differences, you see everything as one. Everything is light. You see only God.

That state must develop within you. But maturity cannot be acquired instantly, just as you cannot make a metal object shine instantly by simply pouring water on it. You have to polish it. Then, to bring out its true beauty, you need to shine a light on it. And if the light is to shine, the current must be connected properly. All these things are needed.

In the same way, to make your life shine, you have to strive hard. And to bring out your true beauty, you need a man of wisdom. Then, if you can connect your heart to his heart, you can come to that state where everything is one light. If you try you can succeed.

June 6, 1979

Session 19

Is it our responsibility to bring others on the path?
217

How can I live a life surrendered to the will of God?
219

*I sent my sister books and pictures, and she intends
to come here. What more should be said to her?*
220

Is it right or wrong to give charity to religions?
221

*What message do you have for some brothers
who are in prison?*
223

Session 19

VERONICA ROTH: What responsibility do we have to bring others on the path?

BAWA MUHAIYADDEEN: We have to do the best we can. To receive our own earnings, however, we must do whatever our duty is. Whether others come or not is their gain or loss. We gain nothing from that. We are not running a business here.

We can tell them, "There is one God. If you go along that path to God, you will reap many benefits in your life." It is our duty to tell them that. But coming or not coming, wanting to come or not wanting to come, is each individual's responsibility. If a person wants to come, it will happen. If he doesn't want to, it will not. We cannot beat him into maturing. Our duty is to say what must be said and to show him love. If he wants to follow the straight path, then show him the map. Following or not following that map is his responsibility. You don't need to advertise; you only need to hold firmly to God's justice and God's truth and make the effort to say what must be said. Anything beyond that is not your responsibility.

If someone has doubt and fear on the path to God, it will be difficult. Doubt is a satanic quality and fear belongs only to ghosts and satans, but faith, certitude, and determination belong to man. In order to reach God, one must want to know the truth with absolute certitude and determination, with $\bar{i}m\bar{a}n$. If a man can establish such $\bar{i}m\bar{a}n$, he can attain wisdom, and having attained it, he can use it to analyze and understand right and wrong. If he knows right from wrong, he can bring his life onto the right path. If he lives his life on that path, he can see the One who drew the map for it.

We must progress in this way; then we will reach the end of the path and know its beauty. We must try to correct our own faults, to eliminate the doubts, anger, and hastiness that are within us. Then we can see God and receive His help. This is what our duty is. To tell

217

others is also our duty, but whether they accept it or not, whether they act on it or not, is their responsibility.

You need not worry or feel sorry about this. You need only speak. Whether they choose to listen is not your responsibility. God has told us, "I will take care of that." All the prophets who came to this world simply related what God told them to. Those who listened progressed, while those who did not listen stayed behind.

One hundred and twenty-four thousand representatives of God came to this world. The lights of God, the messengers of God, the eternal devotees of God, the ones who know the three realms (the world of creation, this world, and the next), and His *qutbs,* who know His names and His powers—all came to convey the commandments of God and to show us how we should act. They came to bring peace and unity to mankind. They called for a state of equality among all lives, but people continued to separate themselves into groups according to various religions, languages, races, and colors. And despite what each prophet said about unity and equality, some people only saw his race, some only saw his color, and others only saw religion.

Every one of the prophets said, "There is just one God. Trust in that One alone. He is the One who gives judgment. He is the Creator and Protector." But instead of following that one God, the people made the prophets into gods, religions into gods, and races into gods. They made all kinds of things into gods, forming numerous divisions and subdivisions. But they did not make the truth into God. They did not worship God with faith, determination, and certitude.

Now all these different languages, colors, races, and religions exist, but the One of equality and peace is the one and only God. Anyone who can trust and follow that one God will live in a state of peace and tranquility. Believing in that One and surrendering to Him is heaven. Man should be aware of this.

There are many diseases that separate man, diseases that kill him, diseases that make one man cause pain to another, diseases that cause one man to murder another or to eat the heart of another. If man can kill all these diseases that are killing him, he will have peace. If he can discard the qualities which cause him to devour others' hearts, the qualities which hurt people and separate them from each other, then all men will live like brothers. And, as children of the same mother, they will see God and accept Him.

There is a path that leads from east to west. We have come from the west to the east, and now we must return to the west. We have come from the place of that One and our goal should be to return to Him. If that is your intention, you will return. On this path, whoever realizes the truth will reach the end. All the others are merely conducting businesses and waging wars. With their envy, murder, sins, and differences, they create the battlefields of hell. One path alone is the straight path. All the rest are battlefields.

Therefore, say what must be said. Whether others listen or not is not your responsibility. That is what God told the prophets. You shouldn't worry. It is your duty to plow the land, to plant the seeds, and to water and fertilize the crops, but it is up to the other person to grow and to flower and bear fruits.

Think about this. Perform your duty to the extent that you can, and don't be sad about it.

QUESTION: How can I live a life of continual sincerity and surrender to the will of God?

BAWA MUHAIYADDEEN: First you must think about what you place your faith in. You should understand through your wisdom that everything in this world which appears will change and that whatever has a beginning also has a time when it must end. Just as the day changes into night, all things change, whether it be the sun, the moon, or the stars. If darkness can come and occlude the sun's power, then the sun has an end, a limit. If sunlight can come and conceal the moon's power, then the moon has an end. If the light of the stars can fade in the daylight or be hidden behind clouds, then the stars also have a limit. Even the water in a well eventually dries up.

Anything that has a beginning is bound to end. It is subject to change. Isn't that so? Your body will also change one day. All these things that change between the time we are born and the time we die are not our real life. They are only lessons, school lessons. We have come to this school of the world, and we must study all the creations that have appeared here. Once we have gained clarity from our study we will arrive at the great realization that there is only one thing which never changes, one thing which exists within everything always. That indestructible and unchangeable thing is truth. Truth never changes. It has neither beginning nor end; it exists within that beginningless Power. It is the fullness of life.

We have to understand this point. The things that change are not our real life. Within us there is another body, another beauty. It belongs to that ray of light which never changes. We must discover how to mingle with it and become one with that unchanging thing. We must realize and understand this treasure of truth. That is why we have come to the world.

While we are here, we must study and learn. Just as we use a book to gain an explanation of something, if we will use the clarity of our wisdom, we can learn from whatever we do, whatever we see, and whatever we are attached to. Everything that we discover in this world can explain some aspect of our life. Our Father has created as His art works all these things that we value and form attachments to: relatives and friends, the study of psychology, school, and all the arts. If we can discover a meaning in each of these things that change, then we can understand the One who does not change.

This is what life is for, to join the unchangeable thing and to become unchangeable, to join our light to that Light which has no end. This is the meaning of life. Everything else is either a duty or a lesson.

QUESTION: Could Bawa say something to my sister who lives in the Dominican Republic? She intends to come here after a while. I have written to her and sent her Bawa's pictures and literature.

BAWA MUHAIYADDEEN: Everything is a picture. But we cannot know the taste of something just by looking at a picture of it. To taste it is to know it. Let her come, and then she will know the taste.

Little brother, in the meantime tell her:
     It's all a dream.
     It's all a lie.
     It's all over.

It's all crazy.

It's all right.

Let us think about this. Let us think about our life and try. You can also tell her:

> Hastiness will kill wisdom.
>
> Impatience will devour wisdom.
>
> Anger is the guru of sin.
>
> Lust is greater than the ocean.
>
> Duty is greater than God.
>
> The actions of one who does not analyze
>
>   and look into things will lead
>
>   to an undying death.
>
> All that glitters is not gold.
>
> A golden pot needs no decoration.
>
> The arrogance of 'I' will hurt oneself.
>
> The possessiveness of 'mine' will
>
>   torture oneself.
>
> With the goad of wisdom control your anger,
>
>   which is like an elephant in musth.

If the duality of the you and the I leaves us, then we will be in a state of absolute oneness; we will obtain the state of God. We will understand that effulgent light, that *jōthi,* through the triple flame of *alif, lām, mīm:* of Allah, the light of wisdom, and the light of the soul. We will understand the *dīn,* the light of perfect purity, which is *ill-Allāhu,* Allah alone. We will know that one and only Treasure.

Tell her that.

KAREEM QUASH: Is it right or wrong to give charity to religions?

BAWA MUHAIYADDEEN: In the world there are millions of religions—many, many paths. All of them are like the roads leading to a city, but they will not take you beyond the city. Reflect upon this with your wisdom.

Now, in Philadelphia there is a city hall where you can get all kinds of documents. Most official papers needed from the time of your birth to the time of your death can be obtained there: birth certificates, work permits, marriage licenses, death certificates, and many other papers. But no certificates can be obtained at city hall giving information about what happened before you were born, where you came from, which group you belong to, where you will go after death, and what will happen on Judgment Day. How can the people at city hall know that? They can only issue the papers to use here in this world.

You yourself have to find out: What is my story? Where was I before I came here? What have I done since I came? What must I do now? Where am I going after this? What will I have to do there? Who is God? Who is my Father? What is His kingdom like? Where does He dwell? We cannot go to city hall to get help with these matters. If you want that information, you must transcend the gates and laws of city hall. There you will find no ready-made path or even a road sign to show you the way. You will have to open up your own subtle path, no matter how difficult it may be. And the only map you will have to help you is the one within you, which exists there as wisdom within wisdom.

Up until that point you will have to go to city hall for whatever you need. They will give you certificates for all sorts of things, and you must pay a fee for each one. Sometimes you may have to slip a little extra to someone to get what you need. Isn't that true? And if you earn an income, you must pay taxes on that. You even have to pay taxes for the roads you use. You have to pay for everything in this world.

But when you go beyond, there will be no fee. The question of payment will no longer arise, for you will have gone beyond all that. Then you will come to a vast open space. If you look, you will know which path to take from there. Of course, if you only want to go as far as city hall, that is all right, too.

KAREEM: On TV we see that people are starving in other countries.

BAWA MUHAIYADDEEN: Yes, aid is being sent to those places. Consider this with your wisdom. In America, how many people are blind? How many people are homeless? How many people are crippled and paralyzed? How many have no mother or father? How many are out in the cold? How many have to sleep in the woods?

There are over 200 million people in America. Many of them

exist in poverty and do not have a place to live or enough to eat. They are undergoing great difficulties. If a person who cannot alleviate the suffering in his own country sets out to help an underdeveloped country, it is like someone wanting to feed another man's wife when his own wife is starving.

People are starving in other countries, and yet, right here there are so many who steal and murder to satisfy their hunger, and then they go to prison for it. You must help them first. Before you assist people in other lands, you must solve the problems in your own community and help your own brothers and sisters. If rain is leaking through a hole in your own roof and you go to other countries to take care of their leaky roofs, that is foolish. That is the way things are done in this world.

Many people have come to America from Africa, Australia, and Europe, from both east and west. Some of them are starving right here. Let us appease their hunger. If we can satisfy the hunger here, if we can develop a state of peace here, there will be no more murder, revenge, separations, or other difficulties. If we can learn to live in peace, then we can help others. But if we ourselves do not even have a loincloth to wear, how can we try to cover the backsides of people in other countries?

Whatever information is presented on television, we must think about it with wisdom. What we are seeing is an advertisement. We should not become involved and concerned. Why should we entangle ourselves with everything that happens in this world? Use your own wisdom and inner patience and carry on your own life.

When your neighbors are starving and going without clothing, when they are in a state of anguish and suffering, you must first lift them up and comfort them. Once that is accomplished, everybody can join together to help other countries.

May God protect you. Help in whatever way you want to.

BAWA MUHAIYADDEEN (to a man on leave from prison): Are you going back today? May God help you.

QUESTION: Is there anything I can take back to the brothers?

BAWA MUHAIYADDEEN: The innermost heart, God, His grace,

and His qualities are what must be given to them. His love must be given to them. Offer that love. Take that back. That is what I can give. I cannot send them fruits or anything else. It is not allowed by the prison officials. I cannot give them the world, I can only give them my heart. Tell them that Bawa offers them his heart. *Āmīn.*

June 10, 1979

Session 20

---·❦·---

How can I readjust my life?
227

What are the lights I see during prayer?
227

*I have realized much inner growth, but
I feel I should be doing more.*
228

Session 20

QUESTIONER: I want to readjust my life and break my attachments.

BAWA MUHAIYADDEEN: Now, you are aware of the faults in your life, aren't you? Once you are aware of your faults, it is easy to correct them. Suppose you are going on a journey, and you find that the bridge is broken. You know better than to drive your car over it. You will start searching for a detour, won't you? But if you persist in saying, "I must go over this bridge," even though you are aware of the danger, then you will fall.

In the same way, the moment you become aware of a fault or a mistake in your life, you must immediately say, "Satan, leave this place!" and then correct yourself, clear your heart, and go on the right path. That is the way to control your life and find peace. That is the exaltedness of a human life. Whenever you anticipate any danger or any obstruction, you must immediately take steps to avoid it. Think about this.

Āmīn.

CLAUDE CRUMPTON: For a year now, sometimes when I say *dhikr*—(*Lā ilāha ill-Allāhu:* There is nothing other than You, O God. Only You are Allah), I see a very brilliant light pulsating before my forehead in the area of the gnostic eye.

BAWA MUHAIYADDEEN: Good. Such experiences can occur, but ultimately the light that you see outside should penetrate and disappear within your *qalb,* your innermost heart, and radiate from that hidden place. Then your meditation and your worship will be exalted.

There are various kinds of lights and forms and sounds that can come to distract you from true worship. If whatever comes disappears when you recite the Third Kalimah, the *Subhānallāhi Kali-*

227

mah, * then it is a glitter from some satan or jinn or from illusion. But what comes from the light of God, from the *Nūr,* which is the resplendence of Allah, will not disappear. It will remain firm.

So recite the Third Kalimah with the intention that anything other than a light from Allah or the *Qutb* will disappear. If you recite with that intention and the light remains steadfast, then that is the light of God, the inner light of devotion, of true worship. That is what you really need for the straight path. That is what *gnānam,* or wisdom, needs. Any other questions?

CLAIRE MAHER: Through the grace of God I have realized so much happiness and inner growth, and my marriage has also been stabilized. I feel very happy about it, but my mind keeps saying that I should be doing more, both in the world and in learning wisdom.

BAWA MUHAIYADDEEN: All right. You have realized a certain amount of peace and happiness in your life. However, it is possible that all this could change, and to the same extent that you feel peace in life now, you could experience difficulties later. The things that you think bring peace now could turn out to cause problems later. Everything that you experience in this world as peace or problems will be reaped together at harvest time. Then what will you do? Will you smile and laugh or will you cry and wail?

Now you feel happy, because you see something growing in your life, a gain in your business. But later you may experience a loss in that same business. Then what will you do? Will you close your stores? Or will you cry because you have met with a loss? What will you do?

CLAIRE: Well, perhaps the peace that I have now is not the true peace of God. If I had the true peace of God, I would not cry.

BAWA MUHAIYADDEEN: The peace you have now is not true peace. The things that you think bring peace and happiness in your life are all things that disappear. You cannot keep them safe forever. They will always say, "I might go. I will go."

In the Tamil language, the word *selvam* means *wealth* and

---

*See Glossary.

selvohm means *we will go away.* The word *tangum* means *gold* and
tangohm means *we do not stay.* So *selvam* and *tangum* are saying
selvohm and *tangohm:*

> Don't try to keep us locked up.
> We are not people who are going to stay,
> We are people who might go away.
> Why are you protecting and guarding us?
> We are people who roam,
> We come and we go.

Now, *tantiram* means *poverty* and *taritirohm* means *we do not
remain in one place. Taritiram* also joins in, saying *taritirohm:*

> I do not remain in one place.
> I am one who roams,
> I am never stationary.

Happiness and unhappiness join in and they all declare:

> We do not stay in one place.
> Happiness and unhappiness,
> Wealth, gold, and poverty,
> All these do not stand still.
> We visit someone and then we leave them.

It is your own folly if you desire these things. You should desire
only that complete treasure, the One that never comes or goes, the
One that never diminishes. That is the treasure of grace and the
happiness of wisdom. That is the happiness of God. Fill yourself
with that. It will never leave or diminish. Only that is true
happiness.

Whatever else you desire will always contain a mixture of joy and
sorrow. Whatever you experience as happiness can suddenly
change and bring you unhappiness. And when you are experiencing
unhappiness, another incident can suddenly occur and make you
happy. That could be followed by still another incident that is a
cause for suffering and that by something which brings you peace
again. These are changing emotions, changing things. That is not
what you need. What you need is to know the true, eternal treasure,
the treasure of grace. If you can search for that and reach it, then all
the other things will tire of you. The world will no longer accept you;
there will be no place in this world for you. Everyone will discard
you, shouting, "Go away from our wealth! Don't come near our

treasure! This is our country and our wealth. You have no share here." Then they will take a big stick and drive you away.

At that stage, when the whole world beats you and rejects you, if you stand firm without faltering or trembling, without allowing your faith, your *īmān*, to waver, and without fear of anything—if you can withstand that beating, then you will experience the state of complete happiness.

Prior to that, whatever you experience as happiness or sorrow might cause you to change or waver. And as one situation follows another, you might even say, "Oh, what is God doing? Who is this God?" You might even begin to doubt God. Your faith might diminish, causing you to suffer. Something might happen to make you so unhappy that you could discard your wisdom or even go crazy.

Please do not accept these changing things that come to you. If you do, at some point they could change your life completely, and then you could change completely, too. So don't accept and follow either happiness or sorrow. They are the sort of people who befriend you, then desert you; they are only visitors who come and go. Instead of letting them change you, change your state. Try to find the Original One who resides within you and fill yourself with that treasure. If you can find that unchanging thing, it will never leave you.

June 11,12, 1979

Session 21

How can I get rid of jealousy?
233

Why is the expression on the face so important?
234

Session 21

DR. ART HOCHBERG: How can I get rid of jealousy?

BAWA MUHAIYADDEEN: Look at this Siamese peach that someone brought. It is like jealousy, which has two heads. If there is
jealousy in you, you should go to a surgeon to have it cut out. The
end result of jealousy is doubt. Doubt, suspicion, jealousy, pride,
and arrogance are all qualities that belong to satan. Vanity and
anger keep us apart from God. Hatred, treachery, cunning, and
hypocrisy lead us automatically to hell. These are the qualities that
separated satan from God and the kingdom of heaven at the time
Adam (☞) was created. When any of these are present in a human
being, it means that he has separated himself from God.

If we want to dwell with God in His kingdom, we must remove
these qualities from ourselves. As soon as we turn toward God, we
must pluck out and throw away whatever evil is in us. That is the
condition laid down by Allah. That is His decree. Nobody can
destroy these satanic qualities for us. We ourselves have to eliminate them. If we allow them to remain within us, then God will banish
us from heaven and say, "O *mal'ūn,* O degenerate one, get out! You
have to leave!" just as He said to satan when He cast him out and
forbade him to go beyond the fourth heaven. And as long as we fail
to get rid of our evil qualities, we too will have to roam around in the
first four heavens, which correspond to earth, fire, water, and air.
As long as we continue to discard the qualities of inner patience,
contentment, and giving all responsibility to God; as long as we do
not embrace His three thousand gracious attributes, His behavior,
His conduct, and all the duties which He performs through His
sovereign powers, Allah will pick us up and fling us far away, and
we will remain banished from His kingdom. We will be unable to
meet and commune with the saints and prophets and *qutbs* and
angels and the other heavenly beings. We will be kept away from

the *'arsh,* the throne of God, and will not be able to merge with Him. Until we realize this and remove our evil qualities, we will remain separated from Him and will be unable to see Him. Every one of us must understand this.

We have to free ourselves from these qualities. How can we obtain that freedom? Through wisdom. Only wisdom enables man to get rid of lust, anger, hatred, miserliness, blood ties, fanaticism, envy, theft, falsehood, murder, intoxicants, drugs, torpor, arrogance, karma, and illusion. The things that are in satan must not be in us. We must escape from such thoughts and actions and qualities. We must escape.

Then we will be in heaven and will dwell with God and His messengers and prophets and saints and all the celestial beings.

Do you understand?

QUESTION: Why is the expression on our face so important?

BAWA MUHAIYADDEEN: We must strive to attain a certain state. When we seek to reach Allah, we must always try to seek Him with a smiling face. When we meet Allah, we must always meet Him with a smiling face. When we understand Allah, we must live with a smiling face which reflects that understanding. When we pray to Allah, we must pray to Him with a beautiful heart. If we are in that state, a flower garden will bloom in our hearts, and the beauty of those flowers will shine in the face. Good thoughts, good intentions, and good actions will blossom into beautiful flowers of love and emit cooling fragrances within our hearts. How beautiful that flower garden is when it blooms in completeness. That is heaven, and the One who dwells in that heaven is Allah.

With a lovely, resplendent, blooming countenance and with a sweet fragrance and beauty in the heart, we must pray to our Creator and praise Him. Our love and our happiness make Him happy, and then He comes to dwell within that beauty and fragrance. As He draws close to us, we can speak to Him.

This is a mystery, a miracle of Allah. He can see the state of the heart by looking at the face. The beauty of the heart is reflected there. If there is no beauty in the heart, then the face that looks at

Him will not be bright. It will not be able to look straight at Allah, it will bend down in shame. That face, which should always look straight at Him and shine with love and faith, will turn aside. No beauty will show there.

Allah knows at once from the face what a person's true state is. His thoughts transform his face immediately. If jealousy, envy, or treachery are in a man's heart, Allah knows. The face changes. Its beauty disappears and it becomes dark. If there is any secret thought in a man's mind, it will make him bow his head down. If good thoughts are not blooming within, he will be unable to hold his head up and look straight at Allah. No matter who he tries to look at, a good man or a bad man, he will have to look aside or look down.

But if there is no jealousy, treachery, cunning, or deceit in a man's heart, he will be able to look everyone in the face without shame. Everybody will notice his lovely countenance and shining face. The clarity and beauty in his heart will make his face cheerful, broad, cool, and smiling. All lives will be entranced by the cool beauty of such a face and by his soft, loving words. Good people and evil people, big people and small people, demons and ghosts and satans will all succumb to that beauty.

The heart and the face are two very important places. The face is a miracle mirror that Allah has placed within each child. The heart is the mercury and light within that mirror. God made the heart into heaven, and the light from that heaven can be seen in the resplendence on the face. That light must come into each face and be seen by all. This is the miracle which each one of you must realize. Then you will be able to see the prophets and Allah face to face.

God has given this explanation of the face.

June 14, 1979

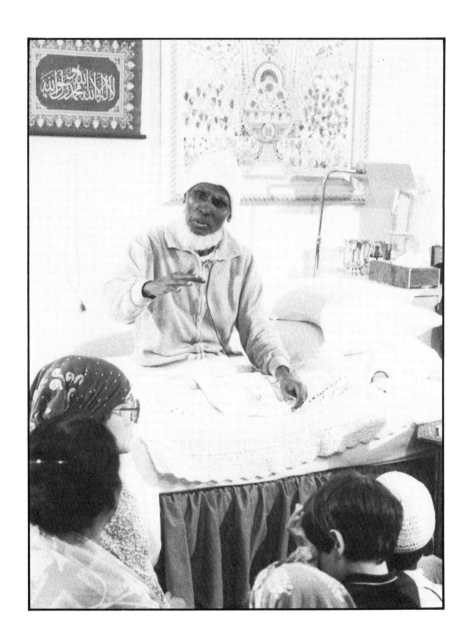

Session 22

Interview for cable television:

Where were you born?
239

How long have you been in the world?
239

How many children can you embrace?
241

*What message would you like to address
to the whole world?*
244

What is the first step to freedom?
245

*How can people understand that all are
God's children?*
246

What should we strive for in life?
246

Session 22

INTERVIEWER: Bawa, I would like to ask a few questions so the television audience can know something about you.

BAWA MUHAIYADDEEN: Very good, please ask.

INTERVIEWER: Were you born in Ceylon?

BAWA MUHAIYADDEEN: I do not know about my birth. I lived in India for some time. I lived in Baghdad for some time. I lived in Jerusalem for some time. I was in Medina for some time. I was in Egypt for some time. I lived in Rome for some time. Later I went to Ceylon, and now I am in America. Whenever I am asked to do a particular duty, I go and perform that duty. That is why I go to each particular place. If I were not commanded to do that duty, I would not go there.

INTERVIEWER: How many years have you been among us, among the people of this world?

BAWA MUHAIYADDEEN: God has let me stay among people of this world for quite a number of years. I stay in one place for a while and then I go to another place. My duties keep changing. I am not in the habit of talking much about these things. At one time I too thought about age and the number of days. Then God gave me this explanation:

"Only God is eternal, unchanging. Everything else is subject to change; there is a limit to its existence. Therefore, if one puts his trust or faith in anything else, when that thing perishes, he will perish with it. When the thing that he trusts and loves reaches its limit, he will too. But if a person were to dwell within Me, he would never perish. Because I am unchanging, he will not change either.

"You must understand that kind of time. One day for Me is equivalent to ten million years for one who does not dwell in that state. But if one dwells within Me, for him too it will be only a day, just one day. Even though many millions of years may pass, if one dwells within Me there will be no counting the years for him. Days and months may pass, even an eon may pass, but still there will be no question of the passage of years.

"Therefore, try to dwell within Me. Then your age will be Mine, and your life will be Mine. On the other hand, if you live with trust in things that are subject to change and have a limit to their existence, then you will too. That is what creates time and age. Understand this, and go on performing the duties you were sent to do."

This is what God told me. Therefore, I do not take stock of the days and months and years. I am only performing the duties that I have been asked to do.

INTERVIEWER: I ask you these questions because people want to know about you. These are the questions that will be in their minds.

BAWA MUHAIYADDEEN: That's all right. This is the world. What you have asked is quite correct. The world will trust the world. The world can trust nothing else. But truth will trust only the truth.

There is only one sun resplending in the skies, the same sun for both east and west. It will be seen in the east, then after a while it will be seen in the west. There will be daylight on one side of the world and darkness on the other. Within the same day, there will be darkness where there was daylight and daylight where there was darkness.

It is the same sun that shines everywhere, but it only benefits those lives that are able to take in its rays of light. All the lives that do not want that light dwell in the darkness of caves and burrows and come out only when it is dark. No matter how often the sun may rise, the lives that like to live in darkness will never come forth into the sunlight, and those that like to live in the sunlight will never retreat into the darkness.

In the same way, there are two kinds of people in the world: those who have faith in the world and whose life is darkness, and those who have faith in God and live in anticipation of truth and light. The first group trusts the world. They trust miracles, mesmerism, occult powers, and worldly praise. These people are like those lives that dwell in dark caves, hidden from the light. But the people who trust God and the truth and act with God's qualities will come out when they see the light of truth. They are always wondering, "When will I ever be able to leave this darkness? It keeps me tossing around, holding me in a state of sleep. How soon will I come out into the light?" These people cannot be forced to enter the darkness; they cannot live in a place which does not suit them. And if we try to get those who live in darkness to come out into the light, what will happen? It will be very difficult for them. The things that they think about and desire cannot be found in the light. Dragging them out would be like tossing a fish from the ocean onto dry land or forcing a land animal to stay under water—both would die. That is the way things are.

Those who have faith in the world are one way, and those who have faith in God are another way.

INTERVIEWER: What about the people who are living in the dark and would like to find the sunshine? How big are your arms? How many children can you embrace?

BAWA MUHAIYADDEEN: Whenever I decide to embrace with my own hands, I can embrace only two, mind and desire. But if God embraces with His hands, then everyone can be embraced. If I were the one teaching, if I were the one embracing, it would not help much. It is God who must teach and God who must embrace. God's breath is the true breath, His word is the true word, and His action is the true action. We must hand over all responsibility and surrender ourselves to Him, for He alone must do those things. I cannot do them.

INTERVIEWER: But these are your children. Aren't they here because they love you and your teachings, and because they love God?

BAWA MUHAIYADDEEN: Are these my children? They are my love. My heart is a flower garden and they are the fragrances of the love that dwells in that flower garden. These are all children of God, and He is the One who is bringing them up. I am only the instrument. When a tree bears fruit, is it the fruit that does the work or the tree? The tree is the one that produces the fruit.

I have many, many children in the world, but God is the Father to all. Even if everyone else lets go, God remains as the Father who never lets go. He embraces anyone who wants Him. His duty is to feed milk to the child that cries. He gives that child whatever he needs and comforts him. With compassion, beneficence, patience, tolerance, peacefulness, and many good actions and beautiful, benevolent qualities, God looks after and protects all His children.

That one treasure has all those qualities, but He has no form. He has no color or shape. He has nothing but His qualities and His state of equality. He does not see any difference between one race or color and another. He does not see any difference between one religion and another. He knows no differences at all. His kingdom is justice.

The wealth of God's children is the love He has for them, and His wealth is the love they have for Him. That is His treasure of grace—their good thoughts, good qualities, good actions, and good conduct. When we think of Him, He thinks of us. When we seek Him, He seeks us. When we need Him, He needs us. When we ask something of Him, He gives what we ask for. He has such beautiful qualities. He is a power without form or shape dwelling right within us, within our heart, within our body. He is the light within our eyes. Within our nostrils He is a tiny piece of flesh which is the sense of smell. He is the sound within our ears, the taste within our tongue, and the gleam in our teeth. With our hands He gives and takes and embraces. He is the completeness within our heart. He is the power which exists as life, as wisdom, as the body, as the light of the eye, as the speech of the tongue, and as good thoughts. It is that power which is called God.

To pray to Him we do not need to pay money. To have faith in Him, we do not need to take anything to Him; we only need to take Him. His qualities are our greatest wealth. His only gain is from our taking His qualities to Him. We must acquire them and take them to Him. To have His qualities must be our constant intention. That is our treasure, our life, our search. That is prayer. That is life.

We must know with certainty that this is the meaning of our life. The love we have for Him and the love He has for us is those good qualities, those good thoughts, and our search for Him.

Love to you.   May God make your life long and help you to do His work.

INTERVIEWER: I'm only a speck . . .

BAWA MUHAIYADDEEN: That is what is best, if we can be a speck of dust. Everything big will perish one day. The huge mountains will be broken down by atom bombs, and the elephants and other large creatures will be destroyed by typhoons and storms. Only the tiny ants and the bits of dust that stay in the earth will escape unharmed.

We must be as tiny as the tiniest ant. God is the Doer, the One who is responsible; we are just instruments, we cannot do anything by ourselves. He does the work and we are His instruments. At all times we must have the intention to be His servants. Our hearts must always be in that place. If we have that thought and establish that state, then we can achieve victory in our lives.

The world is not big, my child. The world is as tiny as an atom, but the mind is vast and desire is enormous. Mind and desire are a huge rock mountain that must be broken down. The big things have to be broken down first. To do this we need God's qualities. We need faith, certitude, and determination. Otherwise, mind and desire will make slaves of us, and then we will not be able to perform our duty toward God.

These things that enslave us will not allow us to work for God. When we want to do something for God, at one time love will beckon us, saying, "You are my slave. Come here." Or gold might shout, "You are my slave. How dare you go there!" Another time lust might call us, "You are my slave. You can't go there." Or earth might pull on us, "Where are you going? You are my slave."

These things will prevent us from praying to God. If we are slaves to all the thoughts we think, if we are slaves to everything our eyes see, if we are slaves to all the music our ears hear, if we are slaves to everything the nose smells and the tongue tastes, if we are slaves to everything the body wants— then how can we ever reach a state of peace? We can never know peace or tranquility this way. We have to escape from this slavery and become a slave only to God.

God is a sun to all the universes. If we can transform ourselves into His son, then we can rule all the universes. As His son and His slave, we can perform our duty toward all kingdoms. That is what we have to do. It is a tiny point.

The world is really very, very small, and only if we can stay small can we hide from it and escape.

INTERVIEWER: Bawa, if at this moment you could speak to the entire world, to the world leaders, the industrialists, to the ill, the afflicted, the poor—if you could speak to them, what would you say?

BAWA MUHAIYADDEEN: Over the past two hundred million years, God has sent many prophets, lights of God, saints, *qutbs,* men of wisdom, messengers, and eternal devotees of God. Why did He send them? Is it not possible for God to reform the people of the world directly? Can't He do that? If He wills something, it will happen. Then why did He have to send all those messengers? It was to demonstrate to the people that there is a power called God, who dwells in a place that cannot be reached by mind and desire. He sent them to help the people form a connection with God and to tell them to have faith in that power, to trust in Him and in the words and commandments He has given.

And to show the people that truth and light do exist, God created evil and darkness. God created many opposites: heaven and hell, right and wrong, things that can be explained and things that cannot be explained. Truth is heaven, evil is hell. God illustrates what one thing is by showing us its opposite. That is why there is good and evil. To prove that good exists, He shows us evil.

Then, to caution us against choosing evil, God appointed 124,000 prophets. He selected twenty-five of them as special, and out of those twenty - five He chose eight exalted ones: Adam, Noah, Abraham, Ishmael, Moses, David, Jesus, and Muhammad , may the peace and blessings of God be upon them all. They belong to one family, the family of the one God. And all of the commandments that they brought belong to that one family. There is only one God, one prayer, one family, and one truth.

If the world leaders had truly accepted the one God within their hearts, they would realize that these different prophets who came, one after another, all belong to the same family, God's family. If the leaders had accepted that, if they were in that state of unity, then all the children of the world would have reached that state too. Everybody would be in that state. There would be no murder and no fighting. There would be no divisions or differences at all. If all the leaders were in the right state, if they would accept the words of the prophets who brought the commandments of God, then everything would be right in the world. There would be one blood, one race, one family, all worshiping the one God. That is the true state. But if the leaders are not in that state, then the whole world will be a battlefield. There will continue to be different castes and religions, divisions, discrimination, and fighting. Everywhere there will be murder.

INTERVIEWER: Will we ever reach the true state in our time?

BAWA MUHAIYADDEEN: If the leaders would change, if they would change and be reborn in that true state, then it would be easy for the people to do the same. If the leaders would desire the wealth of God instead of thinking about business, then they would receive unlimited treasures, and they would give peace and tranquility to all. But as long as they persist in desiring the wealth of darkness, the people of the world will continue to suffer. If the leaders would acquire the undiminishing treasure, on that very day they would have peace and the people would have peace. The whole world would be at peace, with everyone living as one family.

God alone can transform them into that state. If that happens, it will be the day of liberation, the day of freedom for the soul.

INTERVIEWER: But Bawa, does one not keep oneself prisoner?

BAWA MUHAIYADDEEN: Everyone is a prisoner.

INTERVIEWER: A child is not born with prejudice and hate; he is taught that. What is the first step a person can take to free himself?

BAWA MUHAIYADDEEN: There is one very easy thing he can do. It is so easy, my child.

After the age of three, the original shoot is cut away from the child, and the things of the world are grafted on. These grafted shoots grow fast, but because they are not the original, they also die fast. So what must we do? We must cut away all the things which are grafted on and allow the original shoot to grow. All our efforts must be toward nurturing that one shoot.

That original shoot is made of the qualities of God: compassion, equality, loving all lives as our own life, realizing everyone else's suffering as our own suffering and their hunger as our own hunger, understanding other people's illness as our own illness, and seeing others' sorrow as our own sorrow. We must develop those qualities and perform our duties just as God does—impartially, in a state of detachment, without any blood ties, without any distinction between the you and the I, and without any differences between races or religions or philosophies. As soon as we reach this state, the original shoot will begin to grow.

INTERVIEWER: How can we help people to understand that all are God's children, even though they may approach Him in different ways?

BAWA MUHAIYADDEEN: God sent down each of His prophets for a particular reason. Each one came with a special message, and we must understand the meaning of those messages and act accordingly.

Now, at the time when God created Adam ⊛, the one whom we call satan lived in heaven and was the leader of the jinns. But when God commanded him to bow down to Adam ⊛, he became jealous and proud, and three times he refused. His pride, jealousy, vanity, arrogance, conceit, deceitfulness, treachery, and desire for revenge turned him into satan. These qualities caused him and his followers to be thrown out of heaven. It wasn't the jinns that were cast into hell, it was their evil qualities. That is what satan is.

Those same evil qualities are in man, and anyone who has them dwelling within him is satan. Such qualities are not compatible with God's kingdom; that is why they were cast out. They belong to hell. Whoever can remove those qualities from his heart will become a leader in the kingdom of God. God threw away the qualities that could not co-exist with His goodness or His grace, and we must do the same. Anyone who keeps these qualities has no place in the kingdom of God. He is called satan, the one who belongs to hell.

We have to seek wisdom, faith in God, determination, and God's qualities. Once we have these, we can use our wisdom to remove the evil qualities. Then we will become leaders in the kingdom of God, and those castoff qualities will become the leaders in the kingdom of hell. If we can learn this, we will live in peace.

INTERVIEWER: What should we strive for in life?

BAWA MUHAIYADDEEN: My child, there is something very important that we must do in this life. We must overcome a vast battalion of forces that we ourselves have made into forms. All our thoughts and intentions create forms out of whatever we desire, whatever we seek and yearn for, and whatever we want to experience. These forms are the four hundred trillion, ten thousand evil forces within the heart. They are eating us, sucking our blood, and killing us. They make us work for them while they devour us. Every single thought is a form within us: the form of a dog, a fox, a tiger, a lion, an elephant, a crocodile, a pig, a monkey, a snake, or a rat—there are countless millions of animal forms, demonic forms, and ghost forms within us. To overcome these vast battalions of forces is very difficult because they are the very forms that we have created.

Also within us are questions and answers, more questions and more answers. Each question comes out of us and an answer is given. Then another question comes and another answer given. Who is asking these questions? The demonic forces that we ourselves have created. Every one of them keeps asking questions of us.

To eliminate all these forces we must throw out every thought that comes to us. We must take in only God's compassion, His patience, His tolerance, equality, justice, righteousness, and integrity. We must have inner patience, contentment, surrender to God, and praise for Him alone. We must treat all lives as our own life, knowing that they are just as precious. We must see all suffering, all happiness, all hunger, all illness, all health, and all poverty as our own.

We must instill these good qualities and eliminate the bad ones. As soon as we throw away one bad quality, we must replace it with a quality of God. In this way, little by little we can acquire His three thousand beneficent qualities and His ninety-nine actions.* Those actions are the miracles of life, and the heart filled with them will be a garden filled with all the fruits and flowers of heaven. That garden

---

* For further explanation see *Asmā'ul Husnā: The 99 Beautiful Names of Allah,* by M. R. Bawa Muhaiyaddeen.

of the heart is God's kingdom. There you will find so many kinds of sweet honey, nectar, tastes, and fragrances. Wherever His qualities have blossomed and grown plenteous, that will be heaven. That is the kingdom of God, the place of justice where judgment is pronounced. We must decorate and adorn that place with His qualities and actions and fill it with His conduct. We must enrich that place with His wealth. That is our heaven. Our heart is heaven.

If we can achieve this, my child, all questions will stop and our life will be peaceful. That is heaven, where eternal peace exists. We must strive to achieve this.

INTERVIEWER: That's not so easy to do.

BAWA MUHAIYADDEEN: It is easy. It is easy.

INTERVIEWER: If we feel gratified when we experience beautiful qualities in another, aren't we being selfish, because we are getting something from that person?

BAWA MUHAIYADDEEN: No, it is not like that. Anyone who walks along the road can inhale the fragrance from a rose or a jasmine flower. Once that fragrance comes into his nostrils, he relishes it, saying, "What a lovely smell!" He takes in the fragrance and goes on his way. He did not cause any pain to the flower by taking in its fragrance. That fragrance wafts all around, even out to the road. That is not selfishness; that is love, the fragrance of love, which he took with him. Another man might come to that same rose bush and pluck the flower. That would be selfish, because he would spoil the beauty of the flower.

INTERVIEWER: But when we give a material gift with love, are we not selfish because we are gratified by the other person's pleasure in receiving it?

BAWA MUHAIYADDEEN: If a child gives me some fruits or something else in that manner, if he gives it with love, I share it with all the children. I don't take it for myself. Fruits are meant to be shared. But if you give me your heart, I will not share that with anybody else. That is not a thing that can be shared. I will keep it here, within my heart.

INTERVIEWER: Sometimes between two people, one will love

more than the other and feel hurt because the other loves less.

BAWA MUHAIYADDEEN: If he feels pain, he is not in a selfless state.

INTERVIEWER: It's difficult to be selfless.

BAWA MUHAIYADDEEN: When the time comes...

INTERVIEWER: It will happen?

BAWA MUHAIYADDEEN: Yes, it will happen. Much love.
    Open your heart and look within,
    Then all your karma will be dispelled.
    Open your heart and look within,
    Open your heart and look within,
    Then the compassion of God will fill that heart.
    Āmīn.

June 16, 1979

Session 23

Bawa Muhaiyaddeen to a visiting group on
how to treat the illnesses of man.
253

How do fate and destiny relate to doing good works?
255

How does surrender to God fit in with
fate and destiny?
257

What is man-God, God-man?
263

How do we make the connection to God?
267

What is meant by rasūl?
268

Session 23

BAWA MUHAIYADDEEN: Illnesses can be treated in many ways, but no matter how many different treatments are used, they may still fail to heal the patient. In order for a treatment to work, first of all, even if the patient does not have faith in God, he must have faith in the doctor and in whatever treatment he suggests. Secondly, the doctor who is performing the treatment must have faith in God; he must have God's qualities, His love, and His patience. The doctor must give all responsibility to God, instead of thinking that he is the one who is responsible for curing the patient.

When these conditions exist, when the patient has faith in the doctor and the doctor has faith in God, then treatment becomes very easy and the illness will be cured, at least to a certain extent. Sometimes an illness will not be cured because the patient doesn't have faith in himself, in the doctor, or in the medicine, and he doesn't even have faith in God. When such a state exists, a cure is very difficult, perhaps impossible.

All human beings are essentially the same, but their minds differ, and these different thoughts bring about different kinds of illnesses. Each human being has a wide variety of thoughts, qualities, actions, and behaviors. All of these have to be changed, one by one.

Consider the work a tractor does. For each different job you want done, you need to attach a different part. If you want to haul some materials, you must attach a trailer. Even though the tractor does the pulling, it needs the trailer to hold the materials. On the other hand, if you want to cut grass with the tractor, you have to attach a mower to do that. For digging up the earth you need a plow, and to break up what you have plowed, you need a small tiller. For furrowing or breaking up the sod, you need a circular attachment called a disk. If the soil is too high in some places and too low in others, then you need yet another attachment that levels the ground. For each job a different attachment is needed. The tractor itself does not change, but the attachments have to be alternated to suit each different job that must be done.

Just as a farmer knows the tractor parts and can attach whichever one is needed, an *insān kāmil*, a perfected, God-realized teacher, has the wisdom to know the different qualities and potentialities within the heart of a man, and he can attach whatever is required. He will plow up the various qualities that are within a person, then clear them and level them out. To do that, he may have to change parts repeatedly. Sometimes he may have to attach patience, sometimes the inner patience or forbearance known as *sabūr*, and sometimes *shakūr*, or contentment. At other times, he may have to attach *tawakkul 'alallāh*, surrendering all responsibility to God, or *al-hamdu lillāh*, giving all praise to God. He might need to use the part called love, or he might have to attach wisdom. He might also fit on the part called medicine. There are so many parts for treating man's afflictions.

That which has to be treated with wisdom, the *insān kāmil* treats with wisdom. That which has to be treated with love, he treats with love. Whatever has to be treated with faith, he treats with faith. Sometimes his treatment might be a suggestion or thought. In situations where the mind is not functioning correctly, he might have to treat the mind by tricking it. If somebody is possessed by a demon, he might even have to use the magic appropriate to that demon to exorcise it. For every situation, he will use whatever is needed. If the grace of God is the only thing that will treat an illness, then he will use the grace of God to treat it. Sometimes *gnānam*, or divine wisdom, may be the only treatment that will help.

Meanwhile, the patient must have faith. When the doctor feels the need to change the treatment, the patient, with his faith, must cooperate.

The tractor also needs that kind of faith. It should not say, "Oh, why must I have all these different contraptions? Why do I not have just one thing?" The tractor should know that each different attachment serves a particular purpose. That is the faith required of a tractor. It must accept that the farmer, in order to clear the ground and plant his crop, needs to change the parts one by one. Only then will there be a good harvest.

In the same way, if you want to make a man's life better, you need a doctor who has wisdom, an *insān kāmil*, a divinely luminous one. That doctor will know each aspect of the human being he is treating and will apply the different treatments, as required. There are many things inside each human being that have to be changed, one by one. The patient must have faith that the doctor, like the farmer, knows exactly what is required and will change the parts and supply what is appropriate as the need arises. The patient's job is to maintain his faith as the parts are being repeatedly changed.

QUESTION: Could Bawa give me an explanation about *al-qadā' wal-qadar,* or fate and destiny, and how they relate to us doing good works, as we were enjoined to do by *Allah subhānahu wa ta'ālā,* even with our limited knowledge and wisdom?

BAWA MUHAIYADDEEN: God created man. And when He created man, He also created good and evil. These two do exist; they have to exist. This is what the Qur'an says. But people often misunderstand this and say, "Oh, good and evil have both been created by Allah, so whatever is happening has to happen. This is fate, this is what Allah has destined for us." It is not right to say this. It is only an excuse for doing nothing about the evil. If we say that everything is supposed to happen just as it does, then we must ask: What was the reason for sending down 124,000 prophets? Why did these eternal devotees of God, the *rasūls,* have to come? Why were the heavenly messengers sent? What was their purpose?

If everything was destined according to the will of God, and if everything must happen as it has been willed, then there would have been no need for all those messengers to have come. There would be no reason to try to change anything.

Allah created pairs of opposites: *khair* and *sharr,* or what is good and what is evil. He also created *al-qadā' wal-qadar,* fate and destiny. But He created them in such a way that what happens will be the result of man's own actions. He gave man the ability to change what is good or evil. The destiny that each man receives is what he reaps from his own intentions, speech, and actions. That is what Allah has said. That is the word of God.

Just as good and evil are both within man, so man has both *sirr* and *sifat*. What we see outside is the *sifat*, the form, the manifest creation; the *sirr* is the secret hidden within the form. Within man that secret lies hidden as *'ilm*, or divine knowledge. *Insān*, or true man, is a form within the form. Out of all the creations, the one called man is a secret. Within man is another secret, and within that secret is a deeper secret. It is this inner secret that man must understand. Within it is something very mysterious, and within that mystery is *hayāt*, or life. Within that life is another form. Within that form is a resplendent light. Within that resplendent light is the *Nūr*, the completeness. Within that is still another light. And within that light is a power. Within that power is God. It is man's duty to understand this. Then, when good or evil comes he will not simply say, "Oh, this is all the will of God. Both the good and the evil are the will of God," and then keep quiet, without trying to change what is evil. If we can understand the secret that exists within the form, we will realize the error in that way of thinking.

There is a certain fault, or *shirk*, within man. That fault is satan, the qualities of satan. At the time that Adam ⊕ was created, satan became jealous and spat on Adam ⊕. With that spit, satan's qualities entered into man and have stayed within him ever since. The prophets were sent down by God to cut away this fault and to make man realize the secret that is within, the secret that is God.

The Qur'an does speak of destiny, but just repeating the words of the Qur'an is not enough. There are people who can recite its 6,666 verses, but that alone does not benefit them. Every letter in the Qur'an has a secret within it. God's truth exists within every letter, as a secret within the secret, and we must split open each secret, one after another and try to understand them. But it is impossible to ever say that we have completely understood the Qur'an. No matter how many times the world changes, over and over again, the Qur'an will remain as the secret within. And within that secret is another secret.

The Qur'an contains the laws and words of God. Seasons may change and times may change and the world may change, but God and the word of God will never change. Depending upon the conditions in the world at each time, those words will continue to adapt themselves to fit the needs of that time. Therefore, whenever a man opens the book, no matter where he is or what period he lives in, he will be able to find the answer he needs. He will find the secret explanation for what he wants. Depending upon the station he has reached when he opens that book, he will find the appropriate *al-qadā' wal-qadar,* the correct fate and destiny for him. The meaning is written there. That is the Qur'an.

ABOUL'ALA: There is a story about 'Alī (ﷺ) when he was a *khalī-fah,* and God gave him the inner sight of the *sirr.* Once when he was walking with one of his companions, he saw another man, and he said, "This man is going to kill me." His companion replied, "O *Khalīfah* of the *Rasūlullāh* (ﷺ), why don't you capture him and put him in jail?" 'Alī's (ﷺ) answer was, "If I capture him, then who would kill me?" He knew that man was going to kill him, but he was willing to let him do it. "Who else would do it?" he said. How does this kind of surrender to Allah's will fit in with the explanation that Bawa gave about *al-qadā' wal-qadar?*

BAWA MUHAIYADDEEN: There is another story about 'Alī (ﷺ), the cousin of Prophet Muhammad, the *Rasūlullāh* (ﷺ), the Messenger of Allah. One day, while the *Rasūlullāh* (ﷺ) was talking to his followers, a very old man with a long beard came tottering along, barely able to walk. He was leaning on a stick and hopping like a rabbit. The old man came up to the *Rasūlullāh* (ﷺ), offered his *salāms,* and said, "O *Rasūlullāh,* my life is so difficult. Please cut away this knot that is binding me. I cannot bear it."

The *Rasūlullāh* (ﷺ) asked very kindly, "What has happened? What is the matter?"

And the old man told him, "I'm the grandson of the one who was cast out of heaven by God. My grandfather subdued and controlled the people of this world, destroying all their good thoughts and intentions, so I decided to attack and conquer the heavenly beings and those who were serving God. I gathered together my army and was on my way to attack them when I saw a youth approaching on a white stallion. Just one glance from him, and all my forces and all my troops were burnt to ashes instantly. He was only a small boy, but the minute he climbed down from his horse and looked at me, I fell down in a swoon. He picked up something and swiftly tied my two big toes together. My liver trembled, and I became like a corpse! Then he climbed up on his stallion and rode away.

"From that day on, I have been trying in so many ways to cut this knot which binds my toes, but I have not been able to cut even one thread. I went in search of someone who could release me; I petitioned the greatest of beings, but not one knew how to sever this knot. This went on for a long time. Then came the time of Prophet Adam ⒜. I went to him and related my woes, but he said, 'I am not able to cut this knot. Only the one who tied it will be able to cut it.' Then came the time of the Prophet Noah ⒜. I went to him and asked for his help, but he also said, 'This knot can be cut only by the one who tied it, not by anyone else.'"

The old man continued telling his story to the Rasūl ⒮, mentioning the name of every prophet in order: Idris ⒜, Jacob ⒜, and so on. Finally, when he came to the time of Prophet Abraham ⒜, he said, "Prophet Abraham ⒜ also told me, 'I'm sorry, I cannot cut this knot. But there will be one called Muhammad ⒮ who will come as the Final Prophet. Not until his time will you have this knot cut away and finally be released.'"

"Even so," the old man continued, "I persevered and continued to ask every prophet who came, hoping one of them would be able to relieve me. But none of them could. And so, throughout eons of time I have been suffering. In desperation, I cried, 'When will that Final Prophet come?' I was told, 'He will appear in a later time, when man's *imān* wavers and becomes shaky. When faith declines and man begins to forget God, at that time one will come as the Final Prophet. There will be no more prophets after him.'"

"Now, I have been waiting patiently for so long, and just recently I remembered what was foretold earlier about the time of little faith, when the last prophet would come. Then I realized that this period had already been going on in the world for forty-five years! So, I thought, 'The *Rasūlullāh* must have arrived by now!' And at long last I have found you, and I am hoping for release from this knot which has troubled me for all these eons."

After hearing the story, the Prophet ⒮ turned and spoke quietly to one of his followers, who had been seated there listening. Then he turned and asked the old man, "Have you ever seen that boy again?"

"Never again," said the old man. "That was the one and only

time I ever saw him. I have never again set eyes on him.''

"If you saw the boy again, would you recognize him?" the Prophet ﷺ asked.

"No! No!" cried the old man. "I don't want to see him again! The very thought of him sends shivers down my spine. Please don't bring him here.''

The Prophet ﷺ comforted him and said, "Don't worry. Sit down here, and we will see.'' Then he turned to one of his followers and said, "Go and fetch 'Alī. Tell him that I asked him to come.''

Now at that time, 'Alī ﷺ was a thirteen-year-old boy. As soon as he received the message, he stopped playing and grabbed his sword, his lance, and his spear, thinking that the Prophet ﷺ must be calling him to go to war. But the man who had come to fetch him said, "I don't know what he wants you for. He only asked that you come.''

As soon as 'Alī ﷺ came into his presence, the Prophet ﷺ commanded him, "Remove the knot from this old man's toes.''

'Alī ﷺ turned and looked at the old man. Immediately the old man began trembling. "O Prophet, please save me! That is the boy! He is the one! Don't let him come near me!" he cried.

The old man tried to hide behind the Prophet ﷺ, but the Prophet ﷺ consoled him, saying, "Do not be frightened. Wait a moment.''

'Alī ﷺ stood still and gazed at the toes of the old man. The knot was cut at once, and the toes were freed. Then the Prophet ﷺ said, "All right, now you can go.''

But the old man pleaded, "O Prophet of God, please teach me the *kalimah*, the remembrance of God. Or if you think I am not fit enough to repeat those words, at least please bless me so that my faith in Allah will be made strong.''

Then the Prophet ﷺ told him, "In order for you to be able to accept the *kalimah*, you have to be in a determined state. You certainly know that God is a great One, since He bound you with such a tiny knot. For you to intend such a great One, your faith and heart must be strong. So bring yourself to that state,'' and then he sent him away.

After that the followers, who had been listening, began to question the Prophet ﷺ, "What is the meaning of this? 'Alī is only thirteen years old, and yet this man was talking about something that happened eons ago. This is a great wonder. What does it mean?''

The Prophet ﷺ then explained, ''That is a secret known only to Allah. He alone knows the secret of 'Alī.''

Now, regarding the question you asked earlier: Even though 'Alī ﷻ said to his companion, ''That person will kill me,'' was 'Alī ﷻ really going to die? Was it really death that he saw? If 'Alī ﷻ had been living for eons of time, since before the time of Adam ﷺ, was he going to die at that time?

There is another story: When 'Umar 'Ibnul-Khaṭṭāb ﷺ heard people saying that Muhammad ﷺ was dead, he stepped forward and called out, ''Who says he is dead? If Muhammad ﷺ is dead, everything is dead!'' He raised his sword, ready to challenge anyone who said that Muhammad ﷺ had died.

How could Muhammad ﷺ be dead? Muhammad ﷺ is something that never dies, and the one who believes that will also never die. Death comes only to the one who says that Muhammad ﷺ is dead.

That kind of thinking is at the level of *sharī'at*. There are four levels of *īmān*: *sharī'at, tarīqat, haqīqat, ma'rifat.* * Each one has a different *ṣūrat*, or form. The form made of the earth functions at the first level, *sharī'at*, which is a school. The form made of fire functions at the second level, or *tarīqat*, in which one's *īmān* is made direct and straight. The form of Muhammad ﷺ, the *mīm*, functions at the third level, or *haqīqat*, in which one's *īmān* is made strong enough to unite with Allah, and he merges with the body of the resplendence of his own *īmān*. In *ma'rifat*, the fourth level, one strengthens one's *īmān* to the point where he surrenders to God and communes with Him in the form of *Nūr*.

Beyond these four is the level of *ṣūfiyyat*, in which one is in the form of light, and he converses with God without speaking. He has surrendered entirely to God. The first four are levels of *īmān*, of accepting God with perfect faith. The fifth is the level of *ṣūfiyyat*, in which one merges with God and disappears in Him.

What we are doing at present is *sharī'at*, which relates to the

---

*For further information see *Four Steps To Pure Iman*, by M. R. Bawa Muhaiyaddeen.

form made of earth. One who is at the level of *sharī'at* receives no punishment for the faults he commits, since he does not yet understand the difference between right and wrong. He has not yet developed within him the understanding and discrimination with which he could correct his faults or determine the appropriate punishment for them. In this stage, he simply looks at things and copies what he sees. If someone drinks milk, he will watch and drink milk too; if a baby is conceived, he will see that and then conceive a baby too; if one person jumps on another, he will watch it and then jump too. Like a baby, he just goes along copying and repeating what he sees.

When he reaches the second stage, *tarīqat*, he begins to have faith and is able to accept things that he cannot see. He accepts that Allah exists in an unseen place. In the third stage, *haqīqat*, he accepts and understands what he could not understand before—that thing which is within himself. The fourth stage is *ma'rifat*. At that time all attachments leave him and all the ten sins have gone. God is dwelling within him at all times, without speech and without sound. To know that is *ma'rifat*. God knows no night or day, no *waqt*, no specified time for prayer. One who reaches the level of *ma'rifat* accepts that which is not contained by time. The fifth stage is *sūfiyyat*. For one at this stage, all judgment is over; he and Allah are one. Allah is the only true Sufi.

We must continue to progress through these stages, little by little. After all, the Qur'an did not come all at once. Different *sūrats*, or chapters, were given in answer to the circumstances existing at different times. A particular commandment would come to answer a particular need, and then further explanations would follow. In the same way, we must move forward in our lives, one step at a time. If we stop at the stage we are in now, we will not progress. The extent of our experience will be to board the ship on one shore and get out on the other, never knowing any more than those points where we embarked and disembarked. That will be the limit of our knowledge. We will never see the whole ocean.

Let us return for a moment to *al-qadā' wal-qadar*. What each person receives is the result of what he searches for or what he does. Those that die have to die; those that do not die will remain alive forever. That is how it is. That one handful of earth must return to the earth. You are formed in the earth, you grow on the earth, you eat the earth, and finally, you are prey to the energy of the earth. But *insān*, true man, did not come from the earth. His form is not of the earth; his body is a light form composed only of the qualities and actions of God. That is the true body of man. It is the form of *alif*, *lām*, and *mīm*, which are not of the earth. So *insān* does not stay here, his form resides with Allah.

God has said, "I created pairs of opposites: heaven and hell, right and wrong." These pairs or opposites exist within everyone. Has God created a hell somewhere far away? No. Has God created a heaven somewhere far away? It is not like that. Man's heaven and hell consist of the right and wrong he himself does. If a man prepares and fosters hell within himself while here in this world, then he will live in hell. On the other hand, if he prepares and fosters heaven within himself, then that will be his house. There is no fire that burns by itself in hell. Man takes his own fire with him; his anger becomes the fire of hell. There is no special firewood either; man's own body forms the firewood. There are no ghosts and demons to torment him in hell other than what he has cultivated within himself here. The snakes and scorpions which will bite him there are the evil qualities and thoughts he has nurtured here in this world. The elephants, tigers, bears, and all the cruel animals and satans that will attack him in hell are the evil qualities he brought up within himself and kept in the house he built while he was here. These things will take form there and devour him.

But a man who has the grace of God, who lives in this world with the thoughts of God and with God's three thousand gracious qualities and His ninety-nine sovereign powers—such a man will merge with God and live in heaven. If he performs God's duties and God's actions, then that is his heaven. Every one of those good thoughts and qualities he fosters within himself will become angels, saints, heavenly beings, heavenly messengers, and celestial beings who will serve him in heaven. That is the house he built while he was here.

God has not set apart a place called heaven and another place called hell. Both heaven and hell exist within us. *Sharr* and *khair*, or right and wrong, are also within us. The *sirr* and the *sifat*, the secret and the manifestation, are both within us. *Al-qadā' wal-qadar*, fate and destiny, are both within us. Life and death are both within us. This world called *dunyā* and the hereafter known as *ākhirah*, in which you merge with God, are within us too. Good and evil, *halāl* and *harām*, the permissible and the impermissible, heaven and hell, satan and God—all these pairs of opposites already exist within us.

Man has within him both *hayawān* and *insān*, beast and true man. This body of man contains all of the eighteen thousand universes. Everything is within man. The whole story of God exists within man as a great secret.

ABOUL'ALA: Bawa used the words *insān-Allāh*, meaning God-man, man-God. How does the relationship between the Creator and the created work? Man is created and God is the Creator. How do they relate?

BAWA MUHAIYADDEEN: Are you not a *rabb*, a creator? The earth is a creator; it brings forth so much. Haven't you created? Every thought you have takes the form of a statue or an idol that you worship. Who created these forms within you? Who created the wrong and the faults within you? Did Allah create them? Didn't you create your own faults?

Now, if a man and a woman get together, what is the result? Without their joining, will a child come? No. In the same way, if *Rabb*, the Original Creator, and *insān*, the created being, do not join together, will anything result? At the time of creation, God said, "*Kun!* Arise!" and what arose was the created being. God created man, He created beast, He created everything. He is Allah, God, the *Rabb*, the Creator. That which was created and made manifest is the form. The one who has the form is *insān*, man; the one who manifested that form is Allah, the Creator. But the One who creates is not manifest; that One remains hidden, unseen.

There is more than one explanation for the term *insān-Allāh*. One cannot derive the meaning of something written in the Qur'an simply by looking at the words. That is as hopeless as trying to read a message written on water. The one who reads the Qur'an must be the one who will understand the meanings within it—that one is the *Rasūlullāh*, the Prophet Muhammad ﷺ. Therefore, if you want to know the true meaning within the Qur'an, you must become the

Rasūlullāh ⓢ. To do that, you have to acquire wisdom. Only if you transform yourself into a person of wisdom can you look at the Qur'an and find the right inner meaning. When a man with no wisdom looks, at that level he will see only faults, discrimination, and differences. But when a man with wisdom looks at the Qur'an, he will see only the *alif,* Allah. He will see God.

There are three letters in Arabic which represent the triple ray, the triple effulgence: *alif, lām,* and *mīm. Alif* is Allah, *lām* is a light, and *mīm* is Muhammad ⓢ. Who are you? You are Muhammad ⓢ. What is inside you? The light, the *lām.* That is wisdom. What is within that? God, the *alif,* who is without sound. All three are joined together in one form, the body; within the body is the light and within the light is the mystery. All three dwell in the same place.

That is the explanation of the relationship between the *Rabb,* the One who created, and *insān,* the created being. The *Rabb* is the Creator of everything; we are the ones who have been created. He created us and He gives us nourishment. We can be seen, our forms are revealed, but He remains hidden as a mystery.

You must look within everything for the inner mystery. Trying to compare one explanation with another is useless. First, you must throw away everything you have been gathering and building and stacking up. Kill all that you desire, and then go toward God. You have to establish the right connection between yourself and Allah. That connection must be made on the inside.

There is a story that illustrates this point. One time, the *Rasūlullāh* ⓢ said to his daughter, Fatimah ⓡ, "You should not be conceited about being the Prophet's daughter. You should not even have the thought, 'I am the daughter of Prophet Muhammad.' Allah is the only One to whom praise is due. All praise should be given to Him. Allah is the One who is responsible to everyone. Judgment is in His charge. You should not think that you belong to the Prophet or that he is your father. Allah does not have such connections. Therefore, do not feel proud.

"Heaven is within man and so is hell. There are seven hells, which are the seven *nafs,* or base desires, formed by earth, fire, water, air, ether, mind, and desire. We have to transcend and conquer all seven. We have to cross over the trench of fire, which can devour us. We must climb onto the bridge called *sirātul-*

mustaqīm, the straight path. That bridge is as narrow as one hair split into seven and then one of those pieces split into seven again. We have to walk across that very narrow bridge.

"What is that bridge? The seven levels of wisdom, or consciousness: feeling, awareness, intellect, judgment, subtle wisdom, divine analytic wisdom, and divine luminous wisdom, which is the wisdom of God. Using wisdom, we must divide and analyze everything until we reach the sixth level, the level of the *Qutbiyyat.* Then, with that wisdom of the *Qutb,* we have to discard everything other than Allah, accepting with absolute certitude that there is nothing other than Allah. We must go on to the seventh level of total surrender to God, *tawakkul 'alallāh,* using the effulgent light called the *Nūr.* We must accept only the divine luminous wisdom which is Allah, and in that state we can cross over the bridge built out of one section of a hair split into seven.

"We have to give up the other six parts and climb onto that one-seventh of a section. That bridge is just wide enough for one who goes in perfect surrender to God. If we fail in this surrender, if we carry with us even an atomic fraction of anything other than surrender to God, the bridge will collapse and we will fall. Surrender is our path. It is the only path. It is the only way we can reach God. We must accept this. Even if someone is a prophet or the child of a prophet, without the help of Allah, he cannot cross that bridge. Only that which belongs to Allah and to Allah alone can cross it.

"Fatimah, you must realize this," the Prophet (ﷺ) said to his daughter. "Your state should be *tawakkul 'alallāh,* surrender to God, and *in shā'Allāh,* if God wills. If instead you go around thinking, 'I am the daughter of the Prophet,' you will never be able to cross that bridge." Then he told Khadijah (ﮬ), "Do not go around saying proudly that you are the wife of the Prophet. That will not take you across the bridge." And to 'Ali (ﮬ) he said, "Do not feel proud and think, 'I am the son-in-law of the Prophet.' That will not take you across. Fatimah, you are not the daughter of the Prophet. 'Ali, you are not his son-in-law, and Khadijah, you are not his wife. If you carry vanity and pride with you, you will never succeed in crossing. Only one who has perfect surrender to God and follows the will of God can cross that bridge. Only what belongs to God can cross over."

This is what Prophet Muhammad⊕told 'Ali⊕and Fati-mah ⊕. He revealed many things only to 'Ali ⊕, and when we read the traditional stories, or *hadiths,* of 'Ali ⊕, we must read with understanding.

The one who worships and the One who is being worshiped must be one. The one praying and the One who is being prayed to must be Allah. Unless they come together as one, that prayer will not reach fulfillment. It will not be true prayer. One merging with the other and the two becoming one is true prayer. In the way that glue and paper merge to become one, or a flower and its fragrance exist as one, in the same way that a light merges with another light—in that way, truth merges with truth, and the two become one. That is true prayer, *'ibādat.*

Fire and firewood are not the same. As long as the firewood remains out of the fire, it is only wood, and there is no connection between the two. No benefit can come from the cold wood; it cannot be used to heat water, or to cook, or to warm ourselves. But once the firewood enters the fire and burns, it can serve us in all these ways. Like that, only if *insān* merges with God and becomes *insān-Allāh* will there be any benefit. That is prayer, that is worship, that is *'ibādat* and *dhikr.*

In the same way, *'ilm,* or divine knowledge, must merge with *'ilm. Imān,* or true faith in God, must merge with *imān.* Light must enter the light. Prayer must merge with prayer. And God must merge with God.

That which emerged from Allah must go back into Allah, so that they can become one. Whatever came out of God must return to Him. You were in God, then you came out into the world. And since you have been here, you have collected so many things—your body, your muscles, your earth, your fire, your water, and everything— but none of these will go back to God. The body is only a temporary house for you. You cannot carry it back with you. If you try to take anything or anyone with you, you will not reach a state of fulfill-ment. Only that which came out of Allah can go back into Allah.

This body is merely a guest house, a hotel you visit briefly, a school you must attend. It is required for your studies. In this short space of time, you have to learn Allah's secrets. You have to learn about the *rizq,* or nourishment, that He gives to each and every one of His created beings. You have to learn about His compassionate qualities, His *wilāyats,* or sovereign powers, His *daulat,* or wealth, and His *rahmat,* His grace. That is why you came here to the school of your body, to study and learn God's story.

God molded man's form out of the five elements of earth, fire, water, air, and ether. But it is not a permanent form. Look at the way you can make a block of ice out of water. By putting the water into different molds and freezing it, you can even make different shapes. But later on, when air blows over the ice, it will melt and change back into water. In the same way this solidified block, which is the body, will change back into what it came from.

You have to reflect upon this. Do not think that the body is anything permanent or valuable. It is only something we have stored up while we have been here. It has to be left behind. But that which came from God, that which He gave us as a trust, has to return to Him. You must not forfeit that into the hands of satan. Death is only for the body that is acquired here. The trust that came from God has no death. You must understand this.

QUESTION: How do we make the connection to God?

BAWA MUHAIYADDEEN: That message, that telegram, goes instantly if we establish the proper lines of communication for it. But instead, we have created millions upon millions of forms and statues within us, and we worship those statues. We worship our wealth and our riches. We pray to earth, woman, and gold, and to all the things that we love and desire. We have become slaves to them. Those things are not within God; they are what we ourselves have created, and they will end up killing us. We surrender to evil qualities and actions, letting every one of them control us. Instead of becoming slaves to Allah, we have become slaves to everything else. Only if our *niyyat,* our intention, is to worship Allah alone are we performing true prayer. Whatever else we desire or intend becomes our prayer; we are surrendering to that thing.

This is why we say that an *insān* is a *rabb,* a creator. First God is the Creator, then the man whom He created makes himself into a creator and begins creating many different things. He creates things that are opposite to God and then considers them equal to God. In this way, the created becomes the creator. If man would seek only that One who created him, then he would not create anything else.

QUESTION: What is meant by *rasūl?*

BAWA MUHAIYADDEEN: A *rasūl* is one who has the wisdom of *'ilm,* of divine knowledge, within him.

My brother, to understand the Qur'an one has to be a good man. Let me give you an explanation. In what form was the Qur'an revealed by Allah? It first came out of Allah's *rahmat,* His benevolence, as a vibration, as a light from Allah. Then it came to the Angel Gabriel ⊛ as a revelation, a *wahy,* and then to the *Rasūl* ⊛ as a commandment. After that, it came as words from the *Rasūl* ⊛ to the people. Those spoken words were written down on paper, and out of the written words emerged a story. From that story evolved a mode of conduct, which led to the rules regarding good and evil. Those rules eventually brought about separations that led to religions. And what has resulted from all these differences? Fighting and battles.

So, my brother, how can we come to really understand the Qur'an? By retracing the steps back to the original light. We have to start with the story that came from the written words. Then we must search within those words to realize Muhammad ⊛ and to receive the commandments he received. Going back still further, we must understand Gabriel ⊛ and the revelations that came to him. Then we must penetrate those revelations until we reach the resonance and the light that emerged from Allah's benevolence. Beyond the benevolence we must see Allah, who is the plenitude, the completeness, the *Rahmatul-'ālamīn,* the One who rules all the universes. There you will find the power of God. Only if you are in that state when you read the Qur'an will you understand its real meaning and its completeness.

Without realizing that state, if you quote the Qur'an, you will only be talking about the outer forms. Letters and words are just forms. You must go beyond all those forms and see the One who has no form, the formless God. You have to retrace the Qur'an back to its origin. That is *imān-Islām*. If we could truly establish Islam in that way, this would be a very good world.

ABOUL'ALA: 'Umar (ﷺ), one of the caliphs of the Prophet (ﷺ), is reputed to have said, ''If the bird knew what was inside the honeybee, the bird would never have swallowed that bee.''

BAWA MUHAIYADDEEN: That is true. Everything is condensed within what 'Umar (ﷺ) said. If man really understood that the truth exists within all of God's creation, that Allah is intermingled within it, then he would never kill any life. He would not catch hold of any of God's creations and eat them. So what 'Umar (ﷺ) said was perfectly correct.

   Āmīn.

June 21, 1979

Session 24

What does 'Duty is greater than God' mean?
273

How can I make my faith grow?
273

Were you ever born?
276

How do energies attack man?
276

Session 24

QUESTION: What is the meaning of the saying: 'Duty is greater than God'?

BAWA MUHAIYADDEEN: Duty is greater than God. God performs His duties without a body, and so it is very easy for Him, but we have a body, and this body makes it very difficult for us. We have wives and children, blood ties and other attachments; we have hunger, aging, and illness. All these things make it difficult for us to do the duty of God with good thoughts and good intentions. If a man is really able to do God's duty in spite of these hindrances, then that man is in a divine state.

Let Almighty God, who is the responsible One, help you.

My brothers and sisters, what do you want? Is there anything that you need to ask?

QUESTION: How can I make my faith grow?

BAWA MUHAIYADDEEN: There is something called faith. It takes many forms in this world. Man focuses his faith on everything he sees, on whatever is easy. He places his faith on money, on his job, or on love. He also has faith in good and evil. He even believes in murder. He has faith in everything he does.

But all these things are destructible, and man himself is destructible. You must learn to differentiate between things that have an end and the one thing that never ends. In which of these is it good to place your faith? Now, which faith is it that you want to grow?

QUESTIONER: Faith in God.

BAWA MUHAIYADDEEN: Faith in God is a completely different point. God has no form. He was never created. He has neither birth nor death, beginning nor end. He is not a sun or a moon or a star. He is not made of earth, fire, water, air, or ether. God cannot be confined to any single race or religion or color. He has no differences or separations that would make Him say, "My color, your color. My language, your language. My race, your race." He is the One who is beyond all that.

God is a power beyond everything. That power is intermingled in all lives and understood within all lives. It is the power within everything, existing as wisdom within wisdom, as the light within the eyes, and as the life within the body. It dwells within the *qalb,* the innermost heart, as a very, very beautiful form. It is a clear light to which nothing else can be compared. It is a power that can help all lives, lead all lives, and rule all lives. It is that power which gives warning to the conscience and makes us aware of any faults within us.

Everything else changes: that treasure is the only thing which will never change. All creations are destructible; that power alone is indestructible. Oceans may give way to land and land to oceans, jungles may become cities and cities turn into jungles, mountains may become flat lands and flat lands might rise up as mountains. Where a palace once stood a cemetery may now exist, and where a cemetery used to be a palace may be built. All these things are constantly changing. God alone never changes.

That power called God exists in all lives as an atom within an atom: in the creeping ants, in gems, in man, in everything. God rules the kingdom with perfect peacefulness and complete justice. He serves without selfishness and without showing any differences. That almighty power stands alone, changeless and incomparable. That power is God.

God cannot be seen by reciting mantras or by performing magic or tricks or miracles. Even animals can perform these elemental miracles. A snake can keep poison within its fangs without harm to itself, but when it gets angry and digs its fangs into someone's flesh, its fatal poison is released. That is the snake's miracle. An eagle flies very high, maintaining perfect balance, but when it spots its prey on the ground, immediately it darts downward, snatches it up, and flies away. How quickly it shifts from soaring in the sky to descending upon its prey. That is the miracle of the eagle. The elephant travels through the jungle without following any path. The whole jungle is its path—it just crushes the trees that are in its way and moves on. That is the miracle of the elephant. Man cannot do that. He needs a path to make his way through the dense growth. A crane can stand motionless on one leg for eight to nine hours waiting to catch a fish. That is the miracle of the crane. A fish can swim from the ocean floor right up to the surface of the sea, balancing perfectly; when a wave comes, the fish moves forward and maintains its balance. That is the miracle of the fish. But the same wave that the fish is able to resist will beat a man down and throw him ashore. An ant can creep very deftly into a tiny hole. Man cannot do that. A termite builds such a subtle home. Man cannot build a home like that. A honeybee searches for honey, builds a hive, and then stores the honey there. That is the miracle of the bee. Man cannot do that. Each creation has its own miracle.

If we reflect upon each and every thing, we will conclude that the entire world is a miracle. All creations are miracles and all energies are miracles. They are all such wonders. But if man concerns himself with the miracles of animals and birds and tries to perform the same acts, then he is not a man. If he wants to do what a snake does, then he is not a man. Man has to be very careful. Maya, or illusion, can creep into his life and lead him astray. Desire can creep in and distract him. Anger can lead him to murder. Each one of these energies can perform its own miracle. Every creation has its miracles, but we must not look upon any of them as real miracles. And we must not become fascinated with the miracles of ghosts and demons and devils, or we will be in a lower state than they are. The *siddhis,* or occult powers, that we see around us are limited to the world, to earth, fire, water, and air. They are just the acts of the body and of mind and desire, the miracles of the sixty-four arts. God is the One who controls all of these. He controls everything. He is the One who can make the creations move.

We have to understand the miracles of God. God has created everything, and His truth can be seen within each and every thing. Within flowers He has placed a fragrance, and within fruits He has placed a taste. Within one tiny seed He has placed the potentiality of a huge tree and a million more seeds. These are the miracles of God. Neither energies nor animals can perform any of these miracles.

They can only go on changing, like the jungle that gives way to a city and the cemetery that gives way to a palace.

God can do what no creation can do. His miracle exists as wisdom within wisdom, as atom within atom. There is no one equal to Him. We must establish our faith in Him and accept Him with absolute certitude as the one God. We must accept that His miracles are the only true miracles. That is what comforts us. We must bring our innermost hearts to a state of no wavering. We must believe in God with absolute faith and prepare a place for His purity within our pure heart. Once we have established a beautiful heart for Him where we can receive Him, then we must keep Him there. Everything else has to be discarded.

What else do you need, my children?

A SMALL CHILD: Was Bawa ever born?

BAWA MUHAIYADDEEN: Very good question! All creations are born. Whatever you see with your physical eyes has begun from something. Don't rays come from the sun? These rays are born from the sun. Doesn't light come from the moon? That light is born from the moon. Don't you see the beauty of the light from the stars? That light is born from the stars. Don't you see blossoms on a bush? Those blossoms are born from the bush. Aren't there fruits on a tree? Those fruits are born from the tree. Isn't there a fragrance in a flower? That scent is born from the flower.

Like that, whatever you see begins from something. All those things have been born, and all will someday die. I too have been born, and so have you. You must believe this. In all of creation God is the only One who was never born. God has no mother and no father. He never dies, never changes, and has no time limit. He is the unending, original, natural Power.

QUESTION: Can Bawa give an explanation of how the energies come and attack man?

BAWA MUHAIYADDEEN: They are not attacking man, they exist within the earth itself. Isn't your body made from the earth? In that earth there is water and air, in the air there is fire, in the fire there are colors, and in the colors there is a kind of torpor. In that torpor there is desire, and within that desire the mind exists. All of these exist, don't they? Inherent in each of these elements is the quality of arrogance. Each one is antagonistic to the other and says, "I am greater than you." Earth is antagonistic to fire, fire is antagonistic to water, and water is antagonistic to air. These five elements exist within the body, and there is antagonism between them at all times.

Therefore, we have to develop a section within us that can control them. Mind and desire, selfishness, blood ties, racial and color differences, bigotry, the arrogance and egoism of the I, the separations that exist between the you and the I, torpor, fascinations, anger, and sin—we must learn how to control all of these qualities that exist within us.

But also existing within us is a treasure, the good treasure called God. Within God is another good treasure, His benevolence. Within that benevolence are other good treasures, His powers, or *wilāyats.* Within those powers is another good treasure, *'ilm,* which is divine knowledge. Within that knowledge there is wisdom, and within wisdom there is divine luminous wisdom. Within that there is another good treasure, the light. Within that light there is another good treasure, the *Nūr,* the resplendence of God. Within that resplendence there is another good treasure, the plenitude. Within that plenitude there is yet another good treasure, and that treasure is Allah. That is God. It is through God alone that we can control all of these energies. If you can control them, you will become *insān kāmil,* perfected man. You will become the *Nūr,* the resplendence of God.

June 24, 1979

Session 25

What should we do when we see faults in others?
281

*Should we perform duty which
does not come from love?*
282

*If I'm paid to fulfill someone's evil purposes,
am I culpable?*
286

*How should I understand karma, accidents, and
destiny in relation to God's will?*
286

*What does it mean to be with the guru
for twelve years?*
287

Session 25

QUESTION: What should we do when we see faults in others?

BAWA MUHAIYADDEEN: Primarily, we must try to correct our own faults. If we analyze every point within us, we will find that the faults we see in others are really within ourselves. If we look into our own thoughts and intentions, we will find that they are all wrong. Therefore it is those faults that we have to correct, not the faults of others. The wisest thing we can do in this life is to correct all the problems and differences and troubles that we have within ourselves. Then only will we understand the world with clarity. We must examine and correct each one of our thoughts, each one of our intentions, and each one of our qualities.

That is the path to becoming true human beings. It is a most difficult path, but if we really follow it, then we will be the leaders for all three worlds: the world of the souls, this world, and the hereafter. Until that time, we will continue to be the ones among God's creations who find fault with others and hurt them. My children, this is something that we must realize and accept. Each one of us must correct our own thoughts and intentions.

If a beetle sits on a flower, it will always make a hole and spoil the flower's beauty. If a pest crawls on a leaf, it will damage the leaf. If a bug creeps into a fruit, the value of that fruit will be completely lost. If a piece of dirt falls into someone's eye, it can injure the eye. In the same way, if there is a flaw in the innermost heart, the *qalb,* it will ruin the heart completely. We should think about this. All those things that fall into the heart can destroy it, so we must destroy them before they destroy us. We must try to remove all the faults that are within us. That is what a wise man would do. That is the intelligent thing to do.

Whatever we see on the outside is a show, an exhibition. There are six kinds of lives, and each one exhibits whatever is natural for that life. Its color, its shape, the language or sounds it produces, the food it eats, the place where it lives—all these will differ, according to what is suitable for that life. Each one has its own ways.

We must find out the section where man dwells. We have to understand that section and then correct everything within it. That will be very good.

There are so many lessons we have to learn, things that we have to understand about ourselves. Many things are there within us, and we must try to find out what they are. The one who can understand that is a true human being. The one who does not understand will have so many animal qualities within him that he will be worse than a devil, worse than the deadliest of animals. His happiness will be to hurt others. His bliss will be to murder others. Such a state could develop within him. We must use our intelligence and try to avoid being like that. Then we can realize and experience the meaning of *shanti,* of true peacefulness.

We must wash away the dirt from our own garments. We should not try to remove the dirt from another person's garments. If we do, we will only get kicked. A dog likes to clean himself with his tongue, so if we try to wash his backside with water, he will bite us. Instead, we must wash our own backsides very carefully.

<center>~~~~~~</center>

FRAN COHEN: If you have to perform a duty and the love just doesn't come, is it just as well not to perform that duty?

BAWA MUHAIYADDEEN: When you are doing a duty in a loveless state, you must give that state a good beating. Duty should not be performed out of favoritism or as a business. It is said that duty is even greater than God. If you want to perform a duty, you have to do it with an open heart. If you perform a duty without love, that means that there is some doubt within you, or some feeling of differences. There may even be a subtle feeling of revenge because of a fault that someone had committed earlier toward you, or some fault that you had done to him. It could be something like that. Maybe anger, envy, treachery, or some such thing prevents that love from being there. Some reason within us prevents that love from coming. We should not hold onto such a state.

What should the state of a man be? If some dirt or a small splinter should fall into the water, the water will push it away. It will not remain where it landed. It will be carried somewhere else or washed up on the shore or disappear altogether. The splinter will never stay in the same spot. Like that, everything in the world will fall into your heart. But no matter what falls there, you should not keep it. Push it out the next second. As soon as something gets in there, throw it out immediately. The *qalb* should always be clear. No bad thoughts or intentions or anything bad should be there. That is how duty must be done. Just as letters written on water disappear at once, we must immediately erase all the letters the world puts in us. The anger and hurt caused by differences of opinion must be cleared out. Don't give room for any of those feelings.

If you harbor a snake in your house and go on feeding it, the snake's family will multiply and soon the whole house will be filled with snakes. Isn't that true? And you are not the only one who will be bitten; the visitors and all those who come near, good people and bad alike, will be in danger. Therefore, do not allow a snake in your house at all.

Do not give room to doubts, anger, or revenge for things that have been said or done earlier. If a person commits a fault, it is either done through his ignorance, or his arrogance, or through envy or selfishness or pride. Or it could be due to deceitfulness. There is always some reason why he has committed that fault. Whatever a person does, it is lack of wisdom that prompts him to do it. What he does through ignorance should not be considered as enmity by us. If he had wisdom, he never would have done it. Someone without wisdom can do many harmful things for many different reasons. He might even commit murder. But a man who has wisdom and faith in God will never do any of those things.

Therefore, if someone who has wisdom and faith in God is hurt by an ignorant man, he should not keep the hurt within him. He must throw it out immediately and forget it. One who can make the hurt disappear is a wise man, but one who keeps it within him is just as ignorant as the person who committed the fault. Only if we have forgotten our hurt and anger can we love that person and teach him wisdom and help him to reach a good state. Only by showing him in our conduct the love and good qualities that we have can we teach him to become a person with the qualities of God, a person with wisdom.

But to think about harming one who has harmed us is the poisonous quality of the snake. If we think we must beat up a person who beat us, that is the work of satan. If we seek revenge against a person who has hurt us, that is the quality of arrogance, the quality of the elephant. If a person should say, "I will not go to so-and-so's house," then God will send him back to that house seventy thousand times. If one person seeks revenge against another, then God will develop in him a state in which he will end up having to go to that person and beg for help again and again. He will have to ask for friendship from the same person he considered an enemy. Whatever he did earlier, that same thing will be returned to him. God has said, "If one man should hate another, I will send him back to the person he hated and make him subordinate to him." This is the way God works.

The day we are free of these qualities, hell will no longer be in us. When our wisdom grows, that ignorance will leave us completely. We should not have any bad thoughts and intentions; only good thoughts and good intentions must dwell within us. We must remove all hostility and say, *"Al-hamdu lillāh!* O God, for whatever is happening at this moment, we praise You. *Shakūr,* it is enough." And for what is going to happen in the next moment, *"Tawakkul 'alallāh!* O God, we give all the responsibility to You." We cannot know what will happen in that moment. Such trust and surrender must be within us. "It is in Your hands, in Your trust, O Allah. It must be Your action and Your duty. It is You who looks after the state of each person."

My children, you must always remember to be in a good state and perform your duties. You should never do anything expecting help in return. Do not anticipate any reward when you help someone. Suppose a snake gets caught in a trap or a net. If you want to set it free, you have to use your wisdom. You must be aware that the snake has poison in its fangs and be careful not to put your hand too close or it will bite you. Instead, take a long stick and try to open the trap or disentangle the net with that. Duty has to be done with wisdom. Whatever duty you set out to do in the world, do it and then escape. Do not expect help in return. The one you help can only give you what he has. The snake has only poison, and that is what he will give you. Then what will happen to you? You will die.

It is dangerous to expect a reward; simply do your duty. If you help an ignorant person and want something from him in return, he can only give you his ignorance. He will only give what he has in him. If you do someone a favor and hope that he might return it someday, you may get hurt. If you think, "Oh, he fell down and I lifted him up and protected him and took him home, so maybe he will help me sometime," then he might wait until dark and put a stone on the road to trip you. Then when you stumble and fall, he will come running and say, "Oh, have you fallen down? Was it this stone that made you fall?" That is the way he will return your favor.

Therefore, do not expect any favors from those you help. Just perform your duty with wisdom. The moment you have finished, that work is over. Leave it at that and do not think of it again. That is how God performs His duty. He never expects any help or favors from us. Those who have wisdom and truly believe in that one God must perform their duties in the same way.

Let us reflect on this. All that the world offers, both the good and the bad, the karma, the anger, the sin—all this must disappear from your heart like writing on water. Within a second after something happens, you must forget it completely. God alone is the One that you must never forget. Whatever duty you do out of selfishness or because you hope for a favor in return is not true duty, and it could bring suffering to you later. You cannot have faith in what others will do. One day people will praise you, the next day they will blame you. One day they will embrace you, the next day they will beat you. One day they will trust you and treat you with respect, and the next day they will try to destroy you. Therefore, we must completely remove such expectations.

We must live the life of a true human being, a life filled with the qualities of God. That is the duty we have to perform. That is the beauty of the kingdom of God. If we can organize our hearts to perform our duties in the highest and loftiest way, we will know victory.

~~~~~~

JONATHAN GRANOFF, ESQ.: If a person is fulfilling the evil

purposes of another person—acting as a conduit for their vengeance, for their greed, for their desire to cause harm to another—is he culpable? If someone pays me to take revenge on another, and I do it for him, am I culpable?

BAWA MUHAIYADDEEN: If a person accepts the payment, then he is at fault. If he gets paid for it, he is doing it for his own gain. That is a fault.

JONATHAN: That's what I'm afraid of, all the time.

BAWA MUHAIYADDEEN: Are you afraid of that? All right, let me tell you something. A rose has its own sweet fragrance. No matter what foul smell may be near it, or no matter how many sweet fragrances from other flowers surround it, the rose does not take them into itself. It retains its own original scent. Even if the rose is surrounded by the foul odors of fertilizer, cow dung, and compost, none of those smells can penetrate the rose; its own sweet fragrance prevails.

Like that, if a person has his own beauty and his own fragrance within, then no matter how many sweet-smelling flowers or foul odors are around him, he will retain only that original fragrance. Nothing will affect him. If his innermost heart is in that fragrant state, no matter what may surround him, he will not be concerned about it or affected by it. However many worlds may exist in the garden, they cannot obscure his beauty; that beauty will always be with him. If the fragrance of God is there within him, if the light and fragrance of wisdom is there, nothing can hide it, and nobody can overcome it. Everything will bow down to that fragrance. Everything will surrender. All foul odors will leave. That is how it is.

QUESTION: I want to ask about four things that relate to each other. The first is accidents. I have heard Bawa describe some things as accidents. In what sense is anything ever an accident? The next question is about karma, and the third is about our destiny. What is destiny, and what is the connection between karma and destiny? And then finally, how should I understand karma, accidents, and destiny in relation to the will of God?

BAWA MUHAIYADDEEN: If you really understood those three, you would accept with certitude whatever happens at any particular moment. You would have inner patience and contentment and say, *"Al-hamdu lillāh,"* praising God for what has happened. And for what is going to happen in the next moment, you would say, *"Tawakkul 'alallāh.* O God, this is Your responsibility." Once you have acquired wisdom and determination and have placed your faith and certitude in God, then there will be no destiny, no karma, and no accidents. But as long as you have not established that, your ignorance will tend to bring about accidents. It is because of that ignorance that you fail to act correctly and then call the results your fate, your *nasīb.* Therefore, until you have acquired God's qualities and placed God within you for protection, you will continue to be subject to your karma. That is how it is.

RABI'ATUL-'ADAWIYYA MCDEVITT: I have heard it said that you should be with the guru for twelve years. What does that mean?

BAWA MUHAIYADDEEN: It is very good that you asked this. We have studied the world through books, through words, through shows, through the sixty-four arts and sciences, and through races, religions, and philosophies. We have studied everything in the world except ourselves. We have seen so many exhibits, we have learned about all of the things around us and experienced every kind of happiness they contain, but we have not understood our own joy and sorrow. We have not understood our own life, or our own state. We have not learned about our inner world or the totality of what we are. That is why we need a sheikh who is an *insān kāmil,* a perfected man, a teacher of wisdom.

You must find such a man. Go to him and give him the responsibility for your *qalb* and your body. Give him your love. How do you do that? Is it by offering him money or through sexual games? No, all your money, all your sexual arts, all your sciences, all your activities, are useless. It is your *qalb,* your innermost heart, that you must offer him. You must surrender the fragrance of your heart to that teacher of wisdom. He will accept that. Your fragrance must attach itself to him. He will be the flower and you will be the fragrance; or you may be the flower and he the fragrance. The two must be right for each other. Your truth must fit his truth. Your *imān*, your faith, certitude, and determination must be like his. Your duty and his duty, your actions and his actions, your good intentions and thoughts, should be compatible with his. You must create that compatibility. If you can establish such a state, then he will show you the path by which you can learn to know yourself.

If you stay with an *insān kāmil* for twelve years in this state of surrender, he will teach you about the twelve worlds within you. There are two worlds, or openings, in the lower part of the body: first is the opening through which you enter this life; second is the opening of fecal arrogance and karma, which is hell. Another world is the world of poisonous qualities, the world of envy, jealousy, pride, and vanity. These satanic qualities enter through the umbilical cord and are kindled by hunger, lust, passion, and desire. The *insān kāmil* will teach you how to overcome these through *shakūr*, contentment, and by *tawakkul,* surrendering all responsibility to God.

Then there are the sensory worlds in the head. The two openings of the eyes are the two worlds called sun and moon. To learn about these takes two years. He will also teach you about the worlds of the two nostrils, the two breaths. To expel the section of your birth he will show you how to exhale from the left nostril, saying, *"Lā ilāha:* Nothing exists but You, O God. I am not.'' And he will show you how to draw your breath in through the right nostril, saying, *"Ill-Allāhu:* You alone are God,'' thus drawing into yourself the kingdom of God. That takes another two years. He will also teach you about the two ears and show you how to tell the difference between the good sounds and the bad sounds, between the sound of God and the sounds of mind, desire, and craving. He will teach you to distinguish between the sounds of the *rūh* and the *rūhāni,* the soul and the elemental spirits. He will analyze all the sounds and teach you how to identify the source of each one. Is this one coming from the mind? Is this coming from desire? Is this coming from karma? Is this coming from lust? Is this coming from the illusory world of maya? He will show you the meaning of all the sounds.

Then you will come to the world of the mouth. He will teach you about the good words and the evil words that come from the tongue.

One word from someone can make you feel victorious, another can kill you. One word can make you laugh and be happy, another can make you cry. Sometimes the same word can make you laugh or cry. The sheikh will explain how the happiness comes and how the sorrow comes, and then he will make you experience them in your own body. Once you have understood the nature and the taste of both happiness and sorrow, he will encourage you to be happy with the tongue of happiness and to eliminate the tongue of sorrow.

In this way the sheikh will teach you all that has to be learned about the sins that correspond to the ten openings of your body. He will develop in you the initiative needed to discard them, and then teach you how to do it.

Eleventh, he will open your eye of wisdom, the *kursī,* that light in the forehead which resplends as the *Qutbiyyat,* the wisdom that explains. He will make you understand who you are, what your path is, where you were before, what you have done, and where you are now. He will make you realize that you are one of the rays of the *Nūr,* the resplendence of Allah. He will show you that light of *Nūr Muhammad* which has been impressed on the center of your forehead and help you to understand the completeness of that light. That resplendent light is capable of seeing all beings in all universes. With it you can look at the world and the eighteen thousand universes and see your own history, your beginning, your end, your destiny, and where you were before the beginningless beginning. You will see all the changing forms that you have taken and will understand your parents, your country, yourself, your judgment, and your God. All that you want to understand will be revealed to you.

The first eleven years of study with the sheikh represent the eleven different openings, the places where the *Qutb* is born within you as wisdom. These are the eleven incarnations of the *Qutb,* the miraculous incarnations of wisdom. He will appear as wisdom in these eleven places, explain their meaning to you, and teach you how to eliminate whatever is poisonous. He will reveal the meaning of the light of the *Qutbiyyat,* or *Qutb Muhaiyaddeen* as the perfect purity, and show you how he dwells within you, functioning and manifesting there, shining forth from within to point out the way. He will help you to see how the two of you, in unity, stand as one, viewing all the universes at the same time.

Finally, the sheikh will show you the relationship between the *kursī*, the eye of wisdom, and the *'arsh*, the throne of Allah. Here Allah and the *Qutbiyyat* merge into one and the state of *Nurullāh* resplends as one complete effulgence, extending from the *'arsh* to the *kursī*. That is the twelfth state. At this point, the light of the *Qutbiyyat* will dawn in you, and you will understand the meaning of the eleven incarnations. You will see the 124,000 prophets, the angels and heavenly beings, the jinns and fairies, this world and the next, heaven and hell, good and evil, man and animals, and all of everything.

To attain that perfection takes twelve years of study with the sheikh. To make you understand the Qur'an that exists within your body and contains all of *'ālam* and *'ālamul-arwāh* (this world and the world of the souls), and to realize the meaning of the *Sūratul-Fātihah*, the first chapter of the Qur'an, which resplends within that Qur'an, you must be with your sheikh for twelve years. What does it mean to be with him? To surrender your heart to him completely.

After that, what will he teach you? The true meaning of the *Sūratul-Ikhlās:*

"*Qul: huwallāhu ahad:* Say: He is God, the One and only." Everything belongs to Allah.
"*Allāhus-samad:* God, the Eternal, the Absolute." He is present equally within all lives, the lofty, the poor, and the lowly.
"*lam yalid:* He begetteth not." He exists as a beggar to a beggar, as a learned one to the learned, as an ignorant one to the ignorant, as love to one who shows love, as wisdom to the one with wisdom, as a king to a king, and as a slave to a slave. He is everywhere.
"*wa lam yūlad:* Nor is He begotten." He is always on the correct path, on the right side.
"*wa lam yakul-lahu kufuwan ahad:* And there is none like unto Him." He is always within the truth, on the right side. His completeness is always there. Wherever everything else may be, He remains on the right. Everything is His secret. That is His state. That is His mystery.

These are the words your sheikh will teach you. And he will demonstrate for you the state of "I do not exist; nothing exists except God. *Lā ilāha ill-Allāhu.*" To receive this state, you must spend twelve years with the sheikh. To learn about this book of the body, to learn about this world, to study about the hereafter, to understand what heaven is, and to understand what is meant by peace in this world, you must spend twelve years with the sheikh. Bawa Muhaiyaddeen⊚ begins to sing:

> For true meditation only one is needed,
> To increase the world two are needed,
> To carry a corpse four are needed.
> One—for devotion and meditation;
> The one who has not understood this is like a corpse.
> Two—for the world to multiply;
> The one who is immersed in this is in hell.
> Four—to carry a corpse;
> The one who has not clearly understood this is in hell.
> He is in hell.
> To analyze this we have been given wisdom.

> There is a wondrous word:
> *Allāhu, Allāhu,*
> Resonating in your heart,
> Beyond all limits,
> Existing within the grace of Allah,
> Beyond any end.
> It will come to serve us in this world.
> It will bring us great benefit.
> It will be the most useful thing in all the world,
> Speaking to us without our knowing
> And dispelling our ignorance.
> The One who understands this is God,
> The Causal One.
> He is the only One who knows,
> He is the One who comprehends these wonders clearly,
> The One who knows and understands our every intention,
> The One who helps us all.

If we become good, then God will become ours.
He will be the heart within our heart,
The explanation within our thoughts,
The resonance within our wisdom,
Our Primal Father, the Eternal Lord.
If we understand this state,
What else will we need?
If we understand this state,
What want will we ever have?
He is God, the unchanging One,
Our undiminishing wealth,
Our never-ending treasure.
He will stand as the Primal Cause,
Resplending as completeness,
As the truth within our heart.
He is the Creator,
The explanation of divine grace,
The meaning of the triple grace in all three worlds.

If you understand this in your heart,
If you understand the five,
Your poisonous qualities will disappear.
You will know your Lord, your Creator.
He is the Primal Cause
And the completeness of wealth.
He exists in the center of the forehead
As the sharpness of wisdom,
As the brilliant light in our heart,
As the effulgence within.

If we reach this state,
We will be in one place with God.
On that day we will see Him
And talk with Him.
If we can surrender all our intentions
And part with the five companions
That joined us at birth,
If we can banish the tricks of our mind

And free ourselves from our suffering,
Our life will not perish
Nor be destroyed.
God, the Eternal,
Will be seen in our heart.
He will light up the heart,
And that beauty will resplend in the face.

Even if we speak with wisdom
And act with good qualities,
And recite a silent mantra with sincere love,
If we do not have the *jōthi*,
The radiant light of *Ahmad,*
Our heart will never resplend.
The triple grace of the Creator must resonate
In our heart and intentions and dreams.
Then the soul will live forever,
Pure and eternal.

To worship and serve Him,
To see Him as body within body,
As one within the other
Is the joy of all true devotees.
This alone will benefit
The true devotees who serve.
This will take us to God,
It will take us to the throne of God.

That primal *Rahmān,*
The vast flood of compassion,
That precious treasure,
The benevolent God,
Will wash away all our karma.
He is the One without form,
The everlasting One,
Who cannot be controlled by anything.

If we do God's duty in this birth,
If we make our hearts resplend,
His grace will resonate within.
May we receive the grace
To serve our Lord day and night,
To live with Him in this world
And to dwell with Him throughout eternity.

O body, O body of earth,
Incessantly eating the karma of illusion,
Seeing only the earth and fire
And water and illusion
Mingled within you,
This is the state that you dwell in.
You take the forms of so many qualities,
Things both real and unreal
Which you claim as your own.

O body, O body,
Always howling and shouting,
Crying and laughing and praying.
O body, this is the way you are.
If you learn to control yourself
And understand with your wisdom
All the qualities which make you cry,
Then truly, you will be the one
Contained within that One,
Both dwelling together within you as one.
The qualities will then become pure.
His grace will resonate
And darkness will leave you.
You will not be affected
By the state of the here and the hereafter,
And death will fly away.
Then the heart will resplend as heaven.

O body, may you understand this.
O body, dispel your ignorance.

Know this with certainty
And walk on the path of truth.
Then you will be held within that truth
And live to serve that reality always.

O body, you live with five companions
Who take many forms in your heart.
Your intentions roam like animals.
You roam and howl and sing and dance.
You grow and grow in ignorance.
You eat and sleep and then die on this earth.
If you dispel this state of illusion,
Then God will be yours.
God will become yours, O body!

There is a path where neither birth nor death exist,
The path of the word of God.
If you can understand this within yourself,
Then earth and illusion will leave you.
They will die away.

The word of God is *Ill-Allāhu.*
Recite this exalted word.
It will be the treasure of your life.
Recite this word with focus,
Make it grow and see what happens.
Learn it and understand it with wisdom.
It will be good medicine for your life.
It will be the beauty of your life,
That beauty that will lead you to your Lord.

Try to acquire the blissful wealth of compassion.
This is your rightful wealth.
Make it yours forever.
It will be your one treasure,
It will be the medicine for your body,
It will be the essence of your life, your existence.

Analyze your body and see what happens.
Analyze the cage of your body.
Subdue all your mischief and come forward.
Destroy the monkey of the mind
And see what happens.
Your body is entwined with your mind
And your mind is in a state of illusion.
Give up the monkey tricks and come.
Search before your time is up.
Search before your body is destroyed.
Learn before your form changes.

Recite, knowing the truth.
This will elevate you,
Then you can join that One.
The good state will come to you,
And your life in this world will be exalted.
Recite, knowing the truth.
Give up your vain talk
And come forward.
Understand the Good One.
Remove all the evils and come.
Then your life will be one of excellence,
Your life will be most exalted. *Āmīn.*

June 26, 1979

Session 26

How can we better our lives?
299

What does it mean to 'Bend the sky into a bow'?
301

What is the station of the elemental spirits?
303

How do the elemental spirits change?
306

Why is Jesus ﷺ the most celebrated prophet?
307

*What is the difference between
a* qutb *and a prophet?*
311

*Did God create the thymus gland as the
center of energy for the body?*
313

Session 26

QUESTIONER: Bawa, a friend wanted me to ask you how she can better her life.

BAWA MUHAIYADDEEN: No matter how intelligent we are, and no matter how much experience we have had in life, certain obstacles will still come and block us. Sometimes, when the mind goes its own way we meet with a block. Or when we set out to do something, we may come up against an obstacle and find it necessary to ask someone else for help. Or when we go on a journey, even if we carry a map and consult it frequently, we may run into difficulties. We might not be able to identify some places correctly, because they appear the same as others. Then, if we stray off the path, we will lose our way and it will be necessary to stop and get out of the car to ask someone, ''Where are we? What is the name of this place? Where does this road lead? Can you please direct us?'' Only by asking will you be able to find out where you are.

But be careful who you ask, because different people will give you different answers. A man who doesn't really know the area might give you any reply just to please you at the moment. If you follow his directions, you might go round in circles until you finally realize you are on the wrong road. Then you will have to retrace your journey. But if you ask someone who really knows, he will give you clear directions. If you can follow them, you will find the right road.

My children, no matter how much experience you may have, no matter how intelligent you are or how many maps you carry, you still need someone who knows the way. Out of all the people you might ask, there may be one who really knows, one who can give you the right directions. When that person shows you the way, the obstacles will be removed. That is what you need to better your life.

If you don't meet someone who knows, or if there is no one to ask, then you might have to go and stand in front of a tree and ask the tree. You can stand under it and reflect upon your actions. "What am I doing? Where am I going? Is what I am doing right?" If you talk to the tree in this way and then stand there and reflect a little while, then from within yourself a certain vibration will arise. This is because God is within you, and He will caution you. He will tell whether what you are embarking on will reach fulfillment or not. A warning will come from within saying, "This is not good. This is not right," or "Go back home," or some such message. If you disobey that warning and continue in the same direction, you might meet with dangers. If you can't find a tree, then go and stand near a wall and talk to that. Stand there and reflect within yourself for a while and you'll get an answer. If you do that, certain paths will be opened to you in your life.

This is the advice your friend needs. You can also tell her that there is one God, who treats everyone equally, without discriminating between one religion and another or between one color and another. He performs all His duties with utmost love and perfect purity, in a way which knows no comparison. Such a Power does exist. That Power is called God. We must place our faith in Him alone. There is no equal to Him. If we want to work with that Power, if we want to become intimate with it and attune ourselves to it, then we need faith and we need certitude in that faith. Determination must be in our hearts.

The world is only a show. All the things that have been created are bound by certain limitations. They will all change in their own season. They are born and they die. They appear and they perish. These things are temporary. Today they can be seen, tomorrow they cannot be seen. They are here for a while and then one day they are not here. They are visible and suddenly they become invisible. This is the nature of created things, the things that we can see and experience. They are objects of our happiness and sadness. If we desire such things and place our faith in them, we will feel sad when they change or when they leave. And they are bound to do this when their time arrives. We know this, and yet we try to hold on to them, only to feel great pain and sorrow when they go.

There is only One who does not come or go. That is God. He always remains where He is. If we understand this truth, we will realize that everything other than God has to change one day. So, we should place our faith in that One who never changes, the One who will never leave us. It would be good for us to reflect on this.

In this world, all the things we desire are subject to change. Every second, every moment, they are changing. Therefore, for whatever happens we must say, *"Al-hamdu lillāh,* all praise be to God." There is only One who has the responsibility for everything. We must have contentment and gratitude for whatever He has given us. We must praise God every moment of our lives. We must not live with the expectation that we will be alive for even one more breath. We should not anticipate the next second, the next breath, the next meal, the next drink of water, or the next day, because the body changes moment by moment. We should say, "I surrender all responsibility to God." We should praise God for this moment that we are alive and place our faith in Him, surrendering to His responsibility whatever is to happen in the next moment.

If we can open up our lives in this manner, then everything will turn out right. Everything will be peaceful for us. We will be dwelling only with Him, and He will never leave us. We will be with Him always. Then, as the reels of our life continue to play, no matter what we see each second, whether it is good or bad, whether it makes us happy or sad, we will be grateful to God. The next moment may come or it may not. Since we can't see what it will bring, we must have gratitude and surrender it to God. If we can live in this manner, we will have peace, no matter what happens.

Please tell your friend this. In each second of her life let her do whatever her duty is.

QUESTION: I have always wondered what Bawa meant when he said, "Bend the sky into a bow." May I have an explanation please?

BAWA MUHAIYADDEEN: It is said that you can bend the sky into a bow and thread sand into rope. Through scientific methods, people have drawn the sky closer to the earth and have gone beyond the sun and the moon. They are building houses in the sky and many other things like that. You must have seen such things.

It is possible to thread sand into rope. After all, ore extracted from earth is transformed into iron and made into chains. Glass is also made from sand. Even gold, silver, and many other glittering objects are extracted from sand. It is possible to walk on fire or on water. It is possible to remain under water for a long time. You can even make yourself invisible by tying up the eyes of others so they cannot see you. All these things are possible.

Look at a rainbow. Have you seen how it draws water? The rainbow is not a god, is it? No, it is an energy which draws water from the ocean. In the same way, through the energies of illusion, one can perform and demonstrate many things. These *siddhis,* these miracles of the elements, are quite easy to perform.

You may have seen people attach two wings to themselves and then fly. Some fly with wings, some fly in a plane, and some fly in a balloon. It is possible to do these things.

We can fly in the sky or subdue the earth and rule over it. The only thing that is truly difficult is to control one's mind and be still. That is the most difficult thing a person can do. All other things are possible. All the supernatural feats that we admire so much are things that can be done by animals and birds, by the earth, by the sky, by the air, by viruses, insects, fish, and by things that live beneath the earth. The mere fact that a man can do such things is no great wonder. That is no miracle. These are only acts and scenes, dramas which are subject to change. They are all bound to perish at some time.

Man can perform all these tricks through the energies of illusion, but they are not true miracles. They are not lasting or eternal. And just as the clouds and the darkness recede when they see the sun, these elemental miracles and energies vanish when they see the power of God. But His power, His control, and His duty will never vanish. He is One who has created all of these energies, the One who nourishes and protects and controls and subdues them. He has the power to create and to destroy. He controls all of the universes and contains them within Him, all the while standing alone as Himself.

A man who can bring his own state to the state of that Power can rule everything within himself. But it is a rare person who can subdue all the energies within him and control all of his thoughts, desires, miracles, and blood ties. Even more rare is the one who can control and subdue his birth and death and all the things he seeks and yearns for, and then remain still with no thought except the thought of God. And rarest of all is the one who can attain the power of God and rule the way God rules. God alone exists in such a state. That is the point. If you can do this, it will be good.

SONIA GILBERT: Bawa is the only one that I have ever known who made it very clear that the *rūh,* the soul, which is the ray from God, is filled with all that which belongs to God. It is plenitude, clear and untroubled. If that is so, then what is the station of the *rūhāni,* the elemental spirit?

BAWA MUHAIYADDEEN: My child, what is called the *rūh,* the soul, is a ray of light that came from God. In the kingdom of the *rūh,* the souls exist as rays, as magnetic powers. Those rays were dispersed by God and scattered all over, filling all places in creation. They fell upon seven different places—upon earth, fire, water, air, and ether, and upon the light and the plenitude. Those rays, which were constantly in motion, became the countless lives of creation. What kind of life each ray became was determined by where it fell, which energy it fell upon. The rays that fell on the earth became earth lives, and those that fell on fire became fire lives. In the same way, water lives, air lives, and ether lives (lives of illusion) were created.

The rays that fell into the realm of wisdom, into God's kingdom, became the sixth form of life, the light life, the human soul. That soul sees only the One who is God. The rays that returned to Him became the seventh form, the light of plenitude or completeness. Those souls which fell back into God were the 124,000 prophets and the *qutbs.*

God looked deeply at each ray, each soul, in the place where it fell. And out of these rays God made the creations and said, *"Kun!* Arise!"" and they rose up and praised God. And God gazed upon all of them again. Then the *Qutb,* which is divine wisdom, returned to God and said, "O God, everything praises You, everything worships You. Earth worships You, fire worships You, water worships You, air worships You, ether worships You. Everything performs *tasbih* to You, praising Your glory. All lives seek You; they seek Your nourishment alone. If You were not there, they could not live. Therefore O God, please keep Your gaze upon them.''

All lives belong to God. They came as rays from Him. He gave them life, He made them appear and rise up, and He gave each one the necessary food and an appropriate place to live. He is the One who guides and protects them forever, as their leader and chieftain.

This explanation of the six kinds of lives came through the *Qutbiyyat*. That which stayed in the form of wisdom within that *Qutbiyyat* is the *rūh*, the soul, and that is what gives the explanation. The life of plenitude, the state which changed into the prophets, is what goes back and merges with God.

A bulb cannot light up until the current flows into it. Where does the light come from? Is it in the wire that carries the current? Is it in the switch? No, the light is generated from the turbine, which produces the power. In the same way, the power and the completeness reside within God, and the current flows through the *Nūr*. The *Qutbiyyat*, or wisdom, is the switch. This is how the light of God comes into man. This is the way it works. The perfection that is in God comes to the *Nūr*, the completeness of the *Nūr* comes to wisdom, the resplendence of wisdom comes to the soul, and the beauty that is in the soul comes into the body. The body is the bulb. That beauty comes from the light within.

The beauty of the body, the beauty of the heart, the resplendence of wisdom, the completeness of the *Nūr*, the perfection which is God—all these things are mingled together within man. If this light, this power, can be made to resplend within him, then that which came from God will go back and lose itself once again within God. Whatever is connected to God dwells within God and returns to Him. It will never be destroyed. That is what is called a human life. That is the *rūh*, the soul.

The *rūhānī* is different. A man may look like a man, but depending upon where his ray originally fell, he may have, impressed within him, the qualities of a monkey or a lion or some other animal. If the ray fell into water, the qualities of water will be impressed upon him. If it fell into fire, he will have fire qualities, as the jinns do. If it fell into air, the qualities of the angels will be within him. If it fell inside of maya, then the qualities of darkness will enter him. If it fell on earth, he will be filled with many millions of thoughts and qualities, dirt and stench, mud, gold, silver, mercury, copper, lead, oil, and the many colors found in stagnant water. So many qualities will come into the person from wherever his soul fell.

These qualities and the actions that result from them are called *rūhānis*. Whatever a person gives life to within himself—each thought, each mantra, each elemental miracle or magic, whatever he brings to life using the angels of earth, fire, water, air, and ether or maya—these become *rūhānis*. They are in opposition to the *rūh*, the pure soul.

Man gives life to these *rūhānis* and what do they do in return? They turn around and devour him. He has to take care of them and earn for them, and they repay him by destroying his treasures and his property. These *rūhānis* take over his kingdom, his wealth, his property, and his blood attachments and claim them as their own. They keep following him wherever he goes, until finally, having seized and destroyed everything he has, they make him their slave. In the end, the *rūhānis* push him away and send him to the cemetery, where he becomes prey to fire or water or air or to the darkness of the hell of illusion. All of his own thoughts have killed him.

Once in the grave, he must face judgment. Since he did not return to God what belonged to God, he forfeited that real thing of truth, the trust that he brought with him from God. Instead he borrowed and brought up these other things within him and dispersed them among the elements. That is why he must face judgment.

This is the difference between the *rūh* and the *rūhānī:* all the things that we create and foster within ourselves are *rūhānis;* what we brought from God is the *rūh*. We must understand this through our wisdom, through the *Qutbiyyat*. If we reflect upon wisdom and that wisdom within wisdom appears, it will give us the explanations we need to eliminate all the things that set out to kill us.

If we can give up these *rūhānis,* then the miracle called the *Nūr*, the resplendence of Allah, will come into us. When that one true miracle resplends within us, we will know plenitude, and when we look into that plenitude, we will see ourselves within God and God within us. One will be seeing the other; God, the wisdom, and the soul will see each other. *Alif, lām,* and *mīm* will become one, and a complete, indestructible power will emerge. The *rūh* that came from God will go back and lose itself within Him. It will return to the completeness of the divine kingdom from which it came, to the universe of the souls, the place of His power of judgment. That *rūh* will never perish.

But the other energies, the *rūhānīs,* will continue to wander about and haunt the places we once frequented. The thoughts that came from our desires and out of earth, fire, water, air, and the darkness of maya will wander about where we lived and make noises. They are the ghosts and demons and spirits that persist in saying, "My relatives, my house, my food! Give me food!" The bulls and cows and goats and horses and other forms that we created within ourselves will haunt the old places. Those elemental energies called *rūhānīs* will continue to wander around until they are destroyed or changed.

But the *rūh* is indestructible. That is the difference.

DR. MARKAR: How do those *rūhānīs* change?

BAWA MUHAIYADDEEN: My child, when a man dies and leaves this world, he hands over all he possesses to his wife or his children. The wife hands over her portion to her daughter. The daughter, in turn, passes on that portion to her younger brother, who passes it on to his younger brother. He, then, will leave his share to his wife.

In this way, the father divides his wealth among many people. If he gave birth to three children, he will share all that he has earned among them. They, in turn, hand it down, generation after generation, one child to the next. In this way it continues on and on. As long as that happens, the *rūhānīs* will go on following them.

Only when one of them cuts away this connection will the *rūhānīs* change. As long as we divide our property among our blood ties, then the *rūhānīs,* our desires and their connection, will continue from generation to generation. But if a person can eliminate the thoughts within him and cut away the *rūhānīs* in his own lifetime, then those same thoughts will not taint the future generations. The karmic connection will be cut.

These *rūhānis* are the ancestral deities, the things which we have made into gods and worshiped. But in the end, every form, every *rūhāni* that we have created, will turn around and suck our blood. They will demand all sorts of sacrifices and finally take away our very kingdom and murder us.

We have given up the kingdom of the *rūh*, which is the universe of the soul, and instead have captured the kingdom of the *rūhāni*, or hell. If we can transform our state while we are still alive, if we can cut away the *rūhāni* that we have raised and nurtured within, if we can say, "Go away! There is no connection between you and me," then from that very day, the *rūhāni* will destroy itself and change. That is how it is.

Think about this. Try to progress and come forward without that heavy burden on your back. Do not carry a bag around with you intending to fill it with whatever you see. Unload that bag and come alone. It will only become a great weight for you. Whether you carry it on your back or under your arm or on your head, it will still be a very heavy burden. If you want to progress, drop these shopping bags in which you gather all the things you find. Those things that you have collected and then seek to distribute to others are your *rūhānis*. You give life to them and then bring them up, saving them to share with others. You carry them under your arm or on your back or on your head; you hide them inside your shirt or in your pockets. Yet these are the things that will kill you later. Not only do you spoil your own state, you hand over your shares to others and spoil them too. But if you can unload these bags and throw them away, then you can progress and become a little lighter.

Surrender to God and praise Him for your being alive at this moment. Have trust in Him and surrender the next moment to His will, saying, *"Tawakkul 'alallāh."* If we live like that, these *rūhānis* will be cut away from us.

～～～～～

QUESTION: Of all the thousands of prophets sent by God, can Bawa tell us why Christ is the one most celebrated by man?

BAWA MUHAIYADDEEN: That is not so. Each country has its own way. The followers of Islam number over eight hundred million; they believe in someone else. Look how many millions of Hindus there are in the world; they have faith in many different gods. The Jews follow Moses ⊛, and those who accept the religion of Zoroastrianism worship fire. People in different countries put their trust in different gods or prophets.

Some people fashion gods out of stones, and some people make different prophets into gods. But the prophets are not God, they are His messengers, sent to convey His commandments. What was it that Moses ⊛ and Muhammad ⊛ told the people? They said that even though the family of Banu Isra'il and the family of Hāshim were called by different names, they both belonged to the same tribe. Muhammad ⊛ and Moses ⊛ both declared, "There is only one God. He is One who cannot be seen and who exists in a realm which is invisible to the eye. He has no form or color. We must worship only that one God. He is the One without equal, the One without parallel, the One who has no need of help." This is what they said.

Most of the people in times gone by worshiped gods that they could see; they made idols and statues out of them. They prayed to the earth, the trees, the sun, and the stars. They worshiped fire gods, water gods, snake gods, and scorpion gods. But Moses ⊛ and Muhammad ⊛ and their followers could not believe in all the gods that others worshiped. They believed in only one God, who existed beyond anything they could see, beyond mind and desire, beyond lights and glitters.

A great many commandments were sent by God to the tribes of Hāshim and Banū Isrā'il, strict laws concerning their daily life, their food and drink, circumcision, their behavior and conduct, and their methods of worshiping God. Flesh could only be eaten after being slaughtered in the correct way according to the laws of *qurbān*.* Many such conditions were laid down, and adhering to them was extremely difficult. Even today some people follow this path, and it is still very difficult. The other paths are easy.

Many religions do exist. Buddhism is not so much a religion as it is a society that has branched off from Hinduism. Millions belong to that branch, while millions follow the religion of Zoroastrianism. There are also millions who worship Jesus ⊛ as the son of God. It is

*See glossary.

no great wonder that all these beliefs exist. Each person chooses to follow whatever way is suitable to him, whatever way is easy.

But it is not for us to talk about religions here. God accepts every religion. To Him, they are all equal. He accepts anyone who follows the path of truth. If a man opens his heart on the path of truth, he will see God.

We cannot say that only one prophet is God's son. Since God has no attachment to the world, to attribute to Him a son, a wife, property, or livestock is ignorance. And for a baby to be born to one without a wife would indeed be a wonder. Everything God created is a child to Him: the sun, the stars, the earth and sky, and all the other works of His artistry. Whatever has manifested from His creation is His child.

Who are you? You are His child. Who created you? God. Everything that was created by Him is His child, so you too are His child. But to say that you are His child does not mean that He married your mother in order to give birth to you. It was His power that gave birth to you. That power exists in a state without attachment. He created all things, all beings, through that power. He is father to all and mother to all. Everything He created and manifested is His child. You cannot say that He had only one child, one son. He protects and sustains everything.

We must reflect upon this truth. As long as we fail to understand the truth, we are subject to judgment and punishment. When one becomes a true human being, he will accept only God, nothing else. He will see only God and accept only the commandments and the conditions set down by God.

He will also accept the prophets who came by the command of God to show us the way. They came to demonstrate good thoughts and good intentions and to point the way from this world to the place from which we came. From the very beginning, many prophets were sent to reveal the truth to us: Jesus, David, Moses, Ishmael, Abraham, Noah, Adam, Jonah, Job, Jacob, Idris, Joseph, and many others, may the peace and blessing of God be upon them all. The last prophet sent was Muhammad ﷺ. All the prophets came to teach us the commandments of God and to show us the direct connection that exists between God and us. Because we are suffering such torment on this path of hell, they came here to tell us,

"No, this is not your way. You must go on the straight path to God."

They pointed out the path; it is up to us to follow it. They drew the map; it is up to us to use it. They showed us the connection between ourselves and God; it is up to us to go that way. Sometimes the path may not be clear, but if we call out for help, if we hold up our hands and say, "O God, I am following what You said, but the path does not seem clear," then suddenly we will receive instructions from within, telling us, "This is the way." Some indication will be given. This does not mean that the prophets will hold us by the hand and take us all the way. That is not their duty. They will only give us directions.

Different people might follow different paths. They might follow various gods. But this is the point of truth: *Lā ilāha*, there is nothing other than You; *ill-Allāhu*, You are God. That is the only way. Follow that way. That is the instruction we have been given.

This path is certainly difficult. The other paths are easy. They say you can purchase a deed and buy your way into heaven; but you end up in the cemetery, anyway. Or you can give money and be called a saint; but you'll only be parading your title in hell. These deeds and titles are like credit cards. When you want to buy something on loan, you just show your card. "See, I have built up good credit. Look at all that I've done. Here's my card." That card will represent all that you fostered within you in the world. But where will you be showing it? In hell.

You cannot show any credit card to God. There is no deed for the truth. You cannot buy God with your money or your fame or your titles. Nothing can come from such efforts, because God knows everything already. He is the One who has heard what you said. He is the One who has observed what you did and understands why you did it. He is the witness and the lawyer. He is also the judge, who pronounces the verdict and decides where you belong. No one can intervene for you in that place. So whether Jesus (ﷺ) or anyone else comes forward on your behalf, they cannot help you there. No lawyer can do anything for you, because everything is on record: all that you thought, all that you did, every breath you took, and every sound you made. It is all recorded and there is nothing you can do to change it.

The prophets' duty was to give the commandments of God while they were here, and they performed that duty. Our duty is to follow the rules and directions they gave and to go forward on the path. To do this, we need to find a sheikh who is an *insān kāmil,* a perfected, God-realized being. If we can grab hold of his coattails and follow him along while he is here, then it will become easy, and we will be closer to where we need to go. But without such a one, we will find it very difficult.

What do we gain by building great mansions here? Nothing at all. Is that heaven? No. These mansions will crash down when their time is up. No matter how beautiful a building may be, an earthquake or a gale can bring it tumbling down. Buildings are only made out of earth, fire, and water. Such things perish. But God will never perish. Truth will not perish. The presence of God will exist forever. Of that one thing we can be absolutely certain. For that you don't need any money or deeds or credit cards. None of those things will help; they are only good for hell.

DAVID FREUDBERG: What is the difference between a *qutb* and a prophet? And what are your duties? We have a sense that you are doing a lot more than just what we can see.

BAWA MUHAIYADDEEN: My brother, the prophets are those who came and repeated the commandments that God gave them. God said to each prophet, "Go and tell this to the people." And each one came and repeated what he was told. Like a microphone, he took the sound, the message, from God and relayed it to everyone. When the sound first came from God, it came as a secret, but it was then transmitted by microphone so it could be heard everywhere. In this mysterious way the secrets of God were revealed and made manifest to mankind.

The prophets could not say whatever they wanted to; they were limited to saying exactly what God commanded. The power was sometimes greater in one than in another, so the commandments they received varied in strength and in volume according to the station, the actions, and the individual capacities of each. Just as a child is given the appropriate instructions as it grows from one stage to the next, the sound and the commandments that were given by

God varied, from place to place and from time to time, depending upon the capacities of the prophets and the needs of the people. And so, from the very beginning, as wisdom grew, the strength of God's commandments grew.

The duty of the *Qutb* differs from that of the prophets. The prophets revealed the secret commandments given to them by God. What they gave was somewhat like a salve that you apply externally for a pain. But the *Qutb* goes within, as a secret within a secret. As the people change, the *Qutb* notes the change and then gives whatever injection is needed for that particular disease. As the wisdom within wisdom, the *Qutb* goes within and gives the necessary explanation.

The sounds of the prophets reach only the first three levels of consciousness: feeling, awareness, and intellect. For example, when an ant crawls on our skin, first we feel an itch through our feeling, then our awareness tells us where it is, and our intellect tells us to scratch it. In the same way, the words of the prophets come first to feeling, then feeling explains to awareness, and awareness conveys each message to the intellect. Thus the commandments of the prophets come to us on the outside, teaching us through feeling, awareness, and intellect. We receive them with our intellect and then follow them.

The *Qutb*, however, is different. It goes within, beyond intellect to deeper levels, and as we grow, it shows us point by point, the meanings at each different step. First as subtle wisdom and then as divine analytic wisdom, it keeps on discriminating and separating each point and explaining them to us. This is the difference between the prophets and the *Qutb*.

The prophets bring sounds to your feeling, awareness, and intellect. Beyond that is judgment, or estimate, which you use to evaluate your life. The *Qutb* functions as the higher levels of wisdom, first as subtle wisdom which helps you to see and understand the subtlety within each different point. Then the *Qutb* becomes divine analytic wisdom, which explains what this is and what that is and then analyzes the difference between them. Finally it becomes the divine luminous wisdom, the *Nūr*. That is the completeness which says, "This is His power."

So, the station and the function of the *Qutb* is that of the wisdom which works within.

QUESTION: Many ancient civilizations believed that God created the thymus gland as the center of energy for the body. Is this true?

BAWA MUHAIYADDEEN: Did you read this in a book?

QUESTIONER: I've heard some doctors speak on television and I've read about it in books....

BAWA MUHAIYADDEEN: All right, my child, but if we look at all the ideas and acts and dramas that are presented on television, we will see that they are things that will put us in reverse gear and take us backwards. You should not take these things in and accept them as the perfect truth. Even the words of a song might sometimes be altered to suit the actor or the drama. It is not good for you to believe such things or to rely on them to guide you in life. If you do, you will be taken backwards. You should not even trust what is written in books. So many different things are said in so many different ways. The writer might copy from other books or change things around and make them wrong. There could be a mistake in the proofreading, or the translation might be altered. Sometimes the editors will change the words to fit the flow of the story. Even the printer might make a number of mistakes. By the time the book is completed, the truth is destroyed. So it is not wise to accept these things as the truth.

Now, just below the Adam's apple, there is something called the *zamzam* well from which water comes. Above that there is something which perceives taste. There is also a place called *halq* through which air passes. A kind of motor or switch is there which is responsible for making the water and the air flow and which enables us to extract the taste from what we eat.

The energies that dwell in that place are connected to earth, fire, water, air, and ether. Those energies give us what is necessary for the body. They relate only to the body and have nothing to do with wisdom. Wisdom does not come from that area.

QUESTIONER: This is just the physical level. Certain civilizations thought that God made the thymus as a basis for the energy supply.

BAWA MUHAIYADDEEN: What we call energies are things that perish. They will die or be destroyed. Energies are subject to change. You feel an itch somewhere, you scratch, and as soon as you scratch, the itch goes away. An insect creeps on your skin, you brush it away, and at once the sensation is gone. That is what is meant by an energy. Energy is concerned with perception and awareness. It makes us aware of things in the blood, in the skin, in the muscles, and other things relating to the body. But where does truth move? In the heart. There, all energies are closed off. No energies exist there. If the heart stops, all the energies stop. Once the heart is finished, everything is finished.

Within the heart is a great mystery, a very subtle mystery. God's house, the house of the soul, the house of wisdom, dwells there. The judgment of the kingdom of God, the judgment of our life, is within that house. The heart holds the greatest subtlety, a very tiny point which cannot be eaten up by the earth, by fire, by air, by water, or by illusion. Satan cannot touch it. Nothing that is perishable, no *shaktis* (energies), can make contact with it. Nothing has the power to eat it up. Even though everything else will perish, that tiny point inside the heart will never perish. That is God's house, where the power of God resides. That power can make things move and carry them along, but it can also stop them. It can both create and destroy. It is the only true power.

That point inside the heart is what we need to understand. Wisdom, the light, the soul, the *Qutbiyyat,* the completeness of the *Nūr,* and the power called God all reside within that tiny point. We have to reach that point to be able to understand it. If we can do that it will be very good.

QUESTION: Getting back to the physical, which is not as important or valuable, what would Bawa say to do to increase your energy? How would one increase one's energy on the physical level?

BAWA MUHAIYADDEEN: There is a point of energy within a seed which makes it germinate. But the seed has to be planted within a certain time limit, within a year or so. If you fail to plant it within that time, the energy within the seed will perish; its time will have passed. After that it will shrink and shrivel up. Then it is useless to try to plant the seed, for it will not grow.

Similarly, a blossom on a tree receives its water, its food, its air, and its beauty from the tree. Yet within a week after it blooms, it shrivels up and falls away. All the energy of that flower is gone. As the energy subsides, the fragrance dwindles, the beauty lessens, the color fades, and the flower withers. After that the tree cannot go on supplying the flower.

No energy can continue forever. Each one has a specific time limit. Only during the period that it is functioning will it give us any benefit. Once that limit has passed, the power supplying the energy stops, and the energy weakens and subsides. The blood turns to water, the skin that was moist and tight begins to dry and shrivel up, the eyes which were once so bright begin to fade, and the nerves do not work as fast as they used to. The beauty that was there earlier is gone.

Have you not seen this in the world? Whether it is a flower or a fruit or anything else, there is a certain period of maturity when the energy is high, but then it declines. The spirit may be willing and the desire may remain, but the energies slacken.

This is not such a vast matter. All energies are subject to this limit. They grow and become strong within the agreed upon time limit, but then the parts begin to waste away, and it is difficult to reactivate them again. If you reflect on this, you will understand what energies are capable of.

It's two minutes to twelve now, time for you to eat. Love to all the children. May God give us everything good. *Āmīn.*

June 27, 1979 AM

Glossary

(A) Indicates an Arabic word

(T) Indicates a Tamil word

'abd (A) Slave; slave of God; one who is completely surrendered to the service of God.

aiyō (T) An exclamatory expression, ''Oh no!''

ākhirah (A) The hereafter; the next world; the kingdom of God.

'ālam (A) (pl. *'ālamīn*) A world; cosmos; universe.

'ālamul-arwāh (A) The world of pure souls, where all souls are performing *tasbīh,* or prayers of praise to God.

al-hamdu lillāh (A) ''All praise is to You.'' Allah is the glory and greatness that deserves all praise. ''You are the One responsible for the appearance of all creations. Whatever appears, whatever disappears, whatever receives benefit or loss–all is Yours. I have surrendered everything into Your hands. I remain with hands outstretched, spread out, empty, and helpless. Whatever is happening and whatever is going to happen is all Yours.'' Lit.: All praise belongs to Allah!

'Alī ☺ (A) The fourth caliph, son-in-law of the Prophet ☺ , husband of Fatimah ☺ , and father of Hasan ☺ and Husain ☺ . The second convert to Islam, following Khadijah ☺ , the first wife of the Prophet ☺ .

alif (A) The first letter of the Arabic alphabet (|). To the transformed man of wisdom, the *alif* represents Allah, the One. See also: *lām, mīm.*

Allah subhānahu wa ta'ālā (A) Allah, glory is His exaltedness! A spontaneous outpouring of love from a believer's heart upon hearing or uttering the name Allah.

Allāhu (A) God; the One of infinite grace and incomparable love; the One who gives of His undiminishing wealth of grace; the One who is beyond comparison or example; the Eternal, Effulgent One; the One of overpowering effulgence.

Āmīn (A) So be it. May He make this complete; may it be so.

anāthi (T) The beginningless beginning; the state in which God meditated upon Himself alone; the period of pre-creation when Allah was alone in darkness, unaware of Himself even though everything was within Him; the state of unmanifestation, before *āthi,* when the creation came forth.

317

'arsh (A) The throne of God; the plenitude from which God rules. The station located on the crown of the head which is the throne that can bear the weight of Allah. Allah is so heavy that we cannot carry the load with our hands or legs. The *'arsh* is the only part of man that can support Allah.

āthi (T) Primal beginning; the period after *anāthi;* the time when the *Qutb* (the wisdom which explains the truth of God) and the *Nūr* (the plenitude of the light of Allah) manifested within Allah; the time of the dawning of the light; the world of grace where the unmanifested begins to manifest in the form of resonance. In contrast to *awwal,* when the creations became manifest in form, *āthi* is the time when the first sound or vibration emerged.

avathānam (T) Concentration; attentiveness.

awwal (A) The time of the creation of forms; the stage at which the soul became surrounded by form and each creation took shape; the stage at which the souls of the six kinds of lives (earth-life, fire-life, water-life, air-life, ether-life, and light-life) were placed in their respective forms. Allah created these forms and then placed that entrusted treasure which is the soul within those forms.

Bismillāhir-Rahmānir-Rahīm (A) In the name of God, Most Merciful, Most Compassionate.

    Bismillāh: Allah, the first and the last; the One with the beginning and without beginning. He is the One who is the cause for creation and for the absence of creation, the cause for the beginning and for the beginningless. He is the One who is completeness.

    Ar-Rahmān: He is the King, the Compassionate One, and the Beneficent One. He is the One who protects all creations and gives them nourishment. He looks after them, gives them love, takes them unto Himself, and comforts them. He gives them food, houses, property, and everything within Himself. He holds His creations within Himself and protects them. He is the One who reigns with justice.

    Ar-Rahīm: He is the One who redeems, the One who protects us from evil, the One who preserves and confers eternal bliss. No matter what we may do, He has the quality of forgiving us and accepting us back. He is the Tolerant One who forgives all the faults we have committed. He is the Savior. On the Day of Judgment, on the Day of Inquiry and on all days since the beginning, He protects and brings His creations back unto Himself.

caliph (Engl.) Vice-regent; successor to the *Rasūlullāh* ⓐ . Used as the English word in the text.

daulat (A) This has two meanings. One is the wealth of the world, or *dunyā;* the other is the wealth of the grace of Allah. The wealth of Allah is the wealth of divine knowledge (*'ilm*) and the wealth of perfect *īmān* (absolute faith, certitude, and determination).

dharma (T) Teaching of truth; duty; one's rightful duty; right action; law.

dhikr (A) The remembrance of God. It is a common name given to certain words in praise of God. Of the many *dhikrs,* the most exalted *dhikr* is to say, *"Lā ilāha ill-Allāhu*—There is nothing other than You, O God. Only You are Allah." All the others relate to His *wilāyat,* or His actions, but this *dhikr* points to Him and to Him alone. See also: *kalimah, Lā ilāha ill-Allāhu.*

dīn (A) Religion; path; faith; belief. Bawa Muhaiyaddeen ⊕ uses this word to refer to the light or path of perfect purity; the resplendence of perfectly pure *īmān* (absolute faith, certitude, and determination).

dunyā (A) The earth-world in which we live; the world of physical existence; the darkness which separated from Allah at the time when the light of the *Nūr Muhammad* manifested from within Allah.

fikr (A) Contemplation, meditation, concentration on God.

Furqān (A) Islam. This is the fourth step of religion, the religion sent to Moses ⊕ and Muhammad ⊕ , which corresponds to the head. It is the "criterion" which distinguishes between good and evil, right and wrong, lawful and unlawful, truth and illusion.

gnāna guru (T) A perfect spiritual guide; a guru who has attained the state of *gnānam,* or divine wisdom; one who can point the way to God.

gnāni (T) A gnostic; one who has divine wisdom, or *gnānam;* one who has received the qualities and wisdom of God by surrendering to God, and, having received these, lives in a state of peace where he sees all lives as equal; one who has attained the state of peace.

hadīth(A) In Islam, a traditional story or observation related by the Prophet ⊕ . If the words or commands of Allah were received directly by the Prophet Muhammad ⊕ , it is known as a *hadīth qudsī;* sometimes means a story about the prophets.

halāl (A) Those things that are permissible or lawful according to the commands of God and which conform to the word of God.

halq (A) Throat or gullet; slaughtering an animal or cut in *qurban.*

haqīqat (A) The third step of spiritual ascendance, signifying the realization of divinity and the beginning of communication with God. Lit.: the station of truth. See also: *sharī'at, tarīqat, haqīqat, ma'rifat, sūfiyyat.*

harām (A) That which is forbidden by truth, forbidden by justice, and forbidden by the warnings or commands of God. For those who are on the straight path, *harām* means all the evil things, the actions, the food, and the dangers that can obstruct the path.

hayāt (A) The plenitude of man's eternal life; the splendor of the completeness of life; the *rūh,* or the soul, of the splendor of man's life.

hayawān (A) Beast. Bawa Muhaiyaddeen ☺ often uses this to refer to that man whose animal-like qualities dominate him.

'ibādat (A) Worship and service to the One God.

Ikrimah (A) The son of Abū Jahl. For many years, along with his father, he was a determined opponent of Muhammad ☺. However, he later embraced Islam and became a companion of the Prophet ☺.

ill-Allāhu (A) See: *Lā ilāha ill-Allāhu; kalimah.*

'ilm (A) Divine knowledge. Lit.: knowledge.

īmān (A) Absolute, complete, and unshakable faith, certitude, and determination that God alone exists; the complete acceptance by the heart that God is One.

Īmān-Islām (A) The state of the spotlessly pure heart which contains Allah's Holy Qur'an, His divine radiance, His divine wisdom, His truth, His prophets, His angels, and His laws. The pure heart which, having cut away all evil, takes on the power of that courageous determination called faith and stands shining in the resplendence of Allah.

When the resplendence of Allah is seen as the completeness within the heart of man, that is *Īmān-Islām.* When the complete unshakable faith of the heart is directed toward the One who is completeness; when that completeness is made to merge with the One who is completeness; when that heart communes with that One, trusts only in Him, and worships only Him, accepting only Him and nothing else as the only perfection and the only One worthy of worship—that is *Īmān-Islām.*

Injīl (A) Christianity. See also: *Zabūr, Jabrāt, Injīl,* and *Furqān.*

insān (A) True man; a true human being; the true form of man; the form of Allah's qualities, actions, conduct, behavior, and virtues. The one who has realized the completeness of this form, having filled himself with these qualities, is an *insān.*

Insān-Allāh (A) Man-God.

insān kāmil (A) A perfected, God-realized being. One who has realized Allah as his only wealth, cutting away all the wealth of the world and the wealth sought by the mind. One who has acquired God's qualities, performs his own actions accordingly, and contains himself within those qualities.

in shā'Allāh (A) If God has willed it.

Jabrāt (A) Fire worship. See also: *Zabūr, Jabrāt, Injīl,* and *Furqān.*

jinn (A) A genie; a being created from fire. There are two kinds of jinns: light jinns who have accepted God and Islam, and evil, demonic jinns who arose from the connection to *maya,* or illusion. Used as an English word in the text.

jōthi (T) Light; radiance; resplendence.

Ka'bah (A) In Islam, the *Ka'bah* is the most important shrine of worship. The place where the earlier prophets and Final Prophet, Muhammad☺, gathered together in prayer. On the path of *sharī'at,* one of the five obligations, or *furūd,* is the pilgrimage to the *Ka'bah,* known as *hajj.*

   Bawa Muhaiyaddeen☺ also uses it to refer to the innermost heart, or *qalb,* which is the original source of prayer; the place where a true man, or *insān,* meets Allah face to face. Whoever brings his heart to that state of perfection and prays to God from that heart will be praying from the *Ka'bah.*

kalimah (A) The affirmation of faith—*Lā ilāha ill-Allāhu:* There is nothing other than You, O God. Only You are Allah.

   The recitation or remembrance of God which cuts away the influence of the five elements (earth, fire, water, air, and ether), washes away all the karma that has accumulated from the very beginning until now, dispels the darkness, beautifies the heart, and makes it resplend. The *kalimah* washes the body and the heart of man and makes him pure, makes his wisdom emerge, and impels that wisdom to know the self and God. See also: *dhikr; Lā ilāha ill-Allāhu.*

kāmil sheikh (A) Perfect spiritual guide; the true guru; the one who, knowing himself and God, guides others on the straight path, the path to Allah; one who has developed the three thousand gracious qualities of Allah.

   Sitting on the throne of patience, with the quality of compassion, he comforts his children, dispels the karmic evils of this *dunyā,* and teaches them *arivu* (wisdom). He teaches them to see the form, or *sūrat,* and makes them realize the form within the form. This form, or *sūrat,* is the light of the *Nūr.* He also shows his children the form and the light of absolute faith, certitude, and determination (*īmān*) and shows that Allah is that wealth that exists within that faith.

karma (T) The inherited qualities formed at the time of conception; the qualities of the essences of the five elements; the qualities of the mind; the qualities of the connection to hell; the qualities and actions of the seventeen *purānas* which are: arrogance, karma, and maya, or illusion; the three sons of maya, *tārahan, singhan,* and *sūran;* the six intrinsic evils of lust, anger, greed, attachment, bigotry, and envy; and the five acquired evils of intoxication, desire, theft, falsehood, and murder. Used in the text as an English word.

khair (A) That which is right or good; that which is acceptable to wisdom and to Allah, as opposed to *sharr,* that which is evil or bad.

Kun! (A) The word of the Lord meaning, ''Be! Arise!'' with which He caused all of everything to exist.

kunūd (A) Ingrate; a ghoul or large demon.

kursī (A) The gnostic eye; the eye of light; the center of the forehead where the light of Allah's *Nūr* was impressed on Adam's ⊙ forehead. Lit.: the ''footstool'' or seat of the resplendence of Allah.

Lā ilāha ill-Allāhu (A) ''There is nothing other than You, O God. Only You are Allah.'' To accept this with certitude, to strengthen one's *īmān* (absolute faith), and to affirm this *kalimah* is the state of Islam.

There are two aspects. *Lā ilāha* is the manifestation of creation (*sifāt*). *Ill-Allāhu* is the essence (*dhāt*). All that has appeared, all creation, belongs to *lā ilāha.* The One who created all that, His name is *ill-Allāhu.*

Lit.: No God (is), except the One God. See also: *kalimah; dhikr.*

lām (A) The Arabic letter (ل) which correlates to the English consonant 'l'. In the transformed man of wisdom, *lām* represents the *Nūr,* the resplendence of Allah. See also: *alif, mīm.*

mal'ūn (A) Accursed, rejected; a name attributed to satan.

mantra (T) An incantation or formula; the recitation of a magic word or set of words; sounds imbued with force or energy, through constant repetition, but limited to the energy of the five elements. (The *kalimah* is not a mantra.) Used in the text as an English word.

ma'rifat (A) The fourth step of spiritual ascendance; gnosis; the knowledge of the secrets of God. It is the knowledge of God and the state of merging with Him. See also: *sharī'at, tarīqat, haqīqat, ma'rifat, sūfiyyat.*

mīm (A) The Arabic letter (م) which correlates to the English consonant 'm'. In the transformed man of wisdom, *mīm* represents Muhammad ⊙. The shape of *mīm* is like a sperm cell and from this comes the dot, the *nuqat*, which is the form of the world. See also: *alif*, *lām*.

nafs or *nafs ammārah* (A) The seven kinds of base desires. That is, desires meant to satisfy one's own pleasure and comforts. All thoughts are contained within the *ammārah*. *Ammārah* is like the mother while the *nafs* are like the children. Lit.: Person, spirit; inclination or desire which goads or incites toward evil.

nasīb (A) Destiny or fate; also means share or portion.

nīthānam (T) Balance.

nīyyat (A) Intention.

Nūr (A) Light; the resplendence of Allah; the plenitude of the light of Allah which has the brilliance of a hundred million suns; the completeness of Allah's qualities. When the plenitude of all these becomes one and resplends as one, that is the *Nūr*—that is Allah's qualities and His beauty. It is the resplendent wisdom which is innate in man and can be awakened.

Nūr Muhammad (A) The beauty of the qualities and actions of the powers (*wilāyat*) of Allah, the radiance of Allah's essence (*dhāt*) which shines within the resplendence of His truth. It was the light of Muhammad ⊕ called *Nūr Muhammad* that was impressed upon the forehead of Adam ⊙ . Of the nine aspects of Muhammad ⊕ , *Nūr Muhammad* is that aspect which is the wisdom.

Nūrullāh (A) Light of Allah.

purānas (T) Stories, usually referring to the Hindu scriptures; mythologies; legends; epics. The stories of each religion can be described as *purānas*. Some were sent down as commandments from God, others were created through man's intelligence and senses, while still others were created by poets, usually as songs of praise depicting stories.

　　Bawa Muhaiyaddeen ⊙ speaks of the seventeen *purānas* within man as the qualities of arrogance, karma, and maya; the three sons of maya, *tārahan, singhan* and *sūran;* lust, anger, miserliness, attachment, fanaticism, envy, intoxicants, obsession, theft, murder, and falsehood.

al-qada' wal-qadar (A) Fate and destiny.

qalb (A) Heart; the heart within the heart of man; the innermost heart. Bawa Muhaiyaddeen ⊙ explains that there are two states for the *qalb*. In one state the *qalb* is made up of four chambers which are earth, fire, air, and water—representing Hinduism, Fire Worship, Christianity, and Islam. Inside these four chambers is the second state, the flower of the *qalb* which is the divine qualities of God. This is the flower of grace (*rahmat*). It is called the *qalb*. God's fragrance exists within this inner *qalb*.

Qiyāmah (A)   The standing forth; Day of Reckoning; Day of Questioning.

qurbān (A)   Externally, it is a ritual method for the slaughter of animals to purify them and make them permissible, or *halāl*, to eat. Inwardly, it is to sacrifice one's life to the devotion and service of God and to cut away the beastly qualities within the heart of man that cause him to want to slaughter animals. [See *Asmā'ul-Husnā* appendix.]

Qutb ☺   (A)   Divine analytic wisdom, the wisdom which explains; that which measures the length and breadth of the seven oceans of the base desires (*nafs*); that which awakens all the truths which have been destroyed and buried in the ocean of maya, or illusion; that which awakens absolute faith, certitude, and determination (*īmān*) and the boat of life which has been buried in the ocean of maya; that which awakens the twelve gifts, or weapons; that which explains to the *hayāt*, to life, the state of purity as it existed in the beginning of creation (*awwal*); the grace of the essence of God (*dhāt*), which awakens the *hayāt* of purity and transforms it into the divine vibration.

    Qutb is also a name which has been given to Allah. He can be addressed as *Yā Qutb* or *Yā Quddūs,* the Holy One. *Quddūs* is His power or miracle, His *wilāyat*, while *Qutb* is His action. *Wilāyat* is the power of that action. Lit.: axis, axle, pole, pivot. Also, a title used for the great holy men of Islam. The correct Arabic plural form is *aqtāb*, but "*qutbs*" is used in the text.

Qutbiyyat (A)   The wisdom of the *Qutb;* the sixth level of consciousness; divine analytic wisdom; the wisdom which explains the truth of God; the wisdom that is the power (*wilāyat*) of the *Qutb*.

Rabb (A)   God; the Lord; the Creator and Protector.

Rahmān (A)   The Most Gracious, Most Merciful. *Ar-Rahmān:* one of the ninety-nine beautiful names of Allah. He is the King. He is the Nourisher, the One who gives food. He is the Compassionate One. He is the One who protects the creations. He is the Beneficent One.

rahmat (A)   God's grace; His mercy; His forgiveness and compassion; His benevolence; His wealth. To all creations, He is the wealth of life (*hayāt*) and the wealth of absolute faith, certitude, and determination (*īmān*). All the good things that we receive from God are called His *rahmat*. That is the wealth of God's plenitude. Everything that is within God is *rahmat,* and if He were to give that grace, that would be an undiminishing, limitless wealth.

Rahmatul-'ālamīn (A) The Mercy and Compassion of all the universes. The One who gives everything to all His creations.

Rasūl ⓐ (A) Allah's Messenger, Muhammad ⓐ, is His essence *(dhāt)* that is, the resplendence that emerged from His effulgence, shining radiantly as His Messenger. The manifestation of that resplendence discourses on the explanations of luminous wisdom which he imparts to Allah's creations. He is the one who begs for truth from Allah and intercedes with prayers for all of Allah's creations and for his followers. Therefore Allah has anointed His *Rasūl,* the Prophet Muhammad ⓐ, with the title: *The Messenger who is the savior for both worlds.*

The word *rasūl* can be used to refer to any of Allah's apostles or messengers. See also: Muhammad ⓐ; *rasūl.*

rasūl(s) (A) Apostle or messenger; one who has wisdom, faith in God, and good qualities; one who behaves with respect and dignity toward his fellow men. A *rasūl* is one who has completely accepted only God and has rejected everything else; one who has accepted God's divine words, His qualities and actions, and puts them into practice. Those who from time immemorial have given the divine laws of God to the people; those who have such a connection with God are called a prophet *(nabī)* or a *rasūl. Yā Rasūl* is a name given to the Prophet Muhammad ⓐ. See also *rasūl.*

Rasūlullāh ⓐ (A) Prophet Muhammad ⓐ, the Messenger of Allah.

rishi(s) (T) An inspired sage or poet. Bawa Muhaiyaddeen ⓐ explains that *rishis, muktars,* and *siddhars* are all the same—they perform miracles and magics.

rizq (A) Nourishment; food; sustenance; livelihood; that which is given as true food and provision by *ar-Razzāq,* the Provider.

rūh (A) The soul; the light ray of God; the light of God's wisdom. Bawa Muhaiyaddeen ⓐ explains that *rūh* also means life *(hayāt).* Out of the six kinds of lives it is the light-life, the ray of the light of the resplendence of Allah *(Nūr)* which does not die. It does not disappear; it is the truth. The other five lives appear and disappear. That which exists forever without death is the soul. It is Allah's *rahmat* which has obtained the wealth of the imperishable treasure of all three worlds *(mubārakāt).*

rūhānī (A) Elemental spirit arising from desires; the spirit of the elements. There are six kinds of lives within man. One is human life which is the light-life. That is the soul (*rūh*). Associated with this are the lives of earth, fire, water, air, and ether. These constitute the *rūhānī*.

When all the four hundred trillion, ten thousand intentions and thoughts take form, they are called *rūhānīs*. All the things to which the mind roams in its thoughts are called *rūhānīs*. Even after a person dies, his desires bring him back. It is those desires, those *rūhānīs*, that bring him back to be born again.

sabūr (A) Inner patience; to go within patience, to accept it, to think and reflect within it. *Sabūr* is that patience deep within patience which comforts, soothes, and alleviates mental suffering.

Yā Sabūr – one of the ninety-nine names of Allah. God, who in a state of limitless patience is always forgiving the faults of His created beings and continuing to protect them.

salām(s) (A) Peace; the peace of God. Greetings! When one says *salām* to another, it means in God's name or in the presence of God, may both of us become one without any division; both of us are in a state of unity, a state of peace.

sayyid (A) Descendant of Prophet Muhammad ﷺ .

shakti(s) (T) Force or energy.

shakūr (A) Contentment; the state within the inner patience known as *sabūr;* that which is stored within the treasure chest of patience.

Yā Shakūr—One of the ninety-nine beautiful names of Allah. To have *shakūr* with the help of the One who is *Yā Shakūr* is true *shakūr*.

shānti (T) True peacefulness.

sharī'at (A) *sharī'at, tarīqat, haqīqat, ma'rifat, sūfiyyat* (A) The five steps of spiritual ascendance:

sharī'at—the discrimination between good and evil, right and wrong, and the conducting of one's life according to the good. Lit.: the way that leads to water; the law; right conduct; right procedure.

tarīqat—unswerving and complete acceptance of the good, and the carrying out of every action accordingly. The truth of intention, certitude, determination, faith, patience, and duty. Lit.: the path.

haqīqat—the realization of Truth which is the Divinity, and the beginning of communication with God.

ma'rifat—the knowledge of the secrets of God. *Ma'rifat* has no day or night; it is the realization of God mingled within all lives as the Light without shadow, as the Truth within truth, as the Unique One shining without separation in all the worlds.

sūfiyyat—the fifth and ultimate level of spiritual ascendance. It is the state of one who has transcended the four religions and has merged with God.

sharr (A) That which is wrong, bad, or evil, as opposed to *khair*, that which is good.

shirk (A) Idolatry. External *shirk* is creating a picture or idol as a form and worshiping it. Internal *shirk*, Bawa Muhaiyaddeen ⊛ explains, is when the mind creates images and ideas and glorifies them, performs *tasbīh* to them.

siddhis (T) Magic; miracle; supernatural abilities. The capacity to perform miracles obtained by devotion to and control of the elements.

sifat (A) (pl. *sifāt*) That which arose from the word *"Kun!"* (Be!); all that has come into being as form. Depending on the context, the word *sifāt* may mean the creations or manifestations of God or the attributes of God.

singhan (T) See: *tārahan*.

sirātul-mustaqīm (A) The straight path.

sirr (A) Secret; the secret of Allah.

Subhānallāhi Kalimah; Third Kalimah: (A) *Subhānallāhi walhamdu lillāhi wa lā ilāha ill-Allāhu wallāhu akbar wa lā hawla wa lā quwwata illā billāhi wa huwal-'alīyul 'azīm:* Glory be to God, and all praise is to God. And there is nothing other than You, O God; only You are Allah. And Allah is most great, and none has the majesty or the power to sustain except for God, and He is the majesty, the supreme in glory.

A prayer revealed and explained to Prophet Muhammad ⊛ to be said as part of the *qurbān,* for the purpose of removing the beastly qualities of animals about to be slaughtered for food and to kill the beastly qualities within man that cause him to want to hurt other lives.

sūfiyyat (A) The fifth level of spiritual ascendance. The state of one who has transcended the four religions and has merged with God.

In the station of *sūfiyyat,* one speaks without talking, sees without looking, hears without listening, relishes fragrances without smelling, and learns without studying. That knowing cannot be known, and that understanding cannot be acquired by mere study. These and many other such states come with acquiring the qualities of God and losing oneself within those qualities. Although one still exists within the body, he has built within himself the palace of divine luminous wisdom. One who has perfected this state is a sufi. See also: *sharī'at, tarīqat, haqīqat, ma'rifat, sūfiyyat.*

sūran (T) See: *tārahan*.

sūrat (A) A chapter of the Qur'an (spelled with the Arabic letter *sīn*). Lit.: A row or series.

sūrat (A) Form or shape, such as the form of man (spelled with the Arabic letter *sād*).

Sūratul-Fātihah (A) The opening chapter of the Qur'an and the inner form of man; the clarity of understanding the four elements of the body (earth, fire, water, and air), and the realization of the self and of Allah within. The *Sūratul-Fātihah* is recited at the beginning of every prayer. Within man is the *Sūratul-Fātihah,* and within the *Sūratul-Fātihah* is the inner form of man. If we split open that form, we can see within it Allah's words, His qualities, His actions, His three thousand divine attributes, and His ninety-nine powers, or *wilāyats.* That is the *sūratul-insān,* the inner form of man.

The *Sūratul-Fātihah* must be split open with wisdom to see all these within. It must be opened by the ocean of divine knowledge (*bahrul-'ilm*). Opening his heart (*qalb*), opening his form (*sūrat*) and looking within, having his own form looking at his own form—that is the *Sūratul-Fātihah.* What is recited on the outside is the *Al-hamdu Sūrat.* The two meanings differ in this manner: the outer one is a meaning on the level of *sharī'at* (the first level of spiritual ascendance); the inner meaning relates to the essence, or *dhāt. Fātihah* means literally to open out. It is opening the heart and looking within.

Sūratul-Ikhlās (A) *Sūrat* of faith, loyalty; declaration of God's unity.

tārahan, singhan, and *sūran* (T) The three sons of *maya,* or illusion. *Tārahan* is the trench or the pathway for the sexual act, the birth canal or vagina. *Singhan* is the arrogance present at the moment when the semen is ejaculated (karma). It is the quality of the lion. *Sūran* is the illusory images of the mind enjoyed at the moment of ejaculation. It is all the qualities and energies of the mind.

tarīqat (A) The second step of spiritual ascendance; unswerving and complete acceptance of the good and the carrying out of every action accordingly; the truth of intention, certitude, determination, faith, patience, and duty. Lit.: the path. See also: *sharī'at, tarīqat, haqīqat, ma'rifat, sūfiyyat.*

tasbīh (A) To purify the innermost heart (*qalb*) which is the abode of the One of purity; glorification of God; to glorify the name of Allah; offering prayers of praise; recitation; recognition; realization of divine attributes. See also: *Subhānallāhi Kalimah.*

tawakkul or *tawakkul'alallāh* (A) Absolute trust and surrender; handing over to God the entire responsibility for everything. *Al-Wakīl* is one of the ninety-nine beautiful names of Allah: the Trustee, the Guardian.

thānam (T) Surrender.

tiyānam (T) Meditation.

'Umar 'Ibnul-Khattāb ⊚ . The second caliph and a father-in-law to the Prophet ⊕ . At first he was violently opposed to Muhammad ⊕ , but later heard his sister reciting part of the Qur'an and was overcome. Going directly to Muhammad, he professed his belief in Allah and His Prophet ⊕ .

vēdāntas (T) Philosophies of Hinduism.

vēdas (T) Hindu scriptures.

wahy (A) Revelation; inspiration from God; the inspired word of God revealed to a prophet; the commandments or words of God transmitted by the Archangel Gabriel ⊚ . *Wahys,* or revelations, have come to Adam ⊚ , Moses ⊚ , and various other prophets, but most of all to Prophet Muhammad ⊕ . Muhammad ⊕ received 6,666 revelations. The histories of each of the earlier prophets were contained within the revelations given to Prophet Muhammad ⊕ .

waqt (A) Time of prayer. In the religion of Islam there are five specified *waqts,* or times of prayer, each day. But truly, there is only one *waqt;* that is the prayer that never ends, wherein one is in direct communication with God and one is merged in God.

wilāyat (A) God's power; that which has been revealed and manifested through God's actions; the miraculous names and actions of God; the powers of His attributes through which all creations came into existence. See also: *asmā'ul-husnā.*

Zabūr, Jabrāt, Injīl, and *Furqān* (A) The four religions or the four steps of spiritual ascendance. The inner form of man, or *sūratul-insān,* is made up of the four religions. The four religions constitute his body.

First is the religion in which man appeared, the religion in which forms are created. This is *Zabūr,* or Hinduism. In the body, Hinduism relates to the area below the waist.

Second is *Jabrāt,* Fire Worship. This relates to hunger, disease, and old age. This is the area of the stomach.

Third is *Injīl,* Christianity. This is the region of the heart which is filled with thoughts, emotions, spirits, vapors, many tens of millions of forms, the five elements, mind and desire, and four hundred trillion, ten thousand types of spiritual worship.

Fourth is *Furqān,* the religion sent down to Moses ☺ and Muhammad ☺. This corresponds to the head. It is made up of the seven causes (two eyes, two ears, two nostrils, and one mouth), and it gives explanations through these.

Lit.: *Zabūr*—the religion given to David ☺ , the Psalms of David; *Jabrāt (Jabrūt)*—a stage in sufi terminology denoting the sphere of knowledge or station where one discards personal power and becomes assimilated into the power of God; *Injīl* – the Gospels; *Furqān* – the criterion of right and wrong.

zamzam (A) A well found in Mecca near the Ka'bah by Hagar, the mother of Ishmael ☺ , and which is said to flow from the spring of abundance (*kauthār*) in paradise.

Questions by Topic

BAWA MUHAIYADDEEN

Can your students reach a state of oneness with you? What will
happen to that relationship when you die?   12

What is the Bawa Muhaiyaddeen Fellowship?   33

Were you ever in our state?   129

When Bawa Muhaiyaddeen talks, how can we know what
level to tune in on?   135

What message do you have for some brothers who are in prison?   223

Where were you born?   239

How long have you been in the world?   239

How many children can you embrace?   241

What message would you like to address to the whole world?   244

Were you ever born?   276

CONTEMPORARY WORLD

What are the false gods of the contemporary world?   3

What is our duty to the world?   5

Why is man here?   169

What should we strive for in life?   246

DEATH, FATE, AND DESTINY

At the time of death, what happens to the soul and to the body?   107

How much of our lives are predestined?   211

How do fate and destiny relate to doing good works?   255

How does surrender to God fit in with fate and destiny?   257

*How should I understand karma, accidents, and destiny in
relation to God's will?*   *286*

DESTRUCTION

When will destruction come?   *10*

Why does there have to be a day of destruction?   *137*

DUTY/SERVICE

What is our duty to the world?   *5*

How do I obtain the strength to serve God?   *23*

Where does duty for my family lie?   *139*

What does 'Duty is greater than God' mean?   *273*

Should we perform duty which does not come from love?   *282*

EMPLOYMENT/OCCUPATIONS

*Two school teachers ask about controlling children with
strength versus love.*   *57*

I'm out of work and need direction in my life.   *75*

*In my work, the recommendations I make sometimes send
people to jail. Is that passing judgment?*   *99*

*My philosophy is opposite to that of someone I work with, how
should I handle the situation?*   *100*

When students are difficult, what should a teacher do?   *101*

I've studied singing. Should I continue?   *184*

What is the correct way to act when seeking employment?   *203*

If I'm paid to fulfill someone's evil purposes, am I culpable?   *286*

ENERGIES/FORCES

How do energies attack man?   *276*

What does "Bend the sky into a bow" mean?   *301*

What is the station of the elemental spirits? *303*

How do the elemental spirits change? *306*

*Did God create the thymus gland as the center of energy
for the body?* *313*

EVIL

Can political education change the evils of the world? *8*

Does satan exist? *36*

Can satan possess us? *36*

Can satan be exorcised? *37*

Please tell us something about Judas. *91*

A friend was mugged twice. What can you advise her? *125*

How can we escape being food for hell? *147*

How can we cut attachment to things that are wrong? *211*

If I'm paid to fulfill someone's evil purposes, am I culpable? *286*

FAITH

Why does our faith waver? *81*

*The discrepancy between my intentions and actions affects
my faith. What can I do?* *150*

What wisdom will make our faith grow firm? *205*

How can I make my faith grow? *273*

FAMILY RELATIONSHIPS (see also MARRIAGE and PARENTING)

Where does duty for my family lie? *139*

I was hurtful to my parents and now I want forgiveness. *142*

My grandmother is ill. What shall I tell her? *191*

How can I cut the excessive attachment to my mother? *206*

My mother only believes in this world. What shall I tell her? *208*

*I sent my sister books and pictures and she intends to come here.
What more should be said to her?* *220*

GOD

How do we dedicate ourselves to God?   *20*

Is my desire for God just another veil?   *23*

Who is God?   *31*

Can we learn about God's qualities by observing them in one of God's representatives?   *56*

How will the sound of God be heard within us?   *113*

How can I prevent my arrogance from blocking my trust in God?   *159*

How can I overcome anxiety and sorrow to see God's light?   *161*

How can we establish a direct connection to God?   *167*

What man can be righteous before God?   *168*

Why do some not love God?   *170*

Is Jesus (A.S.) *God?*   *170*

What is the Trinity?   *194*

Is it true that no two snowflakes are alike?   *212*

How can people understand that all are God's children?   *246*

What is man-God, God-man?   *263*

How do we make the connection to God?   *267*

What does 'Duty is greater than God' mean?   *273*

How should I understand karma, accidents, and destiny in relation to God's will?   *286*

HEALTH

Does disease come from God?   *26*

How to treat the illnesses of man.   *253*

Did God create the thymus gland as the center of energy for the body?   *313*

JUDGMENT

In my work, the recommendations I make sometimes send people to jail. Is that passing judgment?   *99*

MARRIAGE

Should there be equality between men and women?   9

What is marriage according to the will of God?   35

Is it good to be married?   96

A friend is paying us rent. How much involvement should he have in household decisions?   137

MEDITATION

What are the dangers associated with mantra meditation?   7

An individual's questions on meditation.   41

Is repetitive prayer the way to remember God?   70

What are the lights I see during meditation?   227

NEGATIVE EMOTIONS

What can I do about my self-deprecation?   22

How do I remove doubt from my life?   80

How can I stop being afraid of loneliness?   84

Should we express our anger?   100

How can I overcome fear?   130

Once when I was worried, something just popped inside me and my mind was eased. What was that?   151

How can I get rid of jealousy?   233

What should we do when we see faults in others?   281

PARENTING

How can we reach a balance between giving a child too much exposure to the world and overprotecting them?   49

Are parents responsible for the karma and spiritual attainment of their children?   86

Why should anyone choose to have a child?   140

PERSONAL LIFE

*How does one endure the burdens of life and continue to meet
all of his responsibilities?*   *18*

*We are members of Alcoholics Anonymous and are attempting
to turn our lives and wills over to the will of God.*   *64*

*If we haven't seen the roots of our problems, should we keep on
cutting the branches?*   *99*

What can I do in order to know myself?   *149*

Is it wrong to expect happiness?   *152*

*Things I thought I had finished with keep returning to my mind.
How can I prevent that?*   *152*

*Sometimes one needs to rush, sometimes to go slowly. How can
we be consistent?*   *154*

How can we be trusting in the company of many people?   *154*

Why is man here?   *169*

How can I balance my spiritual life with my physical needs?   *175*

Could I have a name to guide my qualities?   *175*

What message do you have for some brothers who are in prison?   *223*

How can I readjust my life?   *227*

Why is the expression on the face so important?   *234*

What should we strive for in life?   *246*

What should we do when we see faults in others?   *281*

How can we better our lives?   *299*

PROPHETS

*Please explain about the battles that surrounded Prophet
Muhammad* (Sal.).   *76*

Why did God send Jesus (A.S.) *to the world?*   *95*

*Why did wise men even attempt to teach those who would only
cause trouble?*   *96*

Can you tell me who Jesus (A.S.) *is? Why did Jesus* (A.S.) *come?
Is Jesus* (A.S.) *with us now?*   *165*

Is Jesus (A.S.) *God?*   *170*

Should we expect any more prophets?   *182*

Who is the Messiah and has he come yet?   *186*

What is the Trinity?   *194*

Who is Jesus (A.S.)?   *198*

What is meant by rasūl?   *268*

Why is Jesus (A.S.) *the most celebrated prophet?*   *307*

What is the difference between a qutb *and a prophet?*   *311*

RELIGION

Please speak about religious indifference.   *176*

Is it right or wrong to give charity to religions?   *221*

SPIRITUAL PATH (see also BAWA MUHAIYADDEEN)

Is there a point at which God or the spiritual teacher gives up
on someone who is on the path?   *50*

What is meant by the melting heart?   *55*

How can we know if we have spiritually progressed?   *82*

I met a karate teacher earlier and felt a connection toward him.
Is that the right path for me?   *97*

What is the meaning of "a man of wisdom will know all three
time periods"?   *113*

How can a disciple overcome the fear of relinquishing his own
learning?   *119*

How can we tell whether it is wisdom or the illusory mind that
is leading us?   *128*

How can I balance my spiritual life with my physical needs?   *175*

How can we transform our thoughts into thoughts of God?   *186*

Who is the true guru?   *192*

Can determination be nurtured?   *204*

What wisdom will make our faith grow firm?   *205*

How does the disciple see his teacher within?   *209*

How can we cut attachment to things that are wrong?   *211*

Is it our responsibility to bring others on the path?   *217*

How can I live a life surrendered to the will of God?   *219*

How can I readjust my life?   *227*

I have realized much inner growth, but I feel I should do more.   *228*

What is the first step to freedom?   *245*

What should we strive for in life?   *246*

How do we make the connection to God?   *263*

How can I make my faith grow?   *273*

What should we do when we see faults in others?   *281*

What does it mean to be with the guru for twelve years?   *287*

Subject Index

Passim denotes that the references are scattered throughout the pages indicated (e.g. 102–107 *passim*). Numbers in bold denote major references (e.g. **83**).

'Abd; see Slave
Abortion, 91
Abraham, 181, 198, 244
Accident(s), 82, 102, **125–127**, 150, 186, 209, **286–287**
Actions, **21, 83, 95**, 117, **150–151**, 166, 178
  of God; *see* God, actions of
Adam, 179, **244**, 256, 309
  children of, 9, 23, 92, 181
  kalimah of, 198
Addiction; *see* Intoxicants
Adoption, 139
Advice, to man from prison, 223–224
  see also Muhaiyaddeen, M. R. Bawa gives advice
Affirmation of faith; *see* Kalimah
Aging, 69–70, 239, 314–315
Ahmad, light of, 293
Aid, to countries, 222–223
Air, 3, 26–27, 69–70, 109, 113, 116, 176–178, 303–306 *passim*
  analogy of—in tire, 21–22
  passes through *halq,* 313
  soul of, 200
Ākhirah; see Hereafter
Alcoholics, 64–69
Al-hamdu lillāh; see God, praise of
'Alī, 257–260, 265–266
Alif, lām, mīm, 221, 262, 264, 306
  see also Triple flame and Triple ray
Allah; *see* God
Al-qadā' wal-qadar, 257, 261–262
Ambition, 52
America, 10, 222–223
Amusement parks, 49–50
Analyze, one's self, 23, 151–152, 296

Angel(s), 171, 200, 233
  good thoughts become, 262
  of Death, 83, 185, 187–188
  of the elements, 305
  two witnessing, 107–111
  why—had to come, 183
Anger, 57–58, 203, 283
  and applying for jobs, 203–204
  and mental health, 100–101
  and progressing on the path, 82–84
  arising from unfulfilled desires, 27
  as disease, 27
  as manifestation of fire, 27
  expressing, 100
  is fire of hell, 262
  is guru of sin, 221
Animal(s), 19, 31, 34–35, 179, 184, 247
  and Noah, 198
  gods, 20, 76, 171
  have miracles, **274–276**
  have *shaktis,* 274
  in man, 150, 165
  kingdom of, 179–184
  marriage, 35
  qualities; *see* Qualities, animal
  within us, **148–149**
Ant(s), 193, 243
Anxiety, 161
"Arise!", 263, 303
Arising, what to do upon, 20
Arrogance, 23, 26, 57, 77, 95–96, 159–161, 178–179, 283–284
  alcohol of, 64
  and applying for jobs, 203–204
  between elements, 277
  connected to satan, **37**, 233–234
  fecal, 181

of the mind, 169
vanishes with faith, 160
'Arsh; see Throne of God
Asmā'ul Husnā: The 99 Beautiful
    Names of Allah by M. R. Bawa
    Muhaiyaddeen, 247
Atom within an atom, 274, 276 passim
Atomic energy, 11
Attachment(s), 31, 69–70, 83–84, 220,
    261
    breaking one's, 227
    cutting one's, 210–211
    everything has, **206**
    make duty difficult, 273
    one—to be fostered, 63
    to God, 63, 206–209
    to mother, 141, 206–209
    to parents, 139–140
    to wife and children, 119–125,
        passim
    see also Blood ties
Attorney, question of, 285–286
Attributes of God; see God, attributes of
Automobile; see Car
Avathānam, 154
    see also Concentration
Awareness, 86, 117, 151–152, 177, 205,
    209–210, 312
    after death, 107–111
    see also Wisdom, seven levels of
Awwal; see Beginning, the

Baby(ies), 19, 37, 96, 261
Bag(s), 307
Baggage, 203
Baghdad, 239
Balance, 18, 82, 154, 183
    between mind and, 175
    between spiritual and physical
        needs, 175
    between too much world and
        overprotecting child, 49–50
    God's, 177
Bank account, 129–130, 153
Banū Isrā'īl, 308
Bar, man in, 98
Battlefield, 219
Battleground, earth is a, 25

Bawa Muhaiyaddeen; see
    Muhaiyaddeen, Bawa
Bawa Muhaiyaddeen Fellowship, 33–35
Beating, 126–127
Beauty, 107, 214, 286, 292, 295, 304, 315
Bee(s), 210, 269, 275
Begging, 75
Beginning, the, 115–116
Benevolence of God, 277
Betrayal, 94
Bigotry, 8, 23–24, 65, 95–96, 165, 169
Bird(s), 198, 206, 269
Birth, 141, 148, 185, 199, 206, 221–222
    of Bawa Muhaiyaddeen, 239, 276
Birth control, 140–142
Blood, 26, 75, 123, 314–315
    and milk, 80, 86
    connected to satan, 37
    drinking, 91–92
    one, 245
Blood ties, 206, 234, 273, 302
    at death, 108
    story of rich man who had no
        peace, 119–125
Blueprint, 136–137
Boasting, 204
Body, 17–18, 26–27, 75–76, 294–296
        passim
    as house and school, 266–267
    attachment to, 83
    balance between mind and body, 175
    connected to satan, 37
    death of, 107–110, 291
    duty to, 18–20
    energies, 313–315
    is a cross, 94
    like ice, 267
    made of elements, 109–110, 276–277
    makes it difficult to do duty, 273
Book(s) 287
    knowledge, 71, 180, 313
    learning, 119–125, 136–137
Bow, bend sky into a, 301
Branches, cutting, 99
Breath, 20, 71, 241
Breathe, how to, 288
Bridge, 227, 265–266
Buddhism, 308

Building, 311
Bulb, current through, 304
Burdens, 18, 84, 159, **161**, 196
   story of rich man who had no
     peace, 119–125
Business, 196, 219, 228
   guru, 192–194
Butter, churning, 55–56

Caliph of God, 199
Cancer, 27
Castes, 24–25, 245
Cat, of the mind, 151–152
Caves, 240–241
Cells, 19, 26
Cemetery, 184–186, 305, 310
Certitude, 150–151,182–183, 205–206,
    287
   see also Faith, certitude, and
    determination
Change, 8, 65, 219–220, 228–230,
    239–240, 273–276 *passim,*
    300–302, *passim*
   one's qualities, **178–179**
   rūhānīs, **306–307**
Charity, 221–223
Children, 57–58, 86–87, 139–142,
    245–246
   of Bawa Muhaiyaddeen, 194, 241–242
   of God; see God, children of
   raising, 49–50, 57–59, 86–87
   teaching, 101–103
Christ; *see* Jesus
Christianity, 182, 196
Church, 21, 33, 68
City Hall, 182–183, 196–198 *passim,*
    221–222
Comfort, 17, 21, 117, 223
Commandments; *see* God,
   commandments of
Compassion, 31–33 *passim,* 64–65,
    178–179, 196, 295
   of God; *see* God, compassion of
Concentration, 154, 160, 177, 183
Conception, 26, 86
Conduct, 185, 204
Confusion, 149
Connection, 69–70, 306

to God, 24, 64–65, 113–115, 264–268
to the sheikh, 12, 50–52, 56–57,
   116–125, 128–129
Conscience, 19, 91–94, 274
Consciousness, 12, 42
   see also; Wisdom, seven levels of
Consistency, 154–155
Contentment, 32–35, 81, 94, 160, 178,
    199, 233, 254, 287
Contraceptives; *see* Birth control
Control, 277, 302–303
Corpse; *see* Body, death of
Correcting oneself, 33–35, 64–65,
    93–95, 127, 142–143, 168, 182,
    217, 227, 281
Countenance, 32, 34–35, 107–108, 182,
    234–235, 293
Countries, underdeveloped, 223
Court, worker in juvenile, 99
Cows, 25–26, 142
Craziness, kinds of, 66–69, 186
Creation, 3, 169–170, 195, 255–256,
    262–264, 309
   as water, 27
   God as point existing within, 31, 113
   nature of, 300
   of false gods, 267–268
   of souls, 303–306
   secret of, 95, 192–193
   seeing God's—as one, 212–214
Credit cards, 310
Cross, 94–95
Crucifixion, 94–95
Crying, 55
Current, electric, 12, 71, 304

Dancing, 184–186
Danger, 21, 81–82, 148, 227
Darkness, 17, 27, 240–241
Daulat; see Wealth of God
David, 179, 309
   kalimah of, 199
Day of Judgment; *see* Judgment Day
Death, 147, 185–186, 221–222, 267, 291,
    293–296 *passim,* 306
   and Ishmael, 199
   Angel of; *see* Angel of Death
   fear of, 131

judgment after, 305
of body of Bawa Muhaiyaddeen, 12
of time, 107–110
transcending, 200, 239–240
within God, 114–116
within point of truth, 70–71
within the sheikh, **116–119**
Deceit, 235, 246, 283
Deceptions, 27, 147, 187–188
Decision-making, 80
Dedicating our life, 20, 32, 65
Deed, receive on Judgment Day, 83, 109
Demons, 3–4, 37, 94, 180–181
Depression, 149, 151
Desire, 5, 9, 27, 34, 63, 275
    and book learning, 137
    and progressing on the path, 82–84
    as nail of cross in forehead, 94
    base, 188, 264
    creates 400 trillion, ten thousand evil
        forms, 247
    for earth, woman, and gold, 25–26,
        41–42, 267
    for truth, 63
    giving up, 120
    melts away, 213
    nature of, 5–6
    of this body, 178
    rocky mountain of, 150
    sounds of, 288
    stopping the hunger of, 210
Destiny, 109, 255–263, 286–287
Destruction, 10–12, 25, 137
Detachment, 246
Determination, 159–160, 182–183,
    204–206
Devil, 36–37, 76–77
Devotee, true, 293
Devotion, 20, 92, 228
Dhikr; see God, remembrance of
Differences, 23–26, 32, 34, 65, 176, 245
    are satanic, 36
    between man and woman, 9
    between you and I, 65, 179
    connected to evil qualities, 246
    create battlefields of hell, 219
    cutting away, 115
    giving up, 109

gnāni does not see any, 96
    racial, 42, 50, 57
    religious, 8–9, 42, 50, 65, 93, 109
Dīn; see Light of perfect purity
Direction in life, **75–76**, 299
Directions, **299**
    from prophets, 310–311
Dirt, we must wash away our own, **283**
Disaster, 10–12
Disciple, **119–125**, **209–210**
Discrimination, 65, 96, 261
    between sheikh's guidance and the
        world, **128–129**
Disease(s) 6, 21, **26–27**, 63, **191–192**
    caused by thoughts, 253
    curing, **253–255**
    fatal, **26–27**
    in family, 140
    in marriage, 36
    must die, 70
    realizing—of others as our own, 42,
        65, 79, 168, 245–247 passim
    surrendering—to God, 191
    that kill us, 123, 148, 218
Divine analytic wisdom, 267, 312
    see also Wisdom, seven levels of
Divine knowledge, 80, 92, 256, 266,
    268, 277
    see also Wisdom
Divine luminous wisdom, 4, 117, 265,
    277, 312
    see also Wisdom, seven levels of
Doctors, 191, **253–255**
Doctrine, 67
Dog(s), 43–44, 59
Dominican Republic, advice to sister in,
    220–221
Donkey(s), 7
Doubt(s), **80–81**, 193–194, 217, **233–234**
    in God; see God, doubt in
Dreams, 110, 198, 220
Driving a car; see Car
Drugs, 64, 236
Drunkard, story of, **66–69**
Dunyā; see World
Dust, if we can be a speck of, 245
Duty, **5–7**, 17–21 passim, 42, 64–65, 75,
    117, 192–193, 208, 220, 256, 301

is greater than God, 221, **273, 282**
of Bawa Muhaiyaddeen, **239–240**
of God; *see* God, duties of
of man, **32–33,** 36, 124–125, 127–128,
  256
of man to create his destiny, **255–263**
of prophets, **310–311**
of *Qutb,* **311–313**
to bring others to path, **217–219**
to family, 139–140
to follow a God-realized being, 311
to God, 23, 65, 167–168
true, 206–207, **282–285**
without love, 282–285

Eagles, 44, 274
Ears, 18, 288
Earth, 3, 37, 69–70, 83, 91–95 *passim,*
  147, 176, 188, 206, 276–278, 303,
  305
as a god, 6, 20, 308
as nail of cross, 94
desire for, 41–42 *passim,* 63
destruction through, 11
level of *sharī'at,* 260–262 *passim*
lives; *see* Lives, six kinds of
rūhānīs belonging to, 109–110
soul of, 200
Effulgence, triple, 266
Ego in meditation, 7–8
Eighteen thousand universes, 19, 291
Electric current; *see* Current, electric
Elemental energies, 6, 41, 113, 123, 150,
  276–277, 302–306 *passim*
for body, 313–315
Elemental spirit; *see* Spirit body
Elements, five, 3, 26–27, 41, 69–70,
  176–177, 262, 264, 274, 277 *passim,*
  292, 313
as a god, 20, 308
as nails of the cross, 94
bank made of, 129
comprise body, **294–295**
destruction through, 11
life of the, 303–305
see also Elemental energies
Elephant(s), **43–44,** 69, 179, 213, 275,
  284

Employment, **203–204**
Enemies, inner, 126
Energies; *see* Elemental energies
Engines, compared to females, 10
Envy, 65, 138, 153, 178, 213, 234, 235
and progressing on the path, 82
creates battlefields of hell, 219
Equality, 9–10, 17, 24, **33–36,** 177–181,
  198, 200, 212–214
between men and women, **9–10**
prophets taught, 218
Estimate, a level of wisdom, 312
see also Wisdom, seven levels of
Eternal life, 239–240
Eternity, **239–240**
Ether, 3, 26, 69–70, 113, 178, 303
as a god, 20
belonging to earth, 109
body composed of, 41
lives, 212–213
nail in cross, **94**
soul of, 200
Europe, 223
Evil(s), 3–4, 18, 255–256, 263, 268
forces in heart, 247
good and, 165–166
mind of Judas, **91–94**
qualities, 8, **36–37,** 65, **76–80,** 94,
  193, 267
six, 138, 213
thoughts, 27, 247
thoughts bringing, **81**
Excess, 27
Exercise, 75–76
Exorcism, 37
Expectations, 152, 285
Explanations of God, 210, **234–235,**
  239–240
Eye(s), 18, 148, 188, 206, 288
of wisdom; *see* Wisdom, eye of

Face; *see* Countenance
Fairies, 19, 113, 200, 290
Faith, 24, 41, 70, **76–81, 125–127,**
  167–170, 203–206, 219, 261
affirmation of; *see Kalimah*
God is point within, 32
have no—in what others will do, 285

in God; *see* God, faith in
in sheikh, **116–119**
in teacher, **101–103**
in world, 204, 239–241
increasing, 205, **273–276**
Ishmael and firm, 199
lack of, **80–82, 150–151,** 258
legs of perfect, 183
to cure illness, **253–255**
unwavering, 230
Faith, certitude, and determination, 55,
    76–80, 109, 118, 130, 143, **150–
    151,** 217–218, 230, 243, 258–260,
    266, 276, 300–301
    in world, 240
    lack of, **80–82**
    sword and axe of *īmān,* 183
False gods; *see* Gods, false
Falsehood, 3, 65, 153, 165, 178, 192,
    213, 234
Fame, 52, 116, 310
Family, duty, **139–140**
    see also Parenting; Children
Fanaticism, 23, 65, 95, 138, 153, 178,
    179, 234
Farmer, 254
Fate; *see* Destiny
Fatigue, 152
Fātihah; see Sūratul-Fātihah
Fatimah, **264–266**
Faults, 33–35, 95, **166–168,** 260–261,
    283, 285
    correcting our, 227, **281–282**
    entered man through satan's spit, 256
    gnāni has no, 96
    God will find, **187–188**
    seeing—in others, 182, 281
    within man, 256, 260–261
Favors, do not expect from others, 285
Fear, 21, 58, 99, 230
    and losing faith, 11
    and mental health, **100–101**
    belongs to ghosts and satan, 217
    of death, **130–131**
    of loneliness, **84–86**
    of wrongdoing, 11, 177
    overcoming—of surrender, **119–125**
Fecal arrogance, 181

Feeling, 151, 177, **209–210,** 265, 312
    see also Wisdom, seven levels of
Fellowship; *see* Bawa Muhaiyaddeen
    Fellowship
Females, 10, 154
    see also Woman
Fetus, 26, 91–92
Fighting, 8, 25, 58, 160, 176–179,
    182–184, 245
    on the path to God, **76–80,** 82
Fikr, 115
Fire, 3, 26–27, 69–70, 113, 116, 176,
    178, 264, 294, 303–306 *passim*
    as a god, 6, 20, 308
    as nail of cross, 94
    bee in, 210
    belonging to earth, 109–110
    body composed of, 41
    desire for, 63
    destruction through, 11
    has attachments, **206**
    level of *tarīqat,* 260–262 *passim*
    lives, 212–213 *passim*
    manifesting as anger, 27
    punishment by—after death, 109
    soul of, 200
    wood in, 168–169
Fish, 207, 241, 275
    as a god, 171
    bubbles, 209
    devouring another, 184
    fishing, 204
    fishing line, 138
    have attachment to water, 206
    miracle of, 275
Flame, triple, 118
    see also Ray, triple
Flashlight, 161
Flesh, eating, 91–92, 308
Flower(s) 113, 169–170, 192, 315
    becoming, 219
    fragrance intermingled within, 115,
        234, 266, 287
    garden of innermost heart, 45,
        234–235, 241, 248
    of faith and certitude, 205
    see also Heart, innermost
Flying, 302

Food, 27, 113–114, 120, 127, 147, 177
Fools, 11
Force, use of, 57, 241
Forces, 19, 150, 195, 247
Forehead, 94, 292
Forest; *see* Trees
Forgiveness, 142–143, 188
Form(s), 6, 256, 260, 264
  distracting from true worship,
    227–228
  external, 31, 33, 41, 213, 256, 268
  God has no, 113–114, **273–274**
  light, 110, 260, 262
  man created out of water as a, 213
  of man, 267
  of mind, 19
  our—in dreams, 110
  physical—at death, **109–110**
  subtle, 19, 260
  within heart, 247
Fragrance, 23, 48
  and the flower, 115, 177
  of God, 18, 115, 205 286–288 *passim*
  of wisdom, 286
Freedom, 34–35, 69–70, **138–139**, 149,
  245
  absolute, 183
  from qualities of satan, 234
  from suffering, 292–293
  of your life, 124
Friendship, 63
  renting to worldly friends, 137–139
Fruit(s) 55, 169–170, 192, 207, 275–276
  bearing, 219, 241
  parrot waiting for, **187–188**
  taste within, 177

Gabriel, Angel, Qur'an revealed to, 268
Gambling, 91
Games, 102
  sexual, 287
Garden; *see* Flowers
Gases, 19
Gem(s), 50
  light within the, 177
Generations, 306
Generosity, 32
Ghee, 80

Ghost(s), 3–4 *passim,* 19, 34, 41, 94,
  150, 180, 247, 306
  fear belongs to, 217
  qualities of, 181
Giving, 248
Gland; *see* Thymus gland
Gnānam; see Wisdom
Gnāni; see Wise man
Gnostic eye; *see* Wisdom, eye of
Goats, 142, 206
God, actions of, 7, 22–25, 27, 33,
  115–116, 166, 170, 176, 180,
  182, 184, 193–194, 198
  art work of, 220
  as creator, 244, 255, 262, 264
  as father, 195, 242, 309
  as man's secret, 24, 263–264
  as resplendent light, 32, 199
  attributes of, 21, 177, 233, 242, 247
  belief in, 165, 182, 199, 218
  benevolence of, 277
  children of, 79, 309
  commandments of, 91, **165–168,** 196,
    218, 244–245, 268, 308–312 *passim*
  compassion of, 94, 179, 182, 191,
    193–194, 242, 247
  connection to, 24, **115–119,** 244,
    264, 267
  doubt in, **80–81, 230**
  duties of, 27, 31–33, 83, 114, 143, 176,
    178, 193–194, 196–198 *passim*
  dying within, 114–115
  faith in, **31, 49–50, 64, 159–161,** 179,
    182, **191,** 193, 239, 241, 245, **273,**
    283, **300–301**
  family of, **244–246**
  form of, 25, 33, 242, **273–274,** 293
  giving responsibility to, **18–22,** 99,
    243, 288, **301**
  grace of, 49, 56, 119, **212–213,** 223,
    228–230 *passim,* 246, 262, 267, 294
  hands of, **241–242**
  house of, **138**
  how—works, 284
  instruments of, 243
  is always with us, 191
  is medicine for our souls, 191
  is witness, **166**

justice of, 170, 177, 191, 196, 217, 242
kingdom of, **8, 24–25,** 34–35, **42,**
   160, 178–181 *passim,* 196, 222,
   233, 242, 248, 285
knowledge of, 117, **180**
laws of, 196, 199–200 *passim,* 256
light form of, 25
light of, 56, 178, **180, 228**
love of, 25, 94, 223–224, **242**
map to, 217, 222, 310
meditation on, 182–183
meeting, 192
merging with, **113–116, 119–125,**
   260–263, 266, 292, 304
message of, 176
messenger of, 93–94, 115, 195, 244,
   255, 308
miracles of, 192, 234–235, 276
ninety-nine beautiful names of, 247
obsession for, 69
one, 170–171, 179–181, 196, 198–199,
   218, 290
path of, 79, 92, 183–184
peace of, 228–230
plenitude of, 303–305 *passim*
power of, 31–32, 113–119 *passim,*
   171, 176–178, 300
praise of, 81, 116, 301
presence of, 169, 311
properties of, 18–19, 25
qualities of, 33–35, 37, 56, 94–95,
   176–177, 242–243, 246–248, 262
realize, 185, 199
remembrance of, 20, 70, 115, 227,
   259
representative of, 35, 115, 165
resonance of, 56, 180
secret of, 263, 266, 311
seeing, 178–180, 200, 214
separation from, 6, 233
serving, 23, 65
slaves of, 17, 115–117, 243
son of, 195, 243, 309
soul of, 95, 199
sound of, 113–118 *passim,* 180
story of, 24–25, 169–170, 192–193
surrender to, 65, 69, 81, 83–84
throne of, 234, 290, 293

treasure of, 24–25, 160–161
trust in, 50, 92, 191–193 *passim,*
   203, 218
truth of, 26, 191, 217
wealth of, 242, 245, 267
who is, 31–33, 222
will of, 65, 219–220, 256, 286–287
wisdom of, 265, 277
words of, 17, 115, 162, 180, 199, 256
world of, 32
worship of, 9, 75, 179, 303, 310
yearning for, 49–50, 55–56
Gods, false, 3–6, 20, 98, 171, 218
   in the *Ka'bah,* 76–77
   we create, 263, 267
   worship of, 307–308
Gold, 5–6, 64, 83, 120
   desire for, 41–42, 63, 70, 95, 153
Good and evil, 11, 18, 165–166,
   255–256, 263, 268
Good conduct, 49–50
Grace, 11, 292–293
   of God; *see* God, grace of
Grandson of satan; *see* Satan,
   grandson of
Gratitude, 81, 301
Grave, 109, 305
Guru, 97–98, 147
   to be with—for twelve years, 287–296
   true, 192–194

Hadīth; see Stories, traditional
Halq, 313
Hand(s), 241
   holding—of *kāmil sheikh,* 50
Happiness, 152, 191, 228–230, 287, 289
   and Ishmael, 199
   faith reveals our, 205
   regarding—of others as our own,
      42, 93, 247
Haqīqat, 260–261
Harming other lives, 21, 32, 36, 93, 149,
   187–188
Hashim tribe, 308
Hastiness, 57, 70, 203
Hatred, 22, 115, 178, 234
Hayāt, 256
Head, 288–289

Healing, 253–255
Health, 191–192
   mental, 100–101
   realizing—of others as our own,
      178, 247
Heart, 150, 155, 293–294
   flower garden of, 234–235, 241,
      247–248
   forms within, 247
   God understands and answers each,
      92
   growing weak; *see* Exercise
   innermost, 18, 26–27, 45, 49–50, 55,
      115, 148, 223
      destruction of, 281
      fragrance of, 286
      mystery of God within, 314
      surrender of, 287–288
   melting, 55
   open your, 32, 195
   surrender—to God, 65, 113–116
   surrender—to man of wisdom, 220
   surrender—to sheikh, 116–119
   tiny point within, 314
   truth within, 314
   weapons in, 94
Heaven(s), 8, 17, 130, 165, 196, 248,
      262, 264
   and hell, 3, 165
   first four, 233–234
   world of, 32
Hell(s), 4, 17, 141–142, 147, 264
   anger is guru leading to, 203
   battlefields of, 219
   deceiving karma, 188
   gods of, 20, 171
   how to get to, 315
   kingdom of hell, 180, 183, 196
   mind is, 148
   satanic qualities lead to, 233
   seven, 26
   world of, 32, 86, 246
Help, giving and receiving, 222–223,
      284–285
Hereafter, 115–116, 265
High school, 101–103
Hinduism, 25, 307
Hippies, 68

History, 177
   inner meaning of, 80
   of God, 211
   of the world, 24–25
   one's entire—reviewed at death, 108
   our, 141, 149, 152–154, 211
Homelessness; *see* Help one's own
      country
Homosexuality, 11
Honey, 27
Honeybee; *see* Bee
House(s), 17, 262
   body as, 27, 197
   inner, 149–150
   obsession for, 68
   of God; *see* God, house of
   of soul, 314
Human beings, true; *see* Man, true
Human body; *see* Body
Human life; *see* Life
Humble, 203
Hunger, 7, 63, 69, 147
   deceiving *nafs,* 188
   for sheikh, 210
   must die, 70
   regarding—of others as our own,
      32, 42, 65, 79, 93, 165, 168, 178,
      206, 247
   stealing and murdering to satisfy, 223
Hurt feelings, 282–285
Hypnotic fascination, 64
Hypocrites, 91

"I," 169
'Ibādat; see Prayer, true
Ice, 215–216, 269
Idols; *see* Gods, false
Idris, 165, 258, 309
Ignorance, 3, 7, 36, 78, 188, 283–285,
      287
Ikhlās; see Sūratul-Ikhlās
Ikrimah, 77–79
Illness; *see* Disease
Illusion(s), 19, 23, 26, 123, 275,
      294–296, 302
   alcohol of, 64
   as a god, 6, 20
   as sky on the outside, 215

discerning, 230
lives of, 303
quality of satan, 236
three sons of, 178
vanish with faith, 160
see also Maya
'Ilm; *see* Divine knowledge
Īmān; see Faith, certitude, and
    determination
Īmān-Islām, 160, 269
Immodesty, 11
Impatience, 193, 221
Incest, 11
India, 241
Innermost heart; *see* Heart, innermost
In shā' Allāh; see God, will of
Insān; see Man, true
Insān-Allāh; see Man-God, God-man
Insān kāmil; see Teacher, God-realized
Insects, 19, 188, 281
Instructions from God, 310
Instrument(s) of God, 243
Intellect, 86, 151, 154, 312
see also Wisdom, seven levels of
Intentions, 4, 21, 26–27, 92, 120,
    166–167,177, 247, 281, 295
create destiny, 255
discrepancy between—and action,
    150–151
for God, 219, 267
same as sheikh's, 117–118
Intoxicants, 64–69, 234
Isaac, 176
Ishmael, 179, 244, 311
kalimah of, 201
Islam, 182, 269, 307

Jail, 99, 195–198
Jealousy, 57, 233–235, 246
Jesus, 92–95, 170–171, 178–182, 244,
    307–310
as savior, 194–198
reason why—sent to world, 95,
    165–168
return of, 198–200
Jinns, 37, 200, 228, 304
Job (Prophet), 165, 309
Jobs, 68, 75, 184, 203–204

Jonah, 165, 309
Joseph, 309
Judas, 91–94
Judgment, 99, 168, 208, 309, 314
at death, 107–111, 305
Day of, 83, 109–110, 165–166, 181,
    188, 208
level of consciousness, 177–178, 265,
    312
see also Wisdom, seven levels of
Justice, 92, 108
of God; *see* God, justice of

Ka'bah, 76–79
Kalimah, 79, 198–199, 259
first, 288, 291, 295, 310
third, 227–228
Kāmil sheikh; see Teacher
Karate, 97–98
Karma, 22–23, 26, 31, 33, 93, 150, 178,
    188, 210, 213, 285–288 *passim,* 306
connected to satan, 37, 234
of our children, 86–87
rocky mountain of, 150
Khadijah, 265
Khalīfah of the *Rasūlullāh,* 257
Khattāb, 'Umar Ibnul-, 260, 269
Kill; *see* Murder
Kingdom(s), four, 180–184
of God; *see* God, kingdom of
of hell; *see* Hell, kingdom of
Kings, 11, 35, 50, 92,193
see also Rulers
Knife of wisdom, 124–125
Knowledge, book; *see* Book,
    knowledge
Kun; see Arise
Kunūd, 76
Kursī; see Wisdom, eye of

Lā ilāha ill-Allāh; see Kalimah
Lakes, 49–50
Lām; see Alif, lām, mīm
Lamp, lighting a, 27
Land, 25–26, 64, 219
Languages, 23–26
Laws, explained by Muhammad,
    199–200

see also God, commandments of
Lawyer, question of, 285–286
Laziness, 75–76
Leaders, 244–246 *passim,* 281
Learned ones, 11, 92
Learnings, 287–289
   see also Lessons
Lessons, 219–220, 282
   see also Learnings
Level(s), of wisdom; *see* Wisdom, seven
   levels of
   to tune in on when listening to Bawa
     Muhaiyaddeen, 135–137
Lid and pot, 85–86
Lies, telling, 75, 77, 153
   "It's all a—," 220
Life, 221–222, 264, 289–291, 293–298
   conducting your, 203–204
   controlling your, 227
   duty in, 247–248
   eternal, 241–142
   how much are we responsible for
     our, 211–214
   one killing another, 182–184 *passim*
   purpose of, 185–186, 200, 224
   secret of, 186, 258
   sixth form of, 3, 93
   see also Lives; Man, purpose of
Light(s), 3–4, 166, 264, 268, 274
   effulgent, 221, 265
   form, 37
   God is—within heart, 294–295
   in the eyes, 9, 32, 242
   life, 3, 93, 214–215
   living in, 240–241
   of *Ahmad,* 293
   of God, 176, 200, 218
   of lamp in innermost heart, 27
   of *Nūr Muhammad,* 289
   of perfect purity, 223
   of wisdom, *see* Wisdom, light of
   one light, 216
   ray of, 222, 305
   resplendent, 124, 161, 256
   seeing—while meditating, 229–230
   words of God are, 180
   see also God, light of; *Nūr*
Limit(s), 128–129, 171

Lives, seeing all—as your own, 21, 24,
   32, 42, 65, 78–79, 91–94, *passim,*
   206, 212, 247
   six kinds of, 212–213 *passim,*
     281–287, 303–304
   see also Life
Loincloth, 142
Loneliness, 84–86
Love, 33–36, 56, 64–65, 177–178,
   248–249, 282–285
   divine, 56–58, 63–65
   for all, 23–24, 57
   for earth, woman, and gold, 25–26,
     64, 95, 153
   in healing, 100–101, 254–255
   making, 5, 140–142
   murder of—for God, 92
   of God, 6, 45
   of neighbor as yourself, 165, 196, 200
   seeing—in all lives, 181
LSD, 68
Lust, 83, 140–142, 169, 178, 234
   is greater than the ocean, 221

Madness, 3
Magnetism, 177
Makeup, 180, 207
Males and females*; see* Equality
   between males and females
Man and monkey, 135–136
   everything exists within, 3, 41–42,
     147–150, 263, 304–305
   father of—kind, 198
   in animal state, 4, 34, 165
   must rule inward self, 275, 304–305
   potential of, 287, 296
   purpose of, 169–170, 211–214,
     266–267
   reason—came, 169
   secret of, 24, 34, 258–259
   son of, 200–202
   true, 9, 17, 20, 32, 42–44, 94, 176–188,
     196, 256, 282–285
   true, form of, 262–264
   true—will accept only God, 3, 309
   with no peace, 119–125
   see also Duty of man; Life, purpose of
Man-God, God-man, 23–24, 32–33

Mantras, 7–8, 11, 41, 70–71, 274
Map, 299
    to God; *see* God, map to
Ma'rifat, 260–261
Marijuana, 64, 68
Marketplace, 185, 197
Marriage, 35–36, 82, 85–86, 97, 205
Mary, 165, 194
Maturity, 214, 217–219
Maya, 22, 37, 123, 188, 206, 275, 288, 308
    see also Illusion
Meaning, inner, 25, 67, 80
Mecca, 76
Medicine, 253–254
    for our souls, 192, 295
    for this world and the next, 119–125
    to transform karma, 86–87
Medina, 239
Meditation, 7–8, 33, **41–45,** 148, 154
    true, 8, 41–44, 184–185, 227–228, 291
Mendicant, story of Pattanathar,
    126–127
Mental health, **100–101**
Messengers of God; *see* Prophets
    see also God, messenger of
Messiah, 187–188
Microphone, prophets speak like,
    311–312
Milk, 26, 55–56, 80, 86, 205
Mīm; see Alif, lām, mīm
Mind, 63, 147, 151–152, 186, 188, 213,
    243, 299
    and body must be in perfect balance,
        175
    and desire, 9, 55, 137
    as actor on stage, 130–131
    as nail in cross, 94
    control the, 292, 302–303
    discerning between the—and the
        sheikh, 128–129
    giving up, 122–123
    in marriage, 36
    is hell, 148
    miracle of, 275
    monkey of, 135–137, 298
    mountain of the, **50–52,** 150, 243
    nature of, 4–7, 19–22, 44–45
    sounds of, 288

source of, 277
    veils of, 19–20, 45
    weapons of, 65
Mirror of wisdom, 4, 6, 20, 235
Modesty, 11
Money, **129–130,** 153, 159–160, 310
Monkey(s), 4, 20, 147
    of the mind; *see* Mind, monkey of
    story of man with, 135–136
Moon, 192–193, 195, 219
Morning, what to do on rising, 20
Moses, 199, 308–309
Mosque, 21, 33
Mother, attachment to, **206–209**
Mountain(s), 97, 149–150, 194, 245
Mouth, 288
Movies, 153
    see also Shows
Muhaiyaddeen, M. R. Bawa, 27, 56, 140
    biography of, **12–13,** 239–242, 276
    duty of 17, 56, 239
    gives his heart, 223–224, 248
    if—was ever in our state, 129
    learning from, 135–137
    Qutb, 289–290
    state of consciousness inseparable
        from, 12
    see also Qutbs; Qutbiyyat
Muhammad, 179–182 *passim,* **257–269,**
    308–309
    as the last prophet, 182, 258
    battles of, 76–79
    eternal life of, 260
    kalimah of, 199–200
    Nūr, 289
Murder, 9, 25–26, 91–94, 98–99, 153,
    165, 218, 244, 267, 269
    in the name of God, 77–79
    rūhānīs—us, 305–307 *passim*
Mystery of life, 256

Nafs; see Desire, base
Nails of crucifixion; *see* Crucifixion
Names, 175–176
Nasīb; see Destiny
Needle, sewing, 209
Nerves, 37, 75
Ninety-nine powers of God, 7, 247

see also God, attributes of

Nithānam, 154

   see also Balance

Nīyyat; see Intention

Noah, 198

Nose, 18, 22–23

Nūr, 256, 260, 265, 277, 289, 304–305, 312, 314

   see also Wisdom, light of

Nūrullāh, 290

Nursing a baby, 141

Obesity; *see* Exercise

Obsessions, 96 kinds, **66–69**

Obstacles, in life, 299

Occult powers; *see* Powers, occult

Ocean, 70, 82

   analogy of crossing, 97, 196, 206

   "lust is greater than the—," 223

Old age; *see* Aging

One family, 9, 23–24, 79, **92–93,** 181, 200

   and Abraham, 198

One-pointedness, 70–71

Opinions, 168

Opposites, God created, **244, 255–256, 262–263**

Original shoot, an analogy, **245–246**

Outside, what is—is within, 42

Overprotection, in raising children, 49–50

Pain, at loss of temporary things, 302

Palpitations, of heart, 187

Parenting, 59, 68, **86–87,** 100–101, 139–140

   see also Family

Parrots, 21

   on cotton plant, an analogy, **187–188**

Path to God; *see* God, path to

Patience, 31–33, 81, 85–86, 233, 287

   and Muhammad, 199

   inner, 94, 160, 178, 199, 223

   of Allah, 247

   of *insān kāmil,* 254

   prophets taught us to act with, 196

Patient, must have faith in doctor, **253–254**

Pattanathar, 126–127

Payoff, 288

Peace, 3, 17–19, 21, 25–26, 31–33, 63, 113–117, 177–178, 207, 301

   giving, 94

   in your life, 81, 203–204, 223

   story of rich man without, **119–125**

   through meditation, 7–8, 70–71

   true, 227–230, 248, 282

   true sheikh has no, 129

   world, 245

Periods of beauty in life, 107

Philosophies, 24–25, 67, 176, 192, 287

Physical needs, 175

Picture, everything as, 220

Plenitude, of God; *see* God, plenitude of

Poison, 27

Politics, 8–9, 24–25

Pond, 95

Possessions, discard, 83

Pot and lid, 85–86

Poverty, 97, **222–223,** 229–230, 244, 247

Power, of God; *see* God, power of

Powers, occult, 19, 113, 150, 275

Praise, 51, 168, 191

Praise of God; *see* God, praise of

Prayer, 67–68, 70, 114–117, 122, 175, 179, 209,

   in school, 101–103

   repetitive; *see* Mantras

   true, **8–9, 20–21, 42–44,** 154, **266–267**

Predestination, 211–212

   see also Destiny

Prejudices, 8

Pride, 34, 181, 203, 265

   connected to satan, 37, 233

Primal cause, God as—, 292

Primal gaze of God, 303–304

Prince of God, 94

Prison, question of man from, 223–224

Prisoner, 245

Profit, 153

   and loss, 64, 228

   and loss in marriage, 36

Progress on path to God; *see* God, path to

Propagation, 184–185
Property, *rūhānīs* connected to, 305
Prophets, 91–94, 171, 303, 308–312
    beseeched by satan's grandson, 258
    message of, 95–96, **165–167,
        176–182, 195–198,** 218–219
    reasons why they were sent, 24, 183,
        198–200, **244–246,** 255–256
    see also Abraham, Adam, David,
        Ishmael, Isaac, Jesus, Job, Jonah,
        Joseph, Moses, Muhammad, Noah
Punishment, after death, 109
Purity; *see* Light, of perfect purity

Qalb, 19, 55, 148, 227, 274, 281, 283,
    287
    see also Heart, innermost
Qiyamah; see Judgment Day
Qualities, animal, 4, **19–20,** 176,
    180–181, 302
    evil, 65, 77, 94–95, 115, 178, 203–204,
        276–277, 282–285, 288
    of God; *see* God, qualities of
    of man, 234–235, 253–255
    of satan, 36, 233–234, 246
Questions, and answers within us,
    247–248
    answering—on a job interview,
        203–204
    asking, 168
    on Day of Judgment, 188
Qur'an, 255–269 *passim,* 290
Qurbān, 308
Qutbiyyat, 265, **289–290, 304–305,**
    314
    see also Qutbs
Qutbs, 218, 228, 244, 265, 289, 303–305
    reasons they came, 171, 183, **195**
    station and function of, **311–313**

Rabb; see God, as creator
Race, one human, 92–93, 245
Races, 8, 185
Rahmān, 293
Rahmat, 56, 267–268
Rainbow, 302
Rasūl; see Muhammad
Rasūlullāh; see Muhammad

Ray(s), 26, 31, 213, 220, 289, **303–305**
    see also Triple ray
Realization, self-, 184–186
Rebirth, 19–20, 147, 178–179, 188, 245
Record, of one's life, 108, 166, 310
Reels of life, 108–109, 151–154, 211–212,
    301
Religions, 8–9, 185, 218, 221–222, 268,
    307–309
    nature of, 21, 24, 26, **176–182,
        196–198**
Remembrance of God; *see* God,
    remembrance of
Renting to a friend, 138–139
Respresentative of God; *see* God,
    representative of
Resonance of Allah; *see* God,
    resonance of
Respect, 11, 58, 101–103, 160, 203
Responsibility
    for our lives, 211
    to bring others on path, 217
    see also God, give all responsibility to
Resurrection, 94–95
Revelation, 268
Rewards, do not expect, 284–285
Right and wrong, 27, 96, 147–149,
    151–152, 194, 210–211, 217, 261
Rizq, 266
Robbery; *see* Theft
Roots, cutting—of tree, 70, 99
Rope, thread sand into, 301–302
Rose, 23, 286
Rūh; see Soul
Rūhānī; see Spirit body
Rules of conduct; *see* Conduct

Sabūr; see Patience
Sabūr, shakūr, tawakkul, and
    al-hamdu lillāh, 32, **81,** 94, 178, 199
    see also Patience; Contentment; God,
        surrender to; God, praise of
Sacrifice, 8, 199
Sadness, 7–8, 55, 300–301
Sages, 76, 96
    see also Gnānis
Saint(s), 171, 183, 244
    message of, 176

Tamil, 126–127
Salvation, 197–198
Sand, thread into rope, 301–302
Satan, **36–37,** 76, 93–94, 165, 246, 284
   dispelling, 181, 217, **227–228**
   kingdom of, 180, 196
   qualities of, 233–234, 256
   soul of, 200
Satan's grandson, 257–260
Scale, 175
Scholars, 11
Scriptures, 9, 25, 113
Seal of the prophets, 76
Searching for God, 20–21, 126
Secret, of God; *see* God, secret of
   within man, 255–269 *passim*
Seeds, 69–70, 124, 167–168, 192, 275,
   314–315
Self, 8, 149–150, 178
Selfless state, 249
Service to God; *see* God, service to
Sexual conduct, 35–36
Shadow, form of body, 109–110
Shaktis; see Elemental energies
Shakūr; see Contentment
Sharī'at, **260–261**
Sheikh, find and study with, **135–137,**
   287–296, 299, 311
   surrender to, **116–119, 209–210**
   see also Guru
Shirk; see Faults within man
Shoot, original; *see* Original shoot
Shows, 49–50, 289
   see also Movies
Siddhis; see Powers, occult
Sifāt; see Forms
Signs of destruction, 10–12
Sin(s), 187–188, 221
   five heinous, 213
Singing, 184–186
Sirātul-mustaqim; see Bridge
Sirr; see Secret within man
Sixty-four arts, 41, 64, 131, 275
Sky, bend into bow, 301–302
Slave of God; *see* God, slave of
Slavery, 243
Sleep, 159–160
Slippers, 204

Small, becoming, 52, 245
Smells, 18, 243
Snake, 274–275, 283–285
Snowflakes, 212–214
Sorrow, 21–22, 148, 161, 191, 289
Soul, 107–110, 180–181, 288, 303–307
   eternal life of, 293
   house of, 314
   of God; *see* God, soul of
   of man; *see* Man, soul of
Sounds, 18, 35, 50
   distinguish between, 228
   of God; *see* God, sounds of
Space, wide-open, 198
Speech, 18, 288–289
Speed, rates of, 154–155
Spirit body, 109–110, 288, 303–307
Spirits, 37, 76, 180
   elemental; *see* Spirit body
Spiritual advancement, 86–87, 175
Spit, satan—on man, 256
Splinter, 283
Stage, of life, 108, 154
   see also World, stage of the
Starvation, in the world, 222–223
States of consciousness, 178, 214, 223,
   230, 282, 284
   understanding, 185–186
Statues; *see* Gods, false
Stealing; *see* Theft
Stillness, 152
Stomach, one-span, 147, 184–186
Stories, traditional, 266
Storms, 243
Stringhoppers, 206–207
Study, with sheikh; *see* Sheikh, find and
   study with
   yourself, 168, **287–296**
Sūfiyyat, 261
Sun, 9–10, 240–241
Supermarket, 182–183
Sūrat, 261
Sūratul-Fātihah, 290
Sūratul-Ikhlās, 290
Surrender to God; *see* God, surrender to
Sword of *īmān,* 77

Tamil saint, 126–127

Tārahan, singhan, and *sūran,* 178, 213
Tarīqat, 260–261
Taste, 19, 242
Tawakkul-Allāh; see God, trust in
Taxes, 222
Teacher, 57–59, 101–103
   God-realized, 254–255, 277, 311
Tears; *see* Crying
Teenagers; *see* Children
Television, 223, 313
Thānam, 154
   see also Surrender
Theft, 91, 125–127, 159, 203, 223
Throne of God; *see* God, throne of
Thymus gland, 313–314
Time, 5, 188, 239–240
   limit, 314–315
Tongue, 18–19, 32, 288–289
Tractor's work, 253–255
Traditional stories; *see* Stories,
   traditional
Train ride, 159–161
Treasure, eternal, 229–230, 274, 292–295
   passim
   see also God, treasure of
Treating all lives as your own, 21, 31,
   42, 65, 79, 91–94, 178
Tree(s), 99, 170, 193, 297–300, 315
Tribes; *see Banū Isrā'īl* tribe; *see*
   Hashim tribe
Tricks, 147, 302
Triple effulgence, 264
Triple flame, 118
Triple grace, 292–293
Triple ray, 264
True man; *see* Man, true
Trust, in God; *see* God, trust in
   in sheikh; *see* Sheikh, trust in the
Truth, 63, 67, 70–71, 80, 95–96, 193, 296,
   313–314 *passim*
   of God; *see* God, truth of
   realize the, 220, 300, 309–311
   understand the, 309–311
   within all creation, 269, 275
Tune in, on what level, **135–137**

'Umar Ibnul-Khattāb; *see* Khattāb,
   'Umar Ibnul-

Unemployment, **75–76**
Unhappiness, 229–230
Unity, 63, 198, 212–214
Universes, 31, 290, 302

Vampire, 5–6
Vapors, 29, 109–110
Veils, of the mind; *see* Mind, veils of
Vice-regents; *see* Prophets
Vulture, 44

Wahy; see Revelation
War(s), 8, 11, 24–26, 65, 79, 219
   fought by Muhammad, 76–79
   inner, 77–80
Warning, inner, 187–188
Washing machine, 127–128
Water, 109, 176
Waves; *see* Ocean
Wealth, 191, 229, 230
   of God; *see* God, wealth of
   of wisdom, 103, 143
   rightful, 295
Weapons, 9, 65, 93–94
Well, *Zamzam,* 313
Wilāyat, 267, 277
Will of God; *see* God, will of
Wisdom, 22–23, 108–109, 154, 161,
   176–182, 186, 200, 210–211
   do duty with, 283–285
   escape satan with, 234
   eye of, 114, 227, 289–290,
   fragrance of, 286
   learn, 71, 102–103, 137, 211–214,
      264–269, 291–296
   light of, 3–7 *passim,* 32, 63–64
   of a God-realized teacher, 254–255
   of the *Qutb,* 289–290, 303–305,
      312–313
   seven levels of, 34, 117, 177, 265, 312
   within wisdom, 114, 220, 276–277
   see also Divine knowledge
Wise man, **96,** 185
   see also Guru
Woman, 5, 9–10, 25–26, 41–42, 50, 66,
   70, 79
Wood, 71, 168–169
Word, nature of, 288–289

of God; *see* God, words of
Work, need to, 75–76
Works, good, 255
World(s), 49, 115–116, 147–149,
    184–186, 240–241, 243
  changes, 256, 300–301
  destruction of, 10–12,
  duty to, 5–7
  heaven and hell in this, 262–263
  leaders, advice to, 244–245
  marketplace of, 197–198
  rejected by the, 229–230
  school of the, 219–220, 266–267
  stage of the, 42, 99, 130–131
  three, 218, 281
  twelve—within, 288
Worry, question about, 151–152
Worship, 227, 266
  of God; *see* God, worship of
  see also Religions

Zamzam well, 313

BOOKS BY
M. R. BAWA MUHAIYADDEEN

Truth & Light: brief explanations

Songs of God's Grace

The Divine Luminous Wisdom That Dispels the Darkness

The Guidebook to the True Secret of the Heart

God, His Prophets and His Children

Four Steps to Pure Iman

The Wisdom of Man

A Book of God's Love

My Love You My Children: 101 Stories for Children of All Ages

Come to the Secret Garden: Sufi Tales of Wisdom

The Golden Words of a Sufi Sheikh

The Tasty, Economical Cookbook

Sheikh and Disciple

Maya Veeram or The Forces of Illusion

Asma' ul-Husna: The 99 Beautiful Names of Allah

Islam and World Peace: Explanations of a Sufi

A Mystical Journey

Questions of Life/Answers of Wisdom

Treasures of the Heart: Sufi Stories for Young Children

Gems of Wisdom 1: The Value of Good Qualities

Gems of Wisdom 2: Beyond Mind and Desire

To Die Before Death: The Sufi Way of Life

For free catalog or book information call:
(215) 879-8604

The central branch of the Bawa Muhaiyaddeen Fellowship is located in Philadelphia, PA. The Fellowship serves as a meeting house and as a reservoir of people and materials for all who are interested in the teachings of M. R. Bawa Muhaiyaddeen.

For information, write or call:

The Bawa Muhaiyaddeen Fellowship
5820 Overbrook Avenue
Philadelphia, Pennsylvania 19131
Telephone: (215) 879-6300